OXFORD MEDICAL PUBLICATIONS

ICPC

Also available

ICHPPC-2-Defined: International classification of health problems in primary care 3rd edn (1983)

IC-Process-PC: International classification of process in primary care (1986)

ICPC

International Classification of Primary Care

Prepared for the World Organisation of National
Colleges, Academies and Academic Associations of
General Practitioners/Family Physicians (WONCA)
by the ICPC Working Party

Edited by Henk Lamberts and Maurice Wood

Oxford   New York   Tokyo
OXFORD UNIVERSITY PRESS

Oxford University Press, Walton Street, Oxford OX2 6DP
Oxford New York Toronto
Delhi Bombay Calcutta Madras Karachi
Petaling Jaya Singapore Hong Kong Tokyo
Nairobi Dar es Salaam Cape Town
Melbourne Auckland
and associated companies in
Berlin Ibadan

Oxford is a trade mark of Oxford University Press

Published in the United States
by Oxford University Press, New York

© *WONCA, 1987*

First published 1987
Reprinted 1989 (with corrections), 1990

British Library Cataloguing in Publication Data
ICPC – International classification of
Primary Care.—(Oxford medical
publications).
1. Medical care—Classification
I. Lamberts, Henk II. Wood, Maurice
362.1'012 RC48
ISBN 0-19-261633-1

Library of Congress Cataloging-in-Publication Data
ICPC, international classification of primary care.
 Bibliography: p.
 Includes index.
 1. Nosology. 2. Family medicine—Classification.
I. Lamberts, Henk. II. Wood, Maurice. III. World
Organization of National Colleges, Academies, and
Academic Associations of General Practitioners/Family
Physicians. IV. ICPC Working Party.
RB115.I36 1987 616'.0012 87-20237
ISBN 0-19-261633-1 (pbk)

Set by Computerised Typesetting Services, Finchley, London from data supplied
Printed in Great Britain by
Biddles Ltd,
Guildford and King's Lynn

Contents

Members of the ICPC Working Party

Bent G. Bentsen, University of Trondheim, Norway

Charles Bridges-Webb, University of Sydney, Australia

Henk Lamberts, University of Amsterdam, The Netherlands

Sue Meads, National Center for Health Statistics, Hyattsville, USA

Manacadu K. Rajakumar, Family Physician, Kuala Lumpur, Malaysia

Maurice Wood (Chairman), Virginia Commonwealth University, USA

Foreword 1: The international classification of primary care

Classification is a key to knowledge and an international classification makes for comparability between items of new knowledge arising out of work in different environments. It is natural, therefore, for WONCA to have become involved in the task of creating a family of international classifications for primary care.

Family physicians see the widest cross-section of humanity and have, therefore, been preoccupied, more than any other specialty in medicine, with the problems of classification and international comparability. WONCA has brought together an international group of family physician–taxonomers to form an unrivalled group of experts in its Classification Committee. This Committee has already produced the *International Classification of Health Problems in Primary Care*, now in its third edition as *ICHPPC-2-Defined* (1983), and the International Classification of Process in Primary Care, published as *IC-Process-PC*, (1986).

The classification presented in this book arose out of the continued work of the group and others to test a classification of reasons given by patients for each encounter with their physician. The structure of this classification showed promise of a broader application after field testing. It is now presented as the International Classification of Primary Care (ICPC).

The ultimate test of the value of a classification is its relevance in practice in the hands of those who work in primary care. It is now up to family physicians and others in primary care to test this new classification and publish their experiences.

Compatibility with the International Classification of Diseases, ninth edition (ICD-9) has been a fixed objective of the WONCA Classification Committee which has always endeavored to keep in close contact with the relevant experts of the World Health Organization (WHO). ICHPPC, in all its editions, as well as ICPC, are compatible with ICD-9. ICD-9 with all its inadequacies remains the centre around which all new classifications revolve.

The reconsideration of ICD itself is overdue. The development of the tenth revision is under way and its main outlines are now established. Whatever the final form, it is important that this edition should take into account the needs of primary care, to which the WHO has been heavily committed since Alma Ata[1] as well as the opportunities provided by increasing use of computers, the experience of using ICHPPC in practice and the potentialities of the structure offered by ICPC.

WONCA places great importance on its official relations with the World Health Organization. We would like to see the active and continuing involvement of its Classification Committee on the development of a revision of the International Classification of Diseases.

I have had the privilege of working in the Classification Committee to develop and test ICPC. In writing this Foreword, I have more than formal interest in seeing its successful application to the problems of primary care.

Dr M. K. Rajakumar
President, WONCA

Reference

1. World Health Organization. Alma Ata 1978: Primary Health Care. Rep. Int. Primary Health Care, Alma-Ata, USSR, Sept. 1978. Geneva, WHO, 1978: reprinted 1982. Health All SER.1

Foreword 2: The international classification of primary care

The International Classification of Primary Care breaks new ground in the world of classification. For the first time, using a single classification, health care providers can classify three important elements of the health care encounter. These are:

1. Reasons for encounter (RFE)
2. Diagnoses or problems
3. Process of care

The three elements may be used separately or concurrently. Linkage of elements permits categorization from the beginning of the encounter with RFE to its conclusion with disposition plans.

The authors were wise to depart from the traditional International Classification of Disease chapter format where the axes of its several chapters vary, from organ systems (Chapters 3, 4, 5, 6, 7, 8, 9, 12 and 13) to etiology (Chapters 1, 2, 14, 17) and to others (Chapters 11, 15, 16 and 18). This mixture of axes creates confusion and increasing difficulty in organization as diagnostic titles increase in number and specificity with each revision. Instead of conforming to an increasingly clumsy format, the authors chose instead a bold and creative departure with the introduction of a biaxial classification. Clinicians will be pleased with the chapter format, which is primarily oriented towards body systems. The components that are part of each chapter permit considerable specificity for all three elements of the encounter, yet their symmetrical structure and numbering across all chapters facilitate usage even in manual recording systems. The rational and comprehensive structure of ICPC is a compelling reason to consider the classification a model for future international classifications. Although the format of ICPC is new, it is nevertheless compatible with prior WONCA classifications. ICHPPC-2-Defined and IC-Process-PC can be used in concert with ICPC to provide greater specificity in selected areas; in particular for diagnostic inclusion and exclusion criteria as well as for specific drug interventions. The glossary of terms in the manual is a rational extension of the WONCA International Glossary for Primary Care.

WONCA and its Classification Committee are indebted to the editors Professors Wood and Lamberts, their Committee, and to the organizers of the several national field trials for this new and valuable classification.

Jack Froom, M.D.
Chairman, WONCA Standing Committee on Classification

Historical preface

The landmark Dawson Report of 1920 in the United Kingdom introduced the concepts of 'primary' and 'secondary' care and the terms 'primary health centre' and 'secondary health centre'. In turn these two tiers of care were related to the missions of medical consultants and teaching hospitals. With a clarity and specificity unequalled since, the report argued the case for the bottom-up or population-based approach to the organization of health services, the allocation of resources, the generation of essential records and statistics and the training of health personnel for both environmental and personal health services. Dawson and his colleagues stressed that the elements of a logical system should be 'suitably correlated and available to all'[1]

Forty years later the then Director of the World Health Organization's Division of Health Statistics, Yves Biraud, M.D., M.Sc., promulgated a 'System of Medical Records for Clinical and Statistical purposes for Out-Patient Clinics, Medical Outposts and Health Centres'[2]. He re-introduced the term 'primary health centre', which seems to have been forgotten in the intervening period, and set forth in great detail the characteristics of a health information and statistics system 'designed to ensure continuity of treatment of patients, but also to meet the need of the central health administration . . . for information concerning the prevalence of endemic diseases, epidemics and also . . . technical activity'. The needs of both developed and developing countries were covered and his stated objective was compatible with the Dawson Report's injunction that the 'system of records . . . (should) result in knowledge and usefulness rather than accumulation of lifeless statistics'. In setting forth the criteria for a truly functional health statistics system, Biraud recognized the importance of realistically classifying and coding the problems encountered at the primary care level. Accuracy was seen as more important than specificity. In the section on 'Disease, Complaint or Principal Symptom' the document stated that 'according to the prevailing circumstances one may, therefore, expect an explicit statement of diagnosis, or a statement of the principal symptom observed, or even the complaint of the patient, if a diagnosis cannot be reached at once'.

Biraud's paradigm even included instructions for recording demographic data and information on 'treatment and other actions'.

During the next two decades both the concept and term 'primary care' gradually came into wider currency in the United Kingdom[3,4] and the United States[5]. They received brief mention in the 1964 Report of the World Health Organization's Expert Committee on General Practice[6].

In the meantime the International Classification of Diseases (ICD) grew in size, as a consequence of unbalanced pressure from diverse sub-specialist groups, and in rigidity, through control of successive revisions by vital statisticians and epidemiologists who were increasingly removed from the realities of clinical practice and especially from the vast uncharted realm of primary care. In the absence of any organizing principles, the ICD became an unstructured amalgam of chapters based variously on anatomy, clinical manifestations, changing views of 'causation', clinical specialties, and age groups. In trying to accommodate everyone, it pleased few. Dissatisfaction grew and in 1971 a World Health Organization Study Group on Classification of Diseases recommended that WHO 'start an early investigation . . . of classification needs and applications from the 1980s onwards and that by 1976 initiate some basic thinking on alternative structures for the Tenth Revision of the ICD'[7]. This advice appears to have been unheeded and in 1975 the International Conference for the Ninth Revision of the ICD convened by the WHO seems to have recognized belatedly the wisdom of Dawson's and Biraud's proposal. The Conference urged 'an early start in planning the next revision of the classification and discussed a number of questions that needed to be settled before detailed work could begin. The most fundamental point was that the Organization's programme was no longer confined to disease classification alone'[8].

Three years later at Alma Ata the WHO and UNICEF inaugurated a global programme to achieve 'health for all by the year 2000'[9]. Renewed impetus was given to the population-based approach to organizing health services and to the fundamental importance of primary health care and primary medical care enunciated almost sixty years before by Dawson and his colleagues. In the same year in an effort to provide the kinds of health statistics Dawson and Biraud had advocated, the WHO published a manual on lay reporting of health information[10].

Also in 1978, the WHO appointed what became the WHO Working Party for Development of an International Classification of Primary Care. It is the results of this group's efforts over almost seven years that are presented in this volume.

Because this seminal volume has such enormous implications not only for improved care of patients but also for managing, monitoring, and financing health services, allocating resources, stimulating research, and educating health personnel, it has seemed worthwhile to provide a brief history of the ideas, professional initiatives and bureaucratic manoeuvring that have marked its evolution. What Dawson in the United Kingdom and, among others, Andrija Stamper of Yugoslavia, C.C. Chen of China, Joseph Bhore of India, and John Grant of the United States envisaged were systems of population-based services responsive to the individual and collective needs of people. This perspective was in stark contrast to the traditional institution and physician-based services that dealt with overt demand for curative care. The importance of the Alma Ata meeting was the stimulus it gave to this sea-change in viewpoint, and especially to the recognition that well-developed primary care was an essential component in any balanced health care system. Although change has been slow in the developing world there are national examples of the population-based approach to be found, not only in the United Kingdom but, for example, in such diverse countries as Cuba, Finland, The Netherlands, and Sweden, as well as in the several large investor-owned corporations that are organizing population-based or 'market-oriented' Health Maintenance Organizations in the United States. These examples are tangible reponses to the public's increasing insistence that medical science and technology be directed at meeting their needs as they define and describe them.

To accomplish this objective, however, classification and related coding schemes based on the people's own experiences of their health problems are required. How else is the essential clinical, managerial, and political information to be acquired and aggregated? A bottom-up rather than a top-down paradigm is required for ordering and relating the elements involved in providing for an episode of care, including expressions employed by health professionals for manifestations of ill health and disease.

The genius of the new paradigm expressed in this volume is its congruence with the realities of clinical experience in both developing and developed countries. It focuses on helping the living rather than merely counting the dead. Widespread adoption of this classification scheme and its underlying logic will eventually lead to re-structuring of the chapters in the ICD. Some five chapters will require rearrangement: Infectious and Parasitic Diseases, Neoplasms, Congenital Anomalies, Symptoms, Signs, and Ill-defined Conditions and Injuries. Detailed lists at the three- and four-digit levels will undoubtedly be needed for special purposes. In addition, new chapters dealing with Ear Problems, Eye Problems, Pregnancy, Childbearing and Family Planning and Social Problems will be needed. When fully developed the interrelated classifications should make it possible to 'label', classify and code the full range of symptoms, signs, conditions, problems and 'diseases', as well as the diagnostic, preventive, and therapeutic interventions and administrative responses that characterize the provision of care at all levels of a balanced system.

Indeed, it may be argued that to call this volume the International Classification of Primary Care is a misnomer, since it is readily adaptable for use at the secondary and tertiary levels of care. Perhaps it should have been called 'The International Classification for Population-based Care', since in reality that is what it is.

The opportunity now exists for clinicians, teachers, investigators, statisticians, and managers of all persuasions to apply, test, and make suggestions for future refinements of this new ICPC. In addition, they should urge their governments and the WHO to undertake the fundamental revisions in the ICD called for during the past fifteen years. The hour is late if 'health for all by the year 2000' is to be achieved. But how will we know whether it has been achieved without the means to label, classify, code and count the peoples' health problems and the adequacy of our responses to them?

Kerr L. White, M.D.
Stanardsville, Virginia, U.S.A.

References

1. Dawson Report (United Kingdom Ministry of Health, Consultative Council on Medical and Allied Services). Interim Report on the Future Provision of Medical and Allied Services. London, His Majesty's Stationery Office, Parliament Command Paper 693, 1920.
2. Biraud, Y. A System of Medical Records for Clinical and Statistical Purposes for Outpatient Clinics, Medical Outposts and Health Centres, WHO/HS/103, 3 August, 1960.
3. Fox, T F. The personal doctor and his relation to the hospital: observations and reflections on some American experiments in general practice in groups. **Lancet**, 1960, 1, 743–760.
4. White, K L. The medical school's responsibility for teaching family medicine. **Medical Care**, 1963, 1, 88–91.
5. White, K L. General practice in the United States. **J. Med. Educ.**, 1964, 39, 335–345.
6. World Health Organization Expert Committee on General Practice. WHO Technical Report Series No. 267. Geneva World Health Organization, 1964.
7. World Health Organization Study Group on Classification of Diseases. Tenth Revision of the International Classification of Diseases, WHO/ICD 9/71.2 (mimeographed). Geneva, World Health Organization, 1971.
8. World Health Organization. Manual of the International Classification of Diseases, Injuries and Causes of Death (1975 revision) Volume I. Geneva, World Health Organization, 1977.
9. World Health Organization. Alma-Ata 1978: Primary Health Care. Geneva, World Health Organization, 1978.
10. World Health Organization: Lay Reporting of Health Information. Geneva, World Health Organization, 1976.

Introduction to ICPC

Information systems and health statistics deal with data which have been ordered and have a name, so that they can be counted. What has no name cannot be counted and consequently has no impact[46,49]. What has an incorrect or incomplete name leads, when counted, to irrelevant data prohibiting practical use or even a sensible interpretation[15]. Ample support exists for the need for a classification system which allows a shift in the orientation of health information systems and of health services research towards the identification and collection of episode oriented data[6,12,20,21,34]. The International Classification of Primary Care (ICPC) has been developed to allow this shift[30,32,40].

Towards an episode-oriented health information system

Complete episodes of disease offer an attractive way to organize patient-oriented health information systems[18,37]. ICPC can be used to organize the entry and analysis of clinical information on episodes of disease over time. An episode of disease is defined as a problem or illness in a patient over the entire period of time from its onset to its resolution[2]. By this definition, an episode of illness can be expected to include several encounters. Figures 1 and 2 represent these elements of an encounter, and consequently of an episode of illness, which can be classified with the help of ICPC: the reasons for encounter, the diagnoses, and the diagnostic and therapeutic interventions. The health problem and the need for care as they are perceived in the population before the start of an episode of illness can be established by health and household surveys and these data can be linked to episode data if the ICPC is used subsequently.

In episode recording for health services research four issues are important:

1. There can be several stages in an episode each with a different prognosis and an impact on the functional status of patients.
2. The epidemiological orientation of the data (the 'six E's').
3. The statistical orientation of the data (the 'six P's').
4. The major constructs which determine the professional behaviour of family physicians.

Components of Primary Health Care Encounter

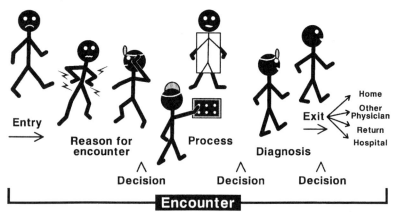

Fig. 1. Components of primary health care encounter.

The first issue was addressed by Kasl, who introduced eight stages in the development of an episode of disease[33]:

1. Asymptomatic status, risk factor(s) absent.
2. Asymptomatic status, risk factor(s) present.
3. Sub-clinical disease (susceptible to detection).
4. Initial symptom experience.
5. Initial event, (i.e., diagnostic criteria for the disease are met).
6. Course of disease (repeat episodes, residual disability, etc.), either as natural course or as treatment-modified one.
7. Irreversible institutionalization.
8. Mortality.

The epidemiological orientation of health care data is characterized by the 'six E's' (see Fig. 2): etiology, efficacy, effectiveness, efficiency, evaluation, and education[63,64]. All of these can be judged more readily in medical audit, quality assessment and quality assurance if the available clinical data are transposed into well structured, classified information[7,8,11,13,58].

The third issue, the orientation of health statistical data (the 'six P's') is particularly important if small area variations and utilization are being considered[12,63,64]. The six requirements for this orientation are that data be:

1. population based;
2. person-specific;
3. problem-oriented;
4. provider-specific;

5. procedure-specific;
6. period-specific.

If health statistics are collected routinely, classified with ICPC and organized in episodes, they allow person-specific, problem-oriented, provider-specific, and procedure-specific analyses. It is an advantage if the population is well-defined and the time period is known[14,61].

The fourth issue is a construct that infers that the professional responses of family physicians to the spectrum of health problems presented by their patients varies with the kind of problem[17]. In fact, there is evidence that at least seven groups of diseases or health problems can be distinguished, each of which requires a specific pattern of professional behaviour by the family physician[39]. These groups are as follows:

- chronic diseases
- psychosocial problems
- frequently occurring diseases
- diseases of children
- diseases of women
- diseases that relatively often evoke defensive behaviour
- diseases that relatively often require specialist care

Again, if the patient information is classified using ICPC, the subsequent grouping of health problems allows better documentation and a more efficient analysis strategy.

Thus patient information which is structured with ICPC, allows four important issues of health services research to be addressed[37–40]:

- the analysis of complete episodes
- a comprehensive epidemiological approach
- an optimal health statistical orientation
- the characterization of the different forms of professional behaviour and clinical judgment by physicians.

ICPC is a widely tested comprehensive classification system to be used by primary care providers[41,45,48,66,67]. Three important aspects of the encounter between the patient and the provider can be classified using ICPC:

1. The reason for encounter or the demand for care as expressed by the patient (and clarified by the provider).
2. The provider's assessment/diagnosis of the patient's health problems.
3. The diagnostic and therapeutic interventions undertaken in the process of care.

Therefore, three of the four parts of a patient's problem-oriented clinical record, which reflects the essential elements of each patient/

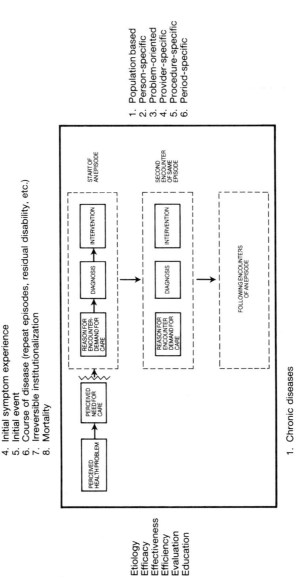

Fig. 2. An episode of disease in relation to four central issues of health service research.

provider encounter (Fig. 1) can be coded using the ICPC. This follows the SOAP acronym[62], namely:

S = Subjective: the patient's reason for the encounter.
O = Objective: this element *cannot* be classified using ICPC.
A = Assessment: the provider's interpretation of the problem in the form of a diagnosis.
P = Plan: the process of care/intervention undertaken by the provider.

The disposition after intervention will normally also be part of the matrix of the health information system[31]. In this manner, ICPC provides a simple and homogeneous framework for primary care providers, and with its index it is compatible with the ICD family of classification systems and fills the major classification needs for primary care. The simplicity of ICPC is based on its bi-axial structure: 17 chapters in one axis, each with an alpha code, and seven identical components with rubrics bearing a two-digit numeric code as the second axis[30] (Fig. 3).

CHAPTERS	A-General	B-Blood, blood forming	D-Digestive	F-Eye	H-Ear	K-Circulatory	L-Musculo-skeletal	N-Neurological	P-Psychological	R-Respiratory	S-Skin	T-Metabolic, Endocrine, Nutr	U-Urinary	W-Pregnancy, Childbearing Family Planning	X-Female genital	Y-Male genital	Z-Social
1. Symptoms and complaints																	
2. Diagnostic, screening prevention																	
3. Treatment, procedures, medication																	
4. Test results																	
5. Administrative																	
6. Other																	
7. Diagnoses, disease																	

(COMPONENTS)

Fig. 3. Biaxial structure of ICPC: 17 chapters and 7 components.

Chapters with Their Alpha Codes

A general and unspecific
B blood and blood-forming organs and lymphatics (spleen, bone marrow)
D digestive
F eye
H ear

K   circulatory
L   musculoskeletal
N   neurological
P   psychological
R   respiratory
S   skin
T   endocrine, metabolic, and nutritional
U   urological
W   pregnancy, child-bearing, family planning
X   female genital (including breast)
Y   male genital
Z   social

Components (standard for each chapter)

1. Complaint and symptom component.
2. Diagnostic and preventive component.
3. Treatment, procedures, and medication component.
4. Test results component.
5. Administrative component.
6. Referral and other reasons for encounter component.
7. Diagnosis and disease component including:

   - infectious diseases
   - neoplasms
   - injuries
   - congenital anomalies
   - other specific diseases

ICPC has a significant mnemonic quality, particularly in components 2–6. This facilitates its day-to-day use both by physicians and other primary care providers and simplifies the centralized manual coding of data recorded elsewhere.

Relation of ICPC to other classifications

WONCA (World Organization of National Colleges, Academies and Academic Associations of General Practitioners/Family Physicians) provides the forum for general practitioners/family physicians to cooperate and conduct research in order to develop well-structured and relevant patient information systems. As a consequence several primary care classifications have been developed and field tested; ICHPPC-1[28], ICHPPC-2-Defined[25,26], and IC-Process-PC[3,31]. These, together with the International Glossary of Primary Care[2], form the basis for ICPC as a comprehensive system. The structure of ICPC was also influenced by other existing major classifications and provides space for incorporating new elements within its system[5,22,29,36] (Fig. 4).

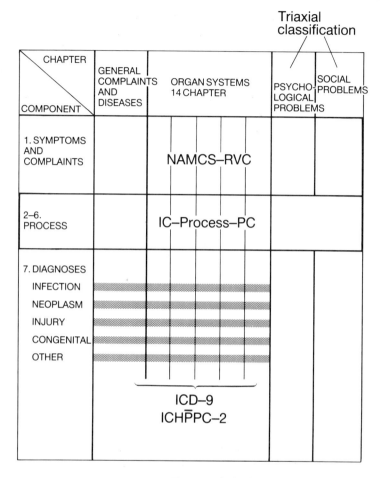

Fig. 4. Format of ICPC.

Component 1 (complaints and symptoms) drew on the existing National Ambulatory Medical Care Survey/Reason for Visit Classification (NAMCS/RFV)[4,53] which has been used successfully in the United States, and also on the Reason for Encounter Classification as developed by a WHO Working Party[44].

Components 2 and 3 (diagnostic, screening, prevention and treatment, procedures and medication) contain categories that correspond broadly with those of the ICD-9 Procedures in Medicine[27] and especially with the newly developed International Classification of Process in Primary Care (IC-Process-PC)[31].

The psychological and social problems developed by the WHO-sponsored Triaxial Classification Group are in essence represented in ICPC in chapters P and Z[47,54].

The ICD-9 [27] was the basis for Component 7 (diagnosis/disease) as it was for the ICHPPC-2[25,26], the version of the ICD-9 modified for primary care which translates readily into this component. Most rubrics in ICPC Component 7 are the same as those in ICHPPC-2 Defined[25]. The rubrics of ICPC have been converted to the corresponding codes of ICD-9, ICHPPC-2, and to the Classification of Diseases, Problems, and Procedures 1984 of the British Royal College of General Practitioners[49]. The results of this conversion will be described in Chapter 12.

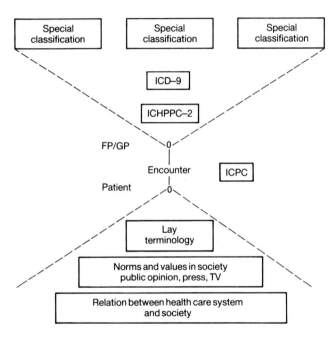

Fig. 5. Position of ICPC between specialized classifications and lay terminology.

Because of its relationship with ICD-9 and its orientation towards identifying subjective information (the patient's reason for encounter), and because of the diagnosis and information on the process of care (provider's interventions and procedures), ICPC is a classification tool which can be used in any setting where a person can initiate an encounter with a provider of care and so begin an episode of illness; namely, the home, the physician's office, the emergency room, the hospital. The nomenclature of ICPC forms a bridge between the more or less specialized ICD-9 derived classification systems on the one hand and lay terminology and common descriptions of symptoms, complaints and health problems in the community on the other hand. (Fig. 5) Thus, the ICPC can be used by primary care providers in four different modes:

- the Reason for Encounter mode, using Components 1–7
- the Diagnosis/Disease mode, using Components 1 and 7
- the Process mode, using Components 2–6
- the Comprehensive mode, using Components 1–7

1 The development of ICPC as a comprehensive classification

At the 1978 World Health Organization (WHO) Conference on Primary Health Care in Alma Ata[55], adequate primary health care was recognized as the key to the goal of 'health for all by the year 2000' WHO and WONCA both recognized that the building of appropriate primary care systems to allow the assessment and the implementation of health care priorities was only possible if the right information was available to health care system planners.

Disease classifications are designed to allow the health care providers' interpretation of a patient's health problem to be coded in the form of an illness, disease, or injury. In contrast, a Reason for Encounter Classification focuses on data elements from the patient's perspective[41,56,66]. In this respect, it is patient-oriented rather than disease- or provider -oriented because the reasons for encounter, (i.e., the demand for care) given by the patient have to be clarified by the physician or other health worker before there is an attempt to interpret and assess the patient's health problem in terms of a diagnosis, or to make any decision about the process of management and care.

White advocates a restructuring of the classification systems used in health care[65]. After commenting on the thousands of different 'labels' available to assign to health problems, he states, 'for our diverse manifestations of ill health and related suffering there are lay and colloquial terms, symptoms, complaints and problems, functional and feeling states, handicaps and disabilities, accidents, injuries and poisonings, fetal deaths and "voodoo" deaths, and finally diseases.' He comments further that the basic and senior classification, the International Classification of Diseases, Injuries and Causes of Death (ICD), has grown in complexity over nine decennial revisions and now has difficulty in satisfying anybody. The classification is without coherent conceptual theme, theory or organization, and it seeks to meet the needs of policymakers, statisticians, third-party payers, managers, clinicians, and investigators in a wide range of socio-economic and cultural settings around the world.

At the time of the Alma Ata Conference, no acceptable international classification system was available to enable the collection of such patient-oriented data, as the reason for encounter. To begin this work,

WHO called together a group of individuals experienced both in the provision of primary health care and in taxonomy. This group first met in Geneva in 1978. After several years' work they first produced the Reason for Encounter Classification (RFEC) in field test form[41,44].

Testing of the RFEC

The first field trial to test the completeness and reliability of the RFEC (the predecessor of ICPC) was a pilot study carried out in The Netherlands in 1980[41]. The results obtained from this pilot study prompted further feasibility testing of the Reason for Encounter Classification, which is now known as the Reason for Encounter mode of ICPC. This was carried out in eight countries, namely, Australia, Brazil, Barbados, Hungary, Malaysia, The Netherlands, Norway, and the United States. The feasibility study began in January 1983 and continued throughout the summer of 1983 in all countries. The entire classification was translated from English into several languages, including French, Hungarian, Norwegian, Portuguese and Russian. The analysis of more than 90 000 reasons for encounter recorded during over 75 000 individual encounters and the collective experience of the participants resulted in the development of a more comprehensive classification[44]. In the course of this feasibility testing, it was noted that RFEC could easily be used to classify simultaneously the reasons for encounter and two other elements of problem-oriented care, namely the process and the assessment. Thus, this conceptual framework allowed the evolution of the Reason For Encounter Classification into the International Classification of Primary Care. The use of ICPC in its comprehensive mode allows the logical relationships between the reason for encounter, the specific processes carried out and the assessment (or diagnosis) of the problem, to be identified (see Figs 1 and 2, pp. 2 and 4).

Results of the field trial with RFEC[41,43,44]

Test sites for the field trial, and details of the organizers and the language used, are given below:

Australia	— Professor Charles Bridges-Webb (in English)
Barbados	— Dr Mike Hoyos (in English)
Brazil	— Dr Maria Lucia LeBrao (in Portuguese)
Hungary	— Dr Marianne Szatmari (in Hungarian and English)
Malaysia	— Dr M. K. Rajakumar (in English)
The Netherlands	— Professor Cees de Geus and Professor Henk Lamberts (in Dutch and English)
Norway	— Professor Bent G. Bentsen (in Norwegian)

United States   Family physicians, Professor Maurice Wood (in English);
                       Nurses, Ms. Sue Meads (in English)

Table 1 shows that the 132 participants on the nine test sites worked very accurately: only 229 codes were invalid, resulting in a total of 90 497 coded reasons for encounter (RFEs). The nominal minimum of 10 000 observations per country was nearly always attained and the average number of observations per participant exceeded 500 in nearly all cases. There was little disparity in the mean number of RFEs per encounter; only in the U.S. was this mean relatively low: evidently here most of the time only one RFE is classified per encounter.

Table 2 shows that the importance of the RFEs classified in the form of a diagnosis (Component 7) is limited to less than 13 per cent. This component is of particular importance for chapters S (skin), T (endocrine system), Y (male genital system), and especially K (circulatory system). Patients with these health problems evidently complain relatively often in the form of a diagnosis.

Most RFEs take the form of a symptom or complaint (Component 1). This is most prominent in Chapters D (digestive system), F and H (sense organs), N (nervous system), L (musculoskeletal system), and R (respiratory system). Most psychological and social problems (P and Z) are likewise expressed in Component 1.

In at least 10 per cent of all cases, patients request a diagnostic or preventive intervention (Component 2). This component encompasses especially the general chapter (innoculations) and the female genital system (smears and pregnancy check-ups). In nearly 9 per cent of all cases patients require a prescription or therapy (Component 3). Chapters B (blood), K (circulatory system), P (psychological), and T (endocrine system) are most prominent here. Apparently people experience health problems such as anemia, hypertension, insomnia, and diabetes often as problems for which they want a prescription.

The differences between countries are illustrated with Table 3, which gives an indication of the relative significance of the different RFEs in the participating test sites. It lists the 20 most common RFEs and also indicates the rank order of the most common RFEs for each test site separately. Cough, fever, and a sore throat unmistakably rank first. They are followed by various aspects of hypertension: diagnosis, therapy, repeat encounters for hypertension, and 'blood pressure problems'.

The various preventive and administrative aspects of primary health care rank third, and in countries, such as Brazil and Malaysia, complaints about the digestive tract rank fairly high. Lower on the list of the most frequent RFEs the picture is more diverse.

The typical distribution of the reasons for encounter over chapters and components has been observed repeatedly in the field trial and in sub-

Table 1. Some quantitative data on the nine field trials.

	Australia	Barbados	Brazil	Hungary	Malaysia	Netherlands	Norway	U.S. Doctors	U.S. Nurses	Total
Total number of accepted RFEs	10863	2109	16271	12654	9518	15070	11785	4041	8131	90497
Number of participants	18	4	23	24	13	8	11	9	22	132
Number of RFEs per encounter and standard deviation	1.47 (0.77)	—	1.70 (0.94)	1.50 (0.84)	1.48 (0.75)	1.69 (0.76)	1.61 (0.78)	1.16 (0.48)	1.09 (0.39)	1.36 (0.69)
Illegitimate codes	13	1	17	29	17	125	5	6	16	229
Number of records to be corrected	116	10	57	47	68	0	0	24	48	370

Table 2. Distribution of 90 497 RFEs over the chapters and components (percentages per chapter)

Components	Chapters																Total number	Component as percentage of total
	A—General	B—Blood, blood-forming	D—Digestive	F—Eye	H—Ear	K—Circulatory	L—Musculoskeletal	N—Neurological	P—Psychological	R—Respiratory	S—Skin	T—Metabolic, Endocrine, Nutr.	U—Urinary	X—Female genital	Y—Male genital	Z—Social		
1. Symptoms and complaints	52.8	19.4	77.7	71.4	70.7	24.0	70.7	79.7	66.2	73.4	54.3	17.0	56.5	49.1	60.8	66.9	53376	59.0
2. Diagnostic, screening, prevention	22.8	17.0	2.7	2.0	6.1	11.7	1.8	1.6	0.9	5.0	1.2	14.4	9.2	32.2	5.4	6.6	9329	10.3
3. Treatment, procedures, medication	5.2	23.1	4.8	3.8	2.9	18.8	8.6	9.1	25.9	4.1	13.2	22.0	4.7	7.2	13.2	3.9	7938	8.8
4. Test results	3.0	22.7	4.7	0.8	0.3	2.2	2.5	0.8	0.5	1.1	0.2	10.3	9.0	2.1	1.3	0.7	2356	2.6
5. Administrative	8.9	0.7	0.6	4.4	0.5	1.0	2.4	1.3	1.7	0.4	0.7	1.7	0.4	0.8	0.8	9.5	2369	2.6
6. Other	4.6	2.0	1.5	1.6	2.3	12.7	2.2	1.4	2.6	2.3	1.9	5.0	4.3	4.5	1.3	12.5	3601	4.0
7. Diagnoses, diseases	2.7	15.2	8.0	16.1	17.2	29.7	11.8	6.1	2.2	13.6	28.6	29.6	15.9	4.1	17.2	—	11473	12.7
Chapter total (absolute numbers)	16805	908	8816	1593	3033	8935	8418	3595	3128	16023	1622	2403	1861	6516	615	1171	90497	
Chapter as percentage of total	18.6	1.7	9.7	1.8	3.4	9.9	9.3	4.0	3.5	17.7	7.3	2.7	2.1	7.2	0.7	1.3		100

Table 3. The twenty most common RFEs per test site (rank numbers).

	Reasons for encounter	Total (abs)	Australia	Barbados	Brazil	Hungary	Malaysia	Netherlands	Norway	U.S.-doctors	U.S.-nurses
1	R17 Cough	4434	2	1	2	6	1	1	1	3	
2	A18 Fever	3633	17	16	1	5	2	3	2	7	
3	R21 Sympt./complt. throat	2206	3	11	7	7	4	5		2	3
4	K83 Uncompl. hypertension	1834	18	2			15	2	16	4	2
5	A30 Examination	1749		6	3					1	6
6	A66 Administrative	1497		3	14	3			5		5
7	K50 Medication	1391	1			2	8				
8	D16 Diarrhea	1312	13		6	18	3				
9	A45 Preventive immunization/med.	1279	8	8	9						1
10	H10 Ear pain, earache	1268	5	17	11			9	7	6	7
11	R15 Head cold NOS	1228			4	19		11	11		
12	N10 Headache	1196		14	10			11	8	9	10
13	N17 Vertigo/dizzyness	1124			10		9	7		12	15
14	K67 Follow up encounter, unspec.	1104					1				
15	D11 Localized abdominal pain	1090		15	13			6	10		
16	D15 Vomiting	1087			5		12				
17	K13 Blood pressure problems	1043		9			4				11
18	A19 General weakness, tiredness	1030		19			10	16	15	6	13
19	S13 Rash skin NOS	1009	7	4			13	7	20	8	19
20	D10 Generalized abdom. pain	836	15				14	13		12	

sequent relevance studies[50], including the pilot study in The Netherlands of the Transition Project[40], which employed the comprehensive mode of ICPC. This study provided a data base of 31 000 encounters collected by 11 general practitioners, covering 10 900 patient years, which was large enough to obtain a distribution of all ICPC rubrics over the three modes of practical use.

Thus, the final version of the ICPC as detailed in this book, which is the version to be used for studies in primary care, is based on the results of the Transition Project and additionally on the insights obtained during the conversion of the ICPC to three other classification systems[30].

2 The practical use of ICPC in the RFE mode

The ICPC was designed to classify the reasons why patients seek care at the primary level. It may be used by any health care provider and should be an important tool to measure and define the demand being made on the health care system. The resulting data will also assist in planning health promotion and disease prevention[40,42,52].

All of the chapters and components of the ICPC can be used to classify the patient's reasons for contacting the health care system as clarified by and agreed with the primary care provider. The ICPC, used in the reason for encounter mode, is patient oriented rather than disease or provider-oriented.

The primary care provider first should identify and clarify the purpose of the encounter as stated by the patient before making any judgments as to the correctness or accuracy of the patient's reasons for encounter. Clarification within the framework of ICPC, of the patient's reason for encounter is necessary so that the most appropriate rubric in the classification can be applied. This practical use of the classification for that reason is guided by two principles:

1. The reason(s) for encounter should be understood and agreed upon between the patient and the provider and it should be recognized by the patient as acceptable descriptions. This can be done in a reliable manner, the reliability of coding the reason for encounter is not less than that of a diagnosis[24]. It is not yet known however whether the use of ICPC in its Reason for Encounter mode provides a valid description of the patient's reasons for contacting the health care system. Its validity from the patient's point of view is not known; its validity from the provider's point of view is reflected in the degree of its relationship with the diagnosis and the interventions which are the consequence of the patient's demand for care as it is understood by the provider. Future research will need to focus on the more general question of to what extent and under which circumstances providers can, with validity, identify the patient's demand and subjectively experienced need for care.

2. The ICPC rubric chosen should be as close as possible to the original statement(s) of the reason(s) given by the patient and must represent a minimal transformation by the provider. The way in which the patient

expresses his/her reason(s) for encounter determines which chapter and which component to use (Fig. 6 and Tables 4 and 5). The entire classification is applicable as patients can describe their reasons for seeking health care, in the form of symptoms, as diagnostic descriptions or as requests for services. The alphabetical index contains approximately 5 000 entries to the main rubrics of ICPC, all carrying the designated three-digit, alphanumeric code.

	CHAPTERS	A–General	B–Blood, blood forming	D–Digestive	F–Eye	H–Ear	K–Circulatory	L–Musculo-skeletal	N–Neurological	P–Psychological	R–Respiratory	S–Skin	T–Metabolic, Endocrine, Nutr	U–Urinary	W–Pregnancy, Childbearing Family Planning	X–Female genital	Y–Male genital	Z–Social
	1. Symptoms and complaints																	
	2. Diagnostic, screening prevention																	
COMPONENTS	3. Treatment, procedures, medication																	
	4. Test results																	
	5. Administrative																	
	6. Other																	
	7. Diagnoses, disease																	

Fig. 6. Biaxial structure of ICPC: 17 chapters and 7 components.

The definition of the reason for encounter consequently is as follows: 'The statement of the reason(s) why a person enters the health care system with a demand for care. The term(s) written down (and classified) by the provider represent the clarification of the reason(s) so that the statement is recognizable by the patient as an acceptable description of his/her demand for care.'

The RFE as an aspect of the patient's demand for care

The patient's reason for encounter, as classified by a provider, using ICPC is the result of a series of steps (see diagram overleaf).

Of considerable importance is the relationship between the provider and the patient and the way in which the provider has previously reacted to health problems of both organic and psycho-social type. This relationship influences the patient's perception of the need for help and the potential source of that help. In other words, the decision to access the

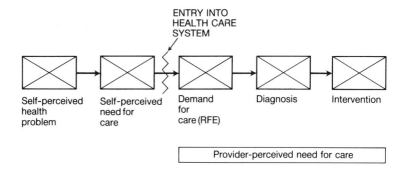

health care system with a demand for care, is influenced by a variety of factors concerned with the setting and the provider.

Demand is not identical with the patient's reason for encounter. The reason for encounter is a part of the patient's demand. The RFE also includes an element of provider input and forms that aspect of demand which can be classified with ICPC. Agreement between the patient and the provider on the patient's reason for encounter, is, therefore, partially dependent on the content of the encounter itself. This classification of the patient's reason for encounter represents the demand of the patient and that aspect of the patient's subjective need to which the provider responds with a diagnosis or definition of the problem and some form of intervention.

Providers will have different levels of skill in clarifying the patient's reason for encounter and this calls into question, the validity of the information produced. However, reliability of coding can be assessed:

(a) by comparing the written medical record with a videotaped observation of what is done for the same patient; for example, as illustrated by the written vignettes in Chapter 6;

(b) by comparing the results of several coders using the ICPC to classify what is done to and for the patient.

How to use the chapters of ICPC (Table 4)

In using ICPC in its Reason for Encounter (RFE) mode, it is necessary first to select the appropriate organ system or chapter, assign the correct alpha code, and then the two-digit numeric code in the relevant component such as a symptom or complaint, a diagnosis, or an aspect of process. The alphabetical index should be used when there is uncertainty about the chapter or the component in which a specific reason for encounter should be placed.

When ICPC is used in the RFE mode five rules apply to the use of chapters, and three rules to the use of components. These rules are listed below with examples of the application of those rules.

Table 4. Chapters and their alpha codes

A General and unspecified
B Blood and blood-forming organs and lymphatics (spleen, bone marrow)
D Digestive
F Eye (Vision)
H Ear (Hearing)
K Circulatory
L Musculoskeletal (Locomotion)
N Neurological
P Psychological
R Respiratory
S Skin
T Endocrine, metabolic and nutritional
U Urological
W Pregnancy, child-bearing, family planning (Women)
X Female genital (including breast) (X-chromosome)
Y Male genital (Y-chromosome)
Z Social problems

A mnemonic alpha code has been used, where possible.

Rule 1

The reason for encounter should be coded as specifically as possible and may require some clarification by the provider.

Example

'Chest pain' can be classified as K0l (pain attributed to heart) or as R0l (pain respiration), or as L04 (chest symptoms/complaints). The decision as to the correct selection is not based on the opinion of the provider as to the type of chest pain but, rather, to the manner in which the patient expresses his reason for encounter following clarification by the provider.

'My chest hurts when I cough' — R0l
'I have chest pain . . . I think it's my heart' — K0l
'I have chest pain after falling down stairs' — L04

Rule 2

Whenever the patient makes a specific statement use his/her terminology.

Example

Jaundice, in the form of a diagnostic descriptive term can be found in Chapter D (digestive) but the patient may present this symptom as a 'yellow discoloration of the skin' (Chapter S). If the patient expresses the problem as 'jaundice', the ICPC code is Dl3. If, however, the patient states 'my skin has turned yellow' the correct code would be S08, regardless of the fact that the health care provider is positive that the diagnosis is a hepatitis of some form.

Rule 3

When the patient is unable to describe his/her complaint, the reason given by the accompanying person is as acceptable as that stated by the patient. (e.g. a mother bringing in a child or relatives accompanying an unconscious patient).

Example

A mother states 'my child has a fever' — A03. 'I have come here with my deaf husband to get a prescription for his heart medicine' — K50.

Rule 4

Any problem whatsoever presented verbally by the patient should be recorded as a reason for encounter. Multiple coding is required if the patient gives more than one reason. Code every reason presented at whatever state in the encounter it occurs.

Example

'I need birth control pills and my breasts are tender and sore' — Wll, Xl8. (A prescription for the pill as a reason for encounter is coded in Wll and not in W50).

Rule 5

It occasionally may seem illogical to code a certain specific reason for encounter in a certain chapter. For example, 'pain in the chest, unspecified' in the Musculoskeletal Chapter. Thus, it may be difficult to find the code in the tabular listing. In these circumstances, use the alphabetical index, remembering that the appropriateness of using that particular rubric will be more visible when the diagnosis and the medical intervention accompany the reason for encounter.

How to use the components (Table 5)

l. Symptoms and complaints

The most common reasons patients give for seeking health care are presented in the form of symptoms and complaints[45,50]. Therefore, it is expected that Component l (symptoms and complaints), will be extensively used. These symptoms are specific for each chapter. Therefore, nausea is found in the Digestive Chapter (D09), while sneezing (R07) is located in Component l of the Respiratory Chapter. While most of the entries in this component are symptoms specific to the chapter in which they are found, some standardization has been introduced for ease of coding.

Table 5. Components (standard for each chapter)

1. Complaint and symptom component
2. Diagnostic and preventive component
3. Treatment, procedures and medication component
4. Test results component
5. Administrative component
6. Referral and other reasons for encounter component
7. Diagnosis/disease component:
   — infectious diseases
   — neoplasms
   — injuries
   — congenital anomalies
   — other

Throughout most of the chapters, with the exception of psychological and social, the first rubric(s) relate to the symptom 'pain.' Examples of this are earache (H0l) and headache (N0l). There are also four standard Component l rubrics in each chapter. They are:

- 26 Fear of cancer
- 27 Fear of having a disease or condition
- 28 Disability/impairment
- 29 Other symptoms/complaints

Codes 26 and 27, and sometimes also a few others, are used when the patient expresses anxiety about or fear of cancer or some other condition or disease. Examples are:

'I'm afraid I have TB' — R27;
'I'm afraid I have cancer of the breast' — X26;
'I'm afraid I have a venereal disease' — Y25.

Even when the provider knows that such an expressed fear is unwarranted or illogical, it constitutes the patient's reason for encounter. When the patient expresses fear or concern about having cancer, code the appropriate chapter using 26. For cancer, an exception to this can be found in Chapter X (X25, fear of genital cancer, while fear of breast cancer is — as might be expected — X26).

Other exceptions to these concerns are:

A25   Fear of death
B25   Fear of AIDS
K24   Fear of Heart Attack
K25   Fear of Hypertension
W02   Fear of Pregnancy

X23   Fear of Venereal Disease (female)
X24   Fear of Sexual Dysfunction (female)
Y24   Fear of Sexual Dysfunction (male)
Y25   Fear of Venereal Disease (male)

Disability/impairment   When the patient's reason for the encounter is expressed in terms of a disability or impairment which affects activities of daily life and social functions, rubric 28 (disability/impairment) should be used[29].

Example

'I cannot climb stairs because of the cast they have put on my leg for my fractured ankle' — L28 (Component 1); L76 (Component 7).
'I can't work in the office because I can't sit for any length of time because of my hemorrhoids' — K28 (Component 1) and K96 (Component 7).

'Catch All Rubric'   In each chapter the component code 29 is the 'catch-all' symptom/complaint category. The index should be checked for synonymous terms before using this rubric, which also contains rarely seen and unusual symptoms and complaints.

2. Diagnostic, screening and preventive procedures

The reasons included in this component are those in which the patient seeks some type of procedure, such as 'I'm here to have some blood work done'. (—34). The patient may request a particular procedure in connection with an expressed problem or as a single demand, such as 'I want the doctor to examine my heart', or 'I think I need to have my urine tested' (—35), or 'I was told to come here today for the result of my X-ray' (—60), or 'I need a vaccination' (—44). Clarification by the provider is necessary to find out why the patient thinks he or she needs a urine test in order to select the appropriate alpha code. The patient wants a urine test and you find out that he thinks that he may have a bladder infection — U35. The results of an X-ray which is being requested refers to a barium meal — D60. A request for a vaccination against *Rubella* — A44.

3. Treatment, procedures and medication

These reasons are expressed when the patient requests a treatment or when the patient refers to the physician's instructions to return for specific treatment, procedure, or medication as the reason for encounter. Further clarification by the provider is often necessary in order to identify the most appropriate code.

Examples

(1) 'I need my medication refilled' (—50).

If the patient expresses the reason why he is taking the medication or the provider knows the reason, select the appropriate alpha code.

If the medication was given for a sinus infection, use the alpha code R, thus the correct code would be R50.

(2) 'I'm here to have my cast removed' (—54).

It is evident that, for instance, the patient suffered a fracture of the left arm and the correct alpha code to select is L.

(3) 'I was told to come and have the stitches taken out today' (—54).

Although at first one might assume that all suture removal would be in the Skin Chapter, the patient might have stitches from cataract surgery (F54) or from a phimosis operation (Y54).

4. Test results

This component should be used when the patient is specifically requesting the results of tests previously carried out. The fact that the results of the test may be negative does not affect the use of this component. Remember, the reasons why people seek medical care are being classified, not the results of the test or treatment or the care provided. Often the patient will request the test result and its consequences and seek more information on the underlying problem. In that case, also consider code —45 (counselling).

Examples

'I was told to come to get the results of my blood test for sugar' (—60).
'I want to know what they found on the X-rays of my stomach that were taken last week' (D60).
'I am supposed to pick up the result of urine test and take it to the urologist. I also want to know what he will do and which examinations and treatment I can expect' (U60, U45).

5. Administrative

Administrative reasons for encounter with the health care system include examinations required by a third party (someone other than the patient), insurance forms which require completion, and discussions regarding the transfer of records:
'I need this medical insurance form completed and mailed to the company' (A62).
'I've come for a certificate so I can return to work: my broken arm has completely healed' (L62).

6. Referrals and other reasons for encounter

This component contains several rubrics which are seldom used or which can be considered 'catch-all' rubrics. If the patient's reason for encounter is to be referred to another provider, —66, —67, and —68 can be used for this purpose. If the patient states his/her reason for encounter is 'being told by you to come back', or 'being sent by someone else', use —64 or —65.

When a provider initiates a new episode or takes the initiative for the follow-up of an already existing episode of a health problem like hypertension, obesity, alcoholism, or a smoking habit, it will be appropriate to code the reason for encounter as —64.

Example

A patient presenting with earwax to be removed has his blood pressure measured because the provider is aware of a previously diagnosed hypertension, and also receives advice on tobacco abuse. The patient's reason for encounter would be classified as follows:

H13 (plugged feeling in ear) — H81 (earwax) — H51 (removal of earwax).

In addition to this, the following will also be coded:
K64 (provider initiated) — K86 (hypertension) — K31 (checking of blood pressure).
and,
P64 (provider-initiated) — P17 (tobacco abuse) — P45 (advice to stop smoking).

7. Diagnosis/disease

Only when the patient expresses the reason for encounter as a specific diagnosis or disease should it be coded in Component 7. The patient who is known to be a diabetic but comes in complaining of a problem such as weakness should not be coded to diabetes but to the problem expressed: weakness (A04).

However, if the patient states that he is seeking care because of diabetes the diagnosis 'diabetes' should be classified as his reason for encounter (T90). It is important to classify the reasons expressed by the patient, even though the practitioner may know that the patient also suffers from a well-established chronic disease.

If the patient names a reason for encounter in the form of a diagnosis which the provider knows is not correct, the 'wrong' RFE of the patient is coded rather than the 'correct' one of the physician (e.g. a patient presenting with a reason for encounter of 'migraine,' when the provider knows it is tension headache, or a patient who is known to have nasal polyps presenting with 'hay fever').

Examples

'I am here because of my Hypertension' (K86)
'I come every month because of the arthritis of my hip' (L89)
In Table 6 some patient presentations are classified using the ICPC in the
reason for encounter mode.

Table 6. Examples of the use of ICPC in the reason for encounter mode

Reason for Encounter	Chapter	Component	ICPC code
Request for heart prescription	Circulatory system (K)	Treatment, procedure, and medication (50 Medication)	K50
Running nose	Respiratory system (R)	Symptoms and complaints (07 Nasal congestion)	R07
Diabetes	Endocrine, metabolic, nutritional (T)	Diagnoses and diseases (90 Diabetes)	T90
Request for pap smear	Female genital system (X)	Diagnostic, screening, and preventive procedures (37 Cytology)	X37
Removal of sutures (skin tumour excised)	Skin (S)	Treatment, procedure, and medication (54 Suture)	S54
X-ray results (previous pneumonia)	Respiratory system (R)	Test results (60)	R60

Several other examples are the following:

(1) A 60-year old lady sees her family physician in his office because of
a plugged feeling in her left ear for two days, plus renewal of the
prescription for hypertension. Hl3, K50.

(2) The family physician examines a l5-year-old boy with pain in his left
knee for the first time. The boy also asks him to fill in a form needed to
attend a boy scout camp. Ll5, A62.

(3) A mother brings in a six-month old girl with diarrhea and a skin rash
of the buttocks. She asks advice about feeding her baby in general: should
she start giving her extra vitamins? Dll, S06, T45.

(4) A 40-year-old man comes into the doctor's office with vague complaints, expressing a fear that he might have cancer. A26.

Rules for use of components

The following rules for the use of each component will reinforce the description of the components.

Rule 1

Components 2, 3, 4, 5, and 6 consist of rubrics with the same number codes throughout the classification. The alpha part of the code will be chosen according to the chapter selected. Whenever a code is shown preceded by a dash (—), select the chapter code (alpha). All codes must begin with an alpha code to be complete.

Example

Biopsy will be coded —52, for digestive system this = D52, for respiratory system = R52.

Medication prescribed will be coded as —50. A patient requesting medication for his/her hypertension = K50.

Rule 2

More than one component, or the same component twice, can be used for the same encounter if more than one reason is presented by the patient.

Example

'I have had abdominal pain since last night and in addition, I vomited several times during the night' = D01, D10.
'I have some abdominal discomfort and I think I may have an appendicitis' = D06, D88.

Rule 3

Rubric —28 in each component stands for 'disability, impairment'. It should be used where the patient complains that he/she is unable to work and also when a limitation of a function is the stated reason for the encounter.

Example

'I cannot climb stairs because of the cast they have put on my leg for my fractured ankle' = L28 (Component 1); L76 (Component 7).
'I cannot work in the office because I can't sit for any length of time because of my hemorrhoids' = K28 (Component 1) and K96 (Component 7).

3 Practical use of ICPC in the diagnostic mode

The basis for the use of ICPC as a diagnostic classification is the application of ICHPPC-2-Defined[25]. Where a rubric is defined in ICHPPC-2, the same inclusion and exclusion criteria are to be used for ICPC. Further, the coding rules of ICHPPC-2, including those for optional hierarchial expansion[1,26] are to be followed.

When ICPC is used in its Diagnostic mode, the first and seventh components of ICPC can be used. Component 7 contains (at least on a one-to-one basis) practically all the defined disease rubrics contained in ICHPPC-2-Defined. Practically all other 'undefined' rubrics of ICHPPC-2-Defined are covered by either Component 1 or Component 7. The table with the conversion from ICPC to ICHPPC-2 (Chapter 12) gives the full details. As a result, ICPC can be used as a diagnostic classification system fully compatible with ICHPPC-2 and consequently with ICD-9 (see Chapter 12 for the conversions). The process components will occasionally be needed (e.g. for a vaccination, a pap smear, or some advice) when ICPC is used in the diagnostic mode.

In this manual, ICHPPC-2 Defined is referred to as the base classification when using ICPC for labelling diagnoses. This is because the inclusion criteria listed for the defined rubrics of ICHPPC-2-Defined have not been incorporated in the ICPC Tabular List. However, in the ICPC listing with short titles (Chapter 12), all rubrics corresponding with a defined ICHPPC-2 rubric carry an *asterisk*. The rubric titles of the defined categories in both classifications are identical, and so the inclusion and exclusion criteria found in the ICHPPC-2 Defined rubrics can be applied to those same rubrics in ICPC. If the alphabetical index does not identify certain specific diagnoses, accessing the inclusion criteria of related diagnoses in ICHPPC-2 Defined may help determine the diagnosis.

General rules for coding diagnosis and diseases

Users are encouraged to record during each encounter, the full spectrum of diagnoses, including organic, psychological, and social health problems. Recording should be at the highest level of diagnostic refinement for which the user can be confident, but never more specific than can be defended by the inclusion criteria for that rubric.

In ICPC, body systems take precedence over etiology so that Chapter A (general) is the *last* chapter to be considered when coding a disease which because of its etiology, can be found in several chapters (for example, tuberculosis). All chapters provide specific rubrics, which include both etiology and the body system or organ involved in that disease. Conditions accompanying pregnancy or the puerperium are usually classified to Chapter W, but a condition affecting pregnancy is coded to the specific chapter representing the body system involved. In using Chapter P remember that the first component is primarily to be used in the RFE mode, while the seventh component is meant to be a diagnostic component. This does not preclude the rubrics in the first component being used in the diagnostic mode if the provider considers them to be relevant. All social problems, whether identified as a reason for encounter or as a diagnosis, are listed in the first component of Chapter Z.

Specific rules for coding diseases and diagnoses using ICHPPC-2-Defined

1. Definitions in ICHPPC-2-Defined contain the minimal number of criteria necessary to permit inclusion in the diagnostic title.
2. For those rubrics labelled 'Inclusion criteria for this rubric are not listed', consult the list of diagnoses included in the rubric or, for a more complete list, refer to the relevant rubrics in ICD-9.
3. Consult the definition *after* the diagnosis has been formulated. If the criteria given in the definition cannot be fulfilled, consult other rubrics suggested by the term 'consider'.
4. The definitions are *not* intended to be used as a guide to therapeutic decisions.
5. Coding of diagnoses should occur at the highest level of specificity possible for that patient encounter.

Optional hierarchical expansion[1]

Clearly, no single international classification can fulfil every need for every user; inevitably users will sometimes want to separate certain problems contained in a single rubric. If this need arises, either because of increased incidence of a condition in one area, or because of the special interests of the recorder, it can be solved by assigning special 'in-house' code numbers to that condition.

All three-digit ICPC codes can thus be expanded to accommodate special needs. It is important that these expansions be documented and that the resulting four-digit code be used consistently thereafter.

Examples

1. D77 Malignant neoplasms other and unspecified sites.
   D77.1   Gallbladder carcinoma
   D77.2   Hepatoma
2. D99 Other diseases of the digestive system
   D99.1   Dumping syndrome
   D99.2   Celiac disease
   D99.3   Gluten enteropathy
3. L72 Fracture: radius, ulna
   L72.1   Fracture, radius, epiphysis
   L72.2   Fracture: radius, styloid process
   L72.3   Fracture: radius, shaft
4. A86 An occupational health adaptation of
   A86   Toxic effect other substances

   A861   Toxic effect accid. expos. alcohol/petroleum prod.
           NEC*
   A862   Toxic effect solvent, non-alcoh./petr. NEC*
   A863   Toxic effect corros./acid/caust. alk NEC*
   A864   Toxic effect of lead NEC*
   A865   Toxic effect of other metals NEC*
   A866   Toxic effect of carbon monoxide NEC*
   A867   Toxic effect noxious subst. eaten NEC*
   A869   Toxic effect other substances NEC*

Residual rubrics

Residual rubrics are found at the end of a section or subsection; their
description includes the word '. . . other. . .'. Clearly, not elsewhere
classified or 'NEC' is implied for all of the terms in these rubrics. A
knowledge of the boundaries of this section or subsection is required for
the best use of the classification. If in doubt, consult the alphabetical
index.

The practice use of morbidity/diagnostic data

During the last 10 years considerable experience has accrued in the use of
ICHPPC-2 both in sentinel practices and in comprehensive morbidity
studies[16,19,39]. Detailed information on the incidence and prevalence
of diseases in primary care is available in many countries. The analysis of
diagnosis-related information from primary care settings results in two
important conclusions:

   A. Problems with the numerator — the upper portion of a fraction used
to calculate a rate or ratio — tend to be underestimated, while denominator problems, the lower portion of the fraction representing the total
population — are overestimated[35,39].

Episode of illness
Patient movement through health care system

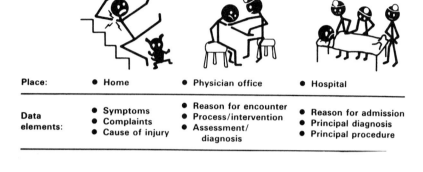

Place:	● Home	● Physician office	● Hospital
Data elements:	● Symptoms ● Complaints ● Cause of injury	● Reason for encounter ● Process/intervention ● Assessment/ diagnosis	● Reason for admission ● Principal diagnosis ● Principal procedure

Source of data:	● Household surveys	● Record files ● Surveys ● Studies ● Reimbursement files	● Hospital record files ● Surveys ● Studies ● Reimbursement files

Fig. 7. Episode of illness: patient movement through health care system.

Episode of illness
Patient continues through health care system

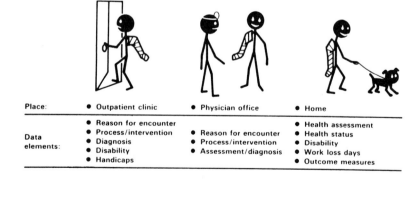

Place:	● Outpatient clinic	● Physician office	● Home
Data elements:	● Reason for encounter ● Process/intervention ● Diagnosis ● Disability ● Handicaps	● Reason for encounter ● Process/intervention ● Assessment/diagnosis	● Health assessment ● Health status ● Disability ● Work loss days ● Outcome measures

Source of data:	● Clinic records ● Surveys ● Reimbursement files	● Record files ● Surveys ● Studies ● Reimbursement files	● Household surveys ● Workmen's Compensation ● Disability insurance files

Fig. 8. Episode of illness: patient continues through health care system.

B. Encounter-based diagnostic information is insufficient to allow the interpretation of the sometimes large variations in results which occur in prevalence and utilization studies carried out within and between the links of the information chain expressed in Figs 7 and 8[40].

To understand these variations resulting from the difference in clinical judgment of primary care physicians and specialists caring for chronic conditions like diabetes, hypertension, depression or chronic respiratory disease, it is necessary to have much more knowledge of the stages of disease known collectively as 'the natural history of disease.'[23,63]. This knowledge can be much more effectively collected during the recording of complete episodes of disease[18,37,57]. In a similar way, the judgment of the quality and appropriateness of medical care will be much more accurate as the transitions in the relationship between the demand of the patient, the diagnostic interpretation by the physician and the medical interventions, are seen as they occur during each phase of an episode. The comprehensive use of ICPC thus can also open a new vista on the long overdue practical use, during the routine of daily work in general practice, of health and functional status measures[7,8,9,51,59].

4 Practical use of ICPC in the process mode

ICPC in the process mode can be used to classify the process of medical care with Components 2, 3, 5, and part of Component 6; however, Component 4 and some rubrics of Component 6, namely, —63, —64, —65, and —69, cannot be used in this way. The classification of the process of medical care may be carried out independently of other uses of ICPC, but preferably it should be carried out simultaneously with the application of the two other modes of ICPC, namely, the reason for encounter mode and the diagnostic mode. The process codes in Components 2, 3, and 5 follow the major headings to be found in the far more detailed IC-Process-PC, which has been developed by the WONCA Classification Committee[3,31]. Three chapters of IC-Process-PC, disposition, site and time of encounter are represented in the data set recommended for use with ICPC and listed in Chapter 7. ICPC and IC-Process-PC are, therefore, compatible one with the other. The details found in IC-Process-PC may be applied to the three-digit ICPC codes by expanding to four or five digits.

In Components 2, 3, 5, and part of Component 6 which can be used to classify the process of care, the rubric codes are standard throughout the chapters at the two-digit level. However, it will often be necessary to refer to the alphabetical index in order to identify the procedure and its correct two-digit code. Sometimes the alpha code of the correct chapter has to be added by the provider who is doing the coding. A limited number of rubrics in the first and seventh components of Chapters W and Y contain procedures such as delivery, abortion, family planning.

The most important principle in coding process is to code all those interventions which take place during that particular encounter and which have a logical relation, either to the reason for encounter or to the assessment (diagnosis) of the health problem, or with both of these elements. As pointed out previously, a fourth or fifth digit may be necessary for increased specificity.

Example 1
—54 Repair/fixation/suture/cast/prosthetic device
 L54.1 Application of casts
 L54.2 Removal of casts

Example 2
—40   Diagnostic endoscopy
D40   Diagnostic endoscopy of the digestive system
D40.1   Gastroscopy

More than one process code may be used for each encounter, but it is extremely important to be consistent. For instance, measuring the blood pressure, which is routine for hypertension, can be coded as K31 on every occasion. Routine examinations, complete or partial, both for body systems or for the general chapter must also be coded with consistency. Below are examples of definitions for complete and partial examinations which have been used in one setting. However, it is essential that each country develops a definition of what constitutes a 'complete examination general' and a 'complete examination — body system' for that culture and that these definitions are used consistently. This will ensure that what is contained in each 'partial examination general' or 'partial examination — body system', in that country, will also have consistency.

Complete examination

The term 'complete examination' refers to an examination which contains those elements of professional assessment which by consensus of a group of local professionals reflects the 'usual standard of care'. This examination will be complete with regard to either the body system (e.g. eye, ear, etc.) or as a complete general examination (Chapter A).

Partial examination

The term 'partial examination' refers to an examination directed to a specific organ (-system) or function or when more than one system is involved in a limited or incomplete examination it is designated 'general' (Chapter A). Most encounters will include a 'partial examination' to evaluate acute and simple illnesses or return visits for chronic illnesses. The following are examples:

Complete examination — general

Example
General check-up A30

Complete examination—Body System

Example
Complete neurological examination N30

Table 7. Standard process components of ICPC

Component 2   Diagnostic and preventive procedures

—30   Medical examination/health evaluation—complete
—31   Medical examination/health evaluation—partial
—32   Sensitivity test
—33   Microbiological/immunological test
—34   Blood test
—35   Urine test
—36   Feces test
—37   Histological/exfoliative cytology
—38   Other laboratory test NEC
—39   Physical function test
—40   Diagnostic endoscopy
—41   Diagnostic radiology/imaging
—42   Electrical tracing
—43   Other diagnostic procedures
—44   Preventive immunizations/medications
—45   Observation/health education/advice/diet
—46   Consultation with primary care provider
—47   Consultation with specialist
—48   Clarification/discussion of RFE/demand
—49   Other preventive procedures

Component 3   Medication, treatment, therapeutic procedures

—50   Medication: prescription/request/renewal/injection
—51   Incision/drainage/flushing/aspiration/removal body fluid (excl. catheterization — 53)
—52   Excision/removal tissue/biopsy/destruction/debridement/cauterization
—53   Instrumentation/catheterization/intubation/dilation
—54   Repair/fixation/suture/cast/prosthetic device (apply/remove)
—55   Local injection/infiltration
—56   Dressing/pressure/compression/tamponade
—57   Physical medicine/rehabilitation
—58   Therapeutic counselling/listening
—59   Other therapeutic procedures/minor surgery, NEC

Component 4   results

—60   Results test/procedures
—61   Results examination/test/record/letter from other provider

Component 5   Administrative

—62   Administrative encounter

Component 6   Referrals and other reasons for encounter

—63   Follow-up encounter unspecified
—64   Encounter/problem initiated by provider
—65   Encounter/problem initiated by other than patient/provider
—66   Referral to other provider/nurse/therapist/social worker (excl. M.D.)
—67   Referral to physician/specialist/clinic/hospital
—68   Other referrals NEC
—69   Other reason for encounter NEC

The dash (—) shown in the first position must be replaced with the appropriate alpha code for each chapter.

Partial examination—General

Example
Limited and incomplete check on several body systems A31

Partial examination—body system

Example
Measuring the blood pressure K31

The following procedures are regarded by the WONCA Classification Committee as included in routine examinations:
— inspection, palpation, percussion, auscultation
— visual acuity
— fundoscopy
— otoscopy
— vibration sense (tuning fork examination)
— vestibular function (excluding calormetric tests)
— digital, rectal and vaginal examination
— vaginal speculum examination
— blood pressure recording
— indirect laryngoscopy
— height/weight
These procedures are to be coded in rubrics —30 and —31.

All other examinations are to be included in other rubrics identified with the help of the index. (See Table 7, which lists the procedures included in Components 2 and 3.)

Component 2 — diagnostic and preventive procedures

Diagnostic and preventive procedures cover a wide range of health care activities including immunizations, screening, risk appraisal, education, and counselling on all diagnostic procedures (see Table 7).

The preventive and screening services are coded when they are provided or ordered during the encounter. Diagnostic procedures are intended to be coded as ordered or performed, regardless of whether the performance is by the provider on site or referred to other providers to be done elsewhere.

Component 3 — medications, treatment, therapeutic procedures

This component is designed to classify those procedures done 'on site' by the coding primary care provider. It is not intended that it be used to document procedures done by providers to whom the patient has been referred. It is necessary to code immunizations in Component 2. Venepuncture, simply to obtain a blood sample for a clinical laboratory assessment, need not be coded; instead, code the laboratory test requested or performed in Component 2.

For medication, the user must decide the criteria for coding 'use', e.g. the issuance of a prescription, or some confirmation by the patient of 'use' of the medication prescribed, e.g. the recording of the fact that the patient was being treated during some phase of an episode, irrespective of whether or not a prescription was issued at each encounter.

Component 4 — results

Component 4 *cannot* be used with ICPC in its process mode.

Component 5 — administrative

This component is designed to classify those instances where the provision of a written document or form by the provider for the patient or other agency is warranted by existing regulations, laws, customs, etc. Writing a referral letter is only considered to be an administrative service, when it is the sole activity performed during the encounter.

Component 6 — referrals

Referrals to other primary care providers, physicians, hospitals, clinics or agencies for therapeutic or counselling purposes, are to be coded in this component. *Do not* code referrals for an X-ray or a laboratory investigation in this component, but in Component 2.

For more specificity, a fourth digit can be added as has been described elsewhere.

Example

—66   Referral to other provider/nurse/therapist/social worker.
    —66.1   Nurse
    —66.2   Physiotherapist
    —66.3   Social worker
    —66.4   Midwife
    —66.5   Psychologist/mental health worker
    —66.6   Dietician/nutritionist
    —66.7   Home help
    —66.8   Health visitor
    —66.9   Community worker

—67.0   Specialist
    —67.01   Internist
    —67.02   Cardiologist
    —67.03   Lung specialist

5 Use of ICPC as a comprehensive classification

If the ICPC is used as a comprehensive classification, covering the reason for encounter, assessment, and process, several extra classification rules (in addition to those previously discussed) are to be observed. This is because the interrelationship between the three modes of ICPC requires adherence to two general principles:

1. When different primary care data elements are to be linked over time involving several encounters, the 'episode of illness' becomes the most logical entity on which to focus[33,57]. An *'episode of illness'* is defined as a health problem or illness occurring in a patient over the period of the time from its onset to its resolution. For the practical use of ICPC, an operational definition of an episode is required. 'An episode of illness is a health problem or illness occurring during the time from the moment of its first presentation to a health care provider until the completion of the last encounter for that same health problem or illness.' Its description includes complaints, concerns, symptoms, investigations, diagnoses, and interventions. This implies that the diagnosis, once established or modified over time, is the most appropriate element available by which to link the sequence of reasons for encounter to each other, to the diagnosis and to the process of care.

2. The reasons for encounter, the process, and the diagnosis, must be coded and recorded in such a way as to maintain the relation between the different elements (Fig. 9). This can be difficult, as many patients have multiple reasons for encounter which can result in two or more distinct diagnoses and processes. Distinction must also be made between several episodes, and each episode must be clearly defined in a predetermined manner.

Example
A 60-year old male patient presents with vomiting and abdominal pain of three day's duration, his fever has subsided but other members of his family have these same symptoms and complaints. He also complains of pain in both knees, in his left wrist and some visible swelling, for which he seeks attention.

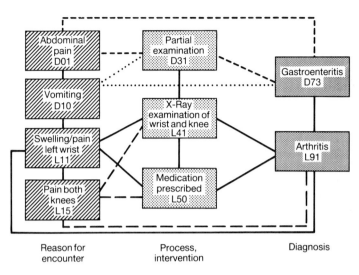

Fig. 9. Data linkage within a single encounter.

Reason for encounter

Abdominal pain — D01
Vomiting — D10
Knee pain — L15
Pain and swelling of wrist — L11

Process

Partial examination of the digestive tract — D31
X-rays of wrist and knee — L41
Medication prescribed for arthritis — L50

Diagnosis

Gastroenteritis — D73
Chronic arthritis — L91

   The correct relationship here is obviously to link the two digestive reasons for encounter with the diagnosis of gastroenteritis (D74) (presumed infection of the digestive system).

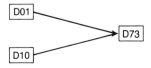

The code for knee pain (L15) should obviously be linked with the diagnosis of chronic arthritis (L91) and with the process/intervention of prescribing medication (L50).

Symptom	Diagnosis	Process
L15 ───────────────→	L91 ───────────────→	L50

It is through such linkages that data can be produced which describe the separation of one episode of illness from another through a number of encounters over time. This allows the study of the relationship between the various reasons for encounter, the processes of care and the assessments within and in between episodes. Figure 10 illustrates an encounter form which is appropriate for comprehensive coding. This is presently being used in the transition project in the Netherlands[37].

Following are a number of other examples which demonstrate the comprehensive use of ICPC.

Example 1

A 65-year-old woman complains of vaginal pain with some bleeding of three weeks' duration. A vaginal inspection shows red dry atrophic walls which bleed easily. The uterus and adnexa are normal. Menses have ceased 10 years previously. A pap smear is carried out, the patient is reassured, and a prescription for estrogen cream is given.

Reason for Encounter	Assessment	Intervention
(1) Vaginal soreness: X01	Senile vaginitis: X11	Partial exam: X31 Pap smear: X37 Medication: X50
(2) Post-menopausal bleeding: X12	Post-menopausal bleeding: X12	Partial exam: X31 Pap smear: X37

Example 2

An 18-year-old woman returns to have sutures removed from a lacerated right hand. The wound has healed nicely. She also complains of drowsiness caused by the antihistamines she is taking for hay fever. Her hay fever has been very bad this last week. The sutures are removed and a prescription for sodium cromoglycate is given instead of the antihistamine.

Reason for Encounter	Assessment	Intervention
(1) Request removal of sutures: S54	Laceration of hand: Sl8	Removal of sutures: S54

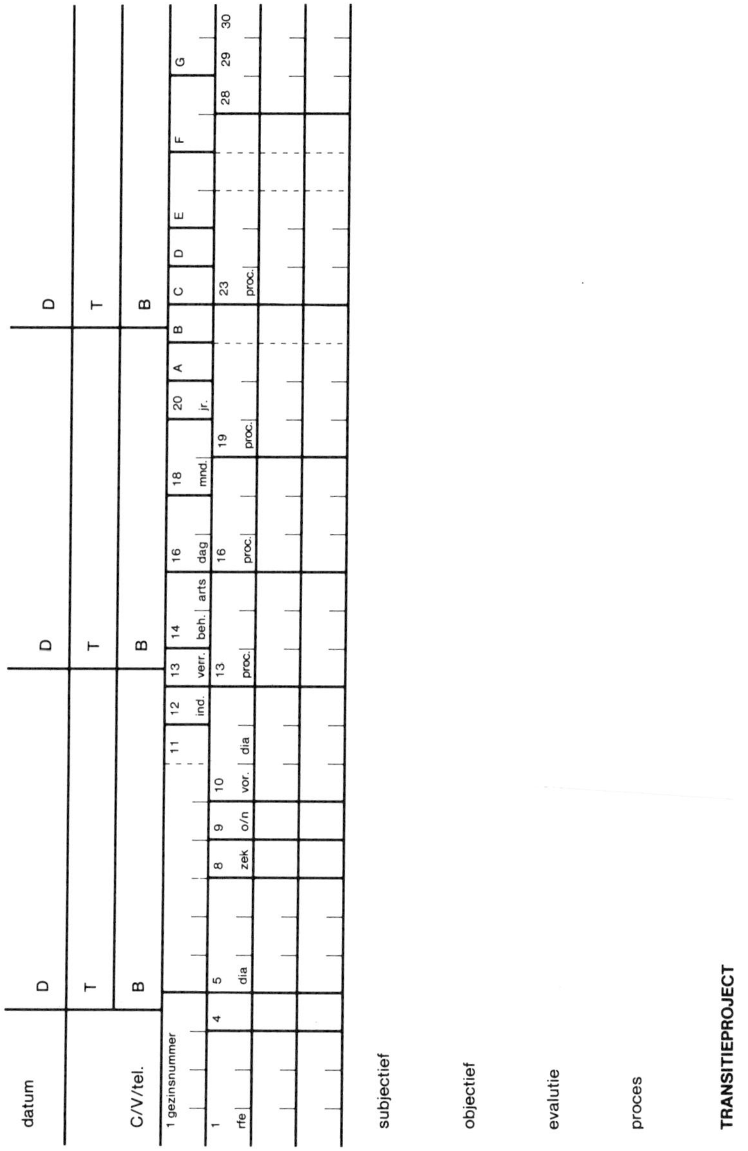

Fig. 10. Example of a self-copying form which allows comprehensive use of ICPC.

(2) Drowsy, sleepy from medication: A85	Adverse effect of medication: A85	
(3) Hay fever: R97	Hay fever: R97	New medication prescribed: R50

Example 3

A labourer, aged 55, weighing 115 kg, presents with a two-week history of increasing cough and shortness of breath. Abnormal findings are a temperature of 38.8°C, red pharynx, moist sounds and wheezes audible in all areas on ausculation of the chest. He is treated with an antibiotic and an expectorant. He is advised to lose some weight.

Reason for Encounter	*Assessment*	*Intervention*
(1) Cough: R05	Bronchitis: R78	Partial exam: R31 Medication: R50
(2) Shortness of breath: R02	Bronchitis: R78	Partial exam: R31 Medication: R50

Additionally, in this case, a diagnosis is coded and a procedure follows on the provider's initiative and no reason for encounter exists for that episode. —64 indicates these occasions.

(3) Problem initiated by provider: T64	Obesity: T82	Diet advised: T45

6 Training in the use of ICPC

There are several ways to train providers in the use of ICPC, depending on the circumstances and also on the aims of the project for which ICPC is being used. If an individual provider wants to become familiar with ICPC and its practical use, this book should be sufficient for this purpose. However, from experience with several recording projects in general practice it is known that most physicians have blind spots when using a classification system. A group of providers, cooperating in the same project, offers a good forum to discuss practical problems with the use of the classification and to prevent the consequences of structural misunderstanding.

Often ICPC will be used in a project where there is a program coordinator or principal investigator (PI) and several collaborating providers. The PI will be the most likely person to become the expert on ICPC and consequently responsible for training the rest of the group in the use of ICPC. Under these circumstances it can be helpful to follow the steps of the training process which by the experience from studies with ICPC have proven to be satisfactory and not too time-consuming.

1. A short introduction is given to the group of participants in the project, not only on the structure of ICPC and its potential, but also on the reasons why the classification system suits the needs of the project. It is pointed out that ICPC is only a feasible tool and not a means in itself, the users should not be intimidated by the sheer volume of the book.
2. The participants are encouraged to study the manual and the classification system and to familiarize themselves at least with the location in the book where specific information can be found.
3. A general discussion in the group gives the opportunity for questions and for more detailed answers and explanations, stressing the fact that it is important to use the classification system correctly in order to guarantee the best possible end results after all the work which has to be done.

4. A series of written vignettes describing patient–physician encounters are presented to the group. All participants are individually encouraged to indicate the essential elements of the encounter and to classify these with ICPC, using the encounter forms designed for the project. The results are discussed in the group, where it usually becomes evident that mistakes are being made, but also that sometimes several different solutions are acceptable. This often happens, either because the vignette itself is not quite clear, or because the limitation in the available information does allow for several plausible interpretations. At the end of this chapter eight vignettes, with their preferred solutions, are presented as illustrations. The encounter form of the Transition Project of the University of Amsterdam is used.

5. The participants now record 10–15 consecutive routine encounters in their own practice on the encounter form and they classify these with ICPC. All forms are scrutinized by the program coordinator and a selection of the forms is discussed in the group.

6. When available, audio or video cassettes with routine encounters, together with the corresponding encounter forms, can be introduced in the group. This approach can be useful when the reliability and the validity of the coding has to be ascertained.

7. Once the project is under way, the coded encounter forms should be checked regularly for completeness and for mistakes. Timely feedback is essential. Especially when the study covers a longer period — for instance one year — regular output from the ongoing analysis of the collected data is very important to motivate the participants. This output can also be discussed in the group in order to prevent the potential fall in the reliability of the coded data and also to ensure an optimal congruence between the potential of ICPC and the goals of the project.

The written vignettes are also coded on the encounter form developed for the Transition Project of the University of Amsterdam[30,37,39]. This form allows three different reasons for encounter, followed by the corresponding diagnoses and interventions. If a diagnosis or intervention is the consequence of more than one reason for encounter, this is indicated with a duplication sign (-). When a reason for encounter forms the start of an episode, a 'N' is written in column 9. An 'R' in this column indicates a repeat (follow-up) encounter. The certainty of the diagnosis is designated with a character in column 8. 'C' stands for certain, if applicable according to the definitions of ICHPPC-2 Defined. 'U' indicates that the coding physician is uncertain whether the diagnosis is correct or whether the necessary inclusion criteria have been fulfilled. If a diagnosis is modified in a later stage during the episode, the former diagnosis which has been modified is repeated in columns 10–12.

Vignettes

1. A woman, aged 18, returns to your office and requests to have the sutures removed from the laceration on her right hand. She also complains that the antihistamine tablets you gave her for hay fever make her very sleepy during the day and the hay fever is troubling her. On examination you find watering eyes, nasal obstruction with a clear nasal discharge, and she sneezes several times. You also examine the laceration on her right hand, which has healed perfectly. You remove the sutures. You replace the antihistamine tablets with a prescription for sodium cromoglycate, after explaining that she may have to compromise on total relief from the symptoms of hay fever as it is better not to overreact in treating the symptoms of the condition (see completed encounter form 1).

D LACERATION R HAND	D ADVERSE EFFECT MEDICATION	D HAYFEVER
T SUTURES REMOVED	T	T NA-CROMOGLYCATE
B	B STOP ANTIHISTAMINICS	B
S 5 4	S 1 8 C R	10 vo dia	S 3 1	S 5 4	19 prx	23 prx
A 8 5	A 8 5 C N		A 4 5			
R 9 7	R 9 7 C R		R 3 1 R 5 0			

Form 1

2. A 23-year old woman working as a typist and also an avid tennis player complains of pain in the left elbow over the last ten days. Her main problem is that she cannot use the left hand during work. On examination you find pain over the left radial epicondyle and the radial muscle group, which feels firmer than on the other side. You diagnose a tennis elbow and you infiltrate the affected area with 1 ml of a corticosteriod solution (see completed encounter form 2).

D TENNISELBOW L	D	D
T LOCAL INJECTION	T	T
B	B	B
1 0	9 3 N	10 vo dia	3 1	5 5	19 prx	23 prx
L 2 8						

Form 2

3. A labourer, aged 55 years and weighing 115 kg, complains of having had increasing bouts of coughing and shortness of breath for one week. When asked, he tells you than he has been sweating and felt feverish for three days. You find a temperature of 38.2°C, a red pharynx, and moist sounds and wheezes are audible in all areas on auscultation of the chest, particularly on the left side. You diagnose an acute bronchitis and you treat him with amoxycillin and an expectorant. You use this opportunity to calculate his Body Mass Index, which is 32.8, and to express your concern with his gross overweight. You advise him strongly to follow the diet you give him and he agrees that his obesity is a real problem. He would like to have some support in his effort to lose weight and you refer him for this reason to a dietitian (nutritionist) who will be able to see him in about six weeks (see completed encounter form 3).

D ACUTE BRONCHITIS	D OBESITY	D
T AMOXYCILLIN	T	T
B	B DIET + DIETICIAN	B
R 0,5	R 7 8 C N	R 3 1 R 5 0	
R 0,2	— — —	— — —	
T 6,4	T 8 2 C N	T 3 1 T 4 5 T 6 6 D	

Form 3

4. You do a house call for a seven-year-old boy, because he has had fever and a sore throat for three days and a rash since early that morning. On examination his temperature is 39.3°C and he has a blush-like erythema of the face and trunk. The tonsillar lymphnodes are markedly enlarged and his throat is bright red with pus on his large tonsils. You diagnose scarlet fever, you prescribe penicillin and arrange a follow-up in a week (see completed encounter form 4).

D SCARLATINA	D	D
T PENICILLIN	T	T
B	B	B
A 0,3	R 7,2 N	R 3 1 R 5 0	
R 2,1	— — —	— — —	
S 0,7	— — —	— — —	

Form 4

5a. A 34-year-old woman comes in for frequency and dysuria. She is also afraid that she suffers from hypertension. In the fresh midstream urine you find 50–60 white blood cells per field (there are no complaints of a vaginitis). You prescribe an antibiotic and you arrange for a urine test in ten days. To your surprise her blood pressure readings are repeatedly 170/100. You decide to measure her blood pressure again when she returns for the results of her urine test in ten days (see completed encounter form 5a).

D CYSTITIS	D ELEVATED BLOODPRESSURE	D
T ANTIBIOTIC	T	T
B URINETEST	B → REPEAT	B

Form 5a

5b. The same patient from encounter 5a returns to get the result of the urine test and to have you check her blood pressure again. The urine test is negative and you tell her that this episode of cystitis is concluded as far as you are concerned and you give her advice on how to deal with a repeat infection. You measure her bloodpressure and the readings are now practically normal: 140/90 and 145/95. You explain the results and advise her not to change her lifestyle and to have her blood pressure checked in 6–9 months (see completed encounter form 5b).

D CYSTITIS	D ELEVATED BP	D
T	T	T
B → OK	B → NOW NORMAL	B

Form 5b

6. A woman, aged 25, who has had two previous babies thinks she may be pregnant again. Her last period was seven weeks previously. The

urine test during consultation confirms the results of the physical examination. She is pregnant. You refer her to a midwife (obstetrician). While you write the referral letter she asks you to remove a mole from in front of her left ear. You have time to do so and you excise the mole. One suture is sufficient to close the wound and you send the mole to a pathologist for further examination (see completed encounter form 6).

D PREGNANT					D MOLE L-EAR				D		
T					T EXCISION				T		
B ➔ MIDWIFE					B ➔ PATHOLOGIST				B		
W‚ 0‚1		dM‚7‚8	C	Nn vo‚dia	Mbc‚3‚1	Mdc‚3‚3	Mc‚6‚6	M prc			
S‚5‚2		S‚8‚2	U	N	S‚3‚1	S‚5‚2	S‚3‚7				

Form 6

7. A 52-year-old man complains that he feels very tired and that he has an urge to cry. He agrees that he feels depressed, but despite all this he has managed to continue to do his job. However, this has become increasingly difficult. He also complains about his working conditions, which are very bad mostly because he cannot cooperate with his boss. You find that your patient is definitely depressed. He is troubled by early morning waking and morning tiredness. He has a decreasing interest in his usual activities. He feels worthless and inappropriate. You diagnose a depression and you propose treatment with an antidepressant. During the 15-minute session you discuss with him both the nature of his depression and how it relates to his working conditions. A prescription for amitryptiline is given and an appointment for next week is made (see completed encounter form 7).

D DEPRESSION					D WORK PROBLEMS				D		
T ANTIDEPRESSANT					T				T		
B PSYCHOTHERAPY ———				B ➔ X				B		
A‚0‚4		P‚7‚6	Cu	oN vo‚dia	Prc‚5‚0	prc‚5‚8	prc				
P‚0‚3			—	—							
Z‚0‚5		Z‚0‚5	C	N		Z‚5‚8					

Form 7

8a. A 42-year-old man complains of having had a plugged feeling in both ears and pain in his right shoulder for ten days. He also wants you to check his bloodpressure. On examination you find wax in both ears, which you remove. You find a limited abduction and limited exorotation of the right shoulder, which is painful. There is local tenderness and you inject corticosteroids after telling the patient that he is suffering from a frozen shoulder. There is elevated blood pressure of 170/105 and you advise the patient to return in ten days (see completed encounter form 8a).

D WAX	D ELEVATED BP	D SHOULDER SYNDROME				
T REMOVED	T	T INJECTION				
B	B RETURN 10 DAYS	B RETURN 10 DAYS				
H 1 3	H 8 1	N	3 1	5 1		
K 3 1	K 8 5	C N	K 3 1			
L 0 8	L 9 2	C N	L 3 1	L 5 5		

Form 8a

8b. Your patient returns for his shoulder. He wants to have a simple analgesic, because although the pain in his shoulder is much better it now bothers him during the night. He also wants to have his blood pressure checked again. You find that there is practically no limitation remaining in the right shoulder and you prescribe two tablets of paracetamol at night. The blood pressure is definitely too high: 180/110 in two readings. You do a partial examination where no other abnormalities are found. Your patient is certainly not overweight and there is no evidence of secondary involvement of heart, kidney, brain, or eye due to hypertension. You order an EKG and some blood tests. You tell him that he suffers from hypertension and you

D SHOULDER SYNDROME	D HYPERTENSION	D				
T PARACETAMOL	T MODURETIC	T				
B	B EKG - BLOOD	B				
5 0	9 2	R	3 1	5 0		
K 3 1	K 8 6	U R	K 8 5	A 3 1	K 3 4	K 4 2

Form 8b

advise him to use a salt-restricted diet during the next two weeks. When he returns for the results you will check his blood pressure again and decide whether or not it is advisable that he be treated with drugs. You ask the patient to return in two weeks (see completed encounter form 8b).

8c. Your patient returns because of his 'hypertension.' He feels all right. He also complains of having had a red and painful nose, for two days. You find his blood pressure is 180/105 and you advise your patient to start using diuretics and to return in four weeks. There is a small boil in the vestibulum of the nose which you open and drain a drop of pus. You prescribe some diachylon ointment (see completed encounter form 8c).

D HYPERTENSION			D BOIL NOSE		D		
T MODURETIC			T DIACHYLON		T		
B			B INCISION		B		
¹ K 8 6	⁴	⁵ K 8 6	⁸ C ⁹ R	¹⁰ vo dia	¹³ K 3 1	¹⁶ K 5 0	¹⁹ proc	²³ proc
R 0 8		R 7 3	C N		R 3 1	R 5 1	R 5 0	

Form 8c

7 Standardized data set for use with ICPC

The use of ICPC as part of a health care information system in primary care settings to record data for subsequent analysis, requires that other basic information must be available in addition to the classification. Any classification is a compromise, its subsequent use in many different settings for slightly different purposes make the need for modifications seem all important. Often, users attempt to modify the structure of the classification; this is inappropriate and in the long run is extremely destructive. Every classification has to be used as one instrument in the health care information system. Inevitably other instruments which record the demography of the population served and of the providers, and which describe the encounters with the patients and the settings in which these occur, are necessary to provide a framework in which the classification can be used[60,64,68].

The following data set is recommended for use with the ICPC.

1. The patient

(a) Age — six digits, date of birth.
(b) Sex — one digit, M/F.

2. The provider type (one digit)

(a) General practitioner/family physician.
(b) Other ambulatory care physician.
(c) Other physicians.
(d) Nurse — community.
(e) Nurse — practice.
(f) Nurse — all others.
(g) Physician's assistant.
(h) Physiotherapist.
(i) Social worker.
(j) Midwife.
(k) Health visitor.
(l) Community health worker.

(m) Lay person acting as the community's health agent.
(n) Other.

3. The encounter

This will always be face-to-face with the provider, which excludes telephone encounters. Separate arrangements can be made to record these, if required.

(a) Date of encounter — six digits, day, month, year.
(b) Site of encounter — one digit.
　　1. Patient's home.
　　2. Physician's office.
　　3. Health centre.
　　4. Ambulatory care health care facility (emergency room, hospital, outpatient).
　　5. Well baby clinic.
　　6. Special clinic site.
　　7. Long stay — hospital or nursing home.
　　8. Other inpatient institution.
(c) Status of the episode to which the reason for encounter and the diagnosis relate:
　　1. Episode presented by the patient for the first time.
　　2. Episode previously presented by the patient to this or another provider, 'follow-up encounter', routine encounter for chronic condition, etc.
　　3. Episode previously presented by the patient to this or another provider but presenting for the first time during a period of continuous registration and coding.
(d) Assessment of the patient's problem, recorded at the highest level of specificity by the provider.
(e) Process of providing primary care.
(f) Referral to:
　　1. Other general practitioner/family physician.
　　2. Other primary care provider:
　　　　— nurse
　　　　— home health worker (health visitor)
　　　　— midwife
　　　　— dentist
　　　　— social worker
　　　　— nutritionist (dietician)
　　　　— physical therapist, occupational therapist
　　　　— mental health worker (psychologist)
　　　　— community agency
　　3. Specialist–ambulatory care (ambulatory surgeon).
　　　　　–hospital.

4. Admission to hospital or other institution.
— Other non-physician provider, including medical institution.

(h) Disposition — The 'disposition' of a patient is a record of the most important communication with regard to follow-up between the individual and the provider of care. Effective recording of dispositions will provide valuable information relating to actual patterns of health care. Many will find that the 2-digit level provides enough specificity, but 3rd and 4th digit rubrics are available to provide more complete information if this is required. A suggested list of more specific rubrics at the 3rd and 4th digit level are available in the IC-Process-PC developed by the Classification Committee of WONCA[31].

When disposition/follow-up is being coded the following rules apply:

1. Code all applicable dispositions, including those made by telephone or staff.
2. At least one disposition should be coded for each encounter.

Dispositions
1. No return appointment.
2. Planned telephone contact.
3. Planned return appointment.
4. Consultation and/or referral to a physician for evaluation or service.
5. Referral to a non-physician or agency.
6. Institutionalization.

(i) Time and/or duration of service — this is specified for an office visit, but these time frames can be applied to other sites.
1. Office encounter — under 6 mins.
2. Office encounter — 6–9 mins.
3. Office encounter — 10–14 mins.
4. Office encounter — 15–29 mins.
5. Office encounter — 30–59 mins.
6. Office encounter — over 1 hr.
7. Office encounter — duration not specified.

8 References

1. Andersen, J E and Lees, E M. Optional hierarchy as a means of increasing the flexibility of a morbidity classification system. **J. Fam. Pract.**, 1978, 10, 1271–1275.
2. An international glossary for primary care. Report of the Classification Committee of the World Organization of National Colleges/Academies and Academic Associations of General Practitioners/Family Physicians (WONCA), 1981. **J. Fam. Pract.**, 1981, 13, 671–681.
3. A process code for primary care (NAPCRG-1). International field trial version, Richmond, VA, North American Primary Care Research Group, 1981.
4. A reason for visit classification for ambulatory care. Hyattsville, MD; U.S. Public Health Service, National Center for Health Statistics, 1979 (DHEW Pub. 79–1352).
5. Bentsen, B G: International classification of primary care, scand. **J. Prim. Health Care,** 1986, 4, 43–50.
6. Bossert, T J and Parker, D A. The political and administrative context of primary health care in the Third World. **Soc. Sci. Med.,** 1984, 18(8), 693–702.
7. Brook, H R and Lohr, K N. Efficacy, effectiveness, variations and quality. **Med. Care** 1985, 23, 710–722.
8. Buck, D, Fry, J and Irvine, D H. A framework for good primary medical care — the measurement and achievement of quality. **J. R. Coll. Gen. Pract.,** 1974, 24, 599–604.
9. Caplan, R M, Bush, J W, and Berry, C C. Health status: types of validity and the index of well being. **Health Services Res.,** 1976, 11, 478–507.
10. Classification of diseases, problems and procedures, 1984. Occasional Paper 26, London, Royal College of General Practitioners, 1984.
11. Donabedian, A. Promoting quality through evaluating the process of patient care. **Med. Care,** 1968, 6, (3).
12. Donabedian, A. The quality of medical care: concept in search of a definition. **J. Fam. Pract.,** 1979, 9, 277–284.
13. Donabedian, A, Wheeler, J R C, and Wyszewianski, L. Quality, cost and health: an integrative model. **Med. Care,** 1982, 20, 975–992.
14. Evans, J L, Hall, H L, and Warford, J. Health care in the developing world: problems of scarcity and choice. **N. Engl. J. Med.,** 1981, 305, 1117–1127.
15. Feinstein, A R. Clinical Epidemiology: the Architecture of Clinical Research. Philadelphia, W B Saunders, 1985.

16. Froom, J. New directions in standard terminology and classifications for primary care. **Public Health Reports,** 1984, 99, 73–77.

17. Froom, J. Primary care classifications: a proposal for ICD-10. In: Role of Informatics in Health Data Coding and Classification Systems. Eds. Cote, R A, Protti, A J, and Scherner, J R. Amsterdam, Elsevier Sci. Publ./JFIP-JMIA, 1985.

18. Gould, M and Azevedo, D. The content of adult primary care episodes. **Public Health Reports,** 1982, 97, 48-57.

19. Green, L A, Wood, M, Becker, L, *et al.* The ambulatory sentinel practice network: purpose, methods and policy. **J. Fam. Pract.** 1984, 18, 275–280.

20. Health Services Research on Primary Care. Program note: National Center for Health Services Research and Health Care Technology Assessment, Washington, D.C., U.S. Department of Health and Human Services, May 1985.

21. Health Services Research 1984. Planning for the third decade of health services research. **Med. Care,** 1985, 23 (Special issue), 377–750.

22. Hjortdahl, P. Medical taxonomy: a general practioner's friend or foe? **Scand. J. Prim. Health Care,** 1986, 4, 1–7.

23. Holland, W W, Ed. Evaluation of Health Care. Oxford, Oxford University Press, 1981.

24. Horst, F, Seelen, A, Vissers, F, Plagge, H, *et al.* Registratie in de Huisarts en Praktijk. **Huisarts Wetensch.,** 1985, 28, 229–234.

25. ICHPPC-2-Defined. Inclusion Criteria for the Use of the Rubrics of the International Classification of Health Problems in Primary Care. Oxford, Oxford University Press, 1983.

26. ICHPPC-2 (International Classification of Health Problems in Primary Care) Oxford, Oxford University Press, 1979.

27. International Classification of Diseases (9th revision). Geneva, World Health Organization, 1977.

28. International Classification of Health Problems in Primary Care (ICHPPC). Chicago, World Organization National Colleges, Academies and Academic Associations of General Practitioners/Family Physicians (WONCA)/American Hospital Association (AHA), 1975.

29. International Classification of Impairments, Disabilities and Handicaps. Geneva, World Health Organization, 1980.

30. International Classification of Primary Care (ICPC). Manual for Use of ICPC and Relevance Studies, as prepared by the WHO Working Party on ICPC. Amsterdam, Department of General Practice, University of Amsterdam,1985.

31. International Classification of Process in Primary Care (IC-Process-PC), Oxford, Oxford University Press, 1986.

32. International Conference on Health Statistics for the Year 2000. Report of WHO on a Bellagio conference. WHO Statistical Publishing House, Budapest, 1984.

33. Kasl, S V. How can epidemiology contribute to the planning of health services research? **Med. Care.,** 1985, 23, 598–666.

34. Kohn, R and White, K L, Eds. Health Care: An International Study. London, Oxford University Press, 1976.

35. Kilpatrick, S J and Boyle, R M, Eds. Primary Care Research. Encounter Records and the Denominator Problem. New York, Praeger, 1984.
36. Kupka, K. International Classification of Diseases: ninth revision. **WHO Chronicle,** 1978, 32, 219–225.
37. Lamberts, H. Aan de diagnose gebonden informatie uit de huisartspraktijk; van een op de prevalentie naar een op de episode georieenteerde epidemiologie. **Ned. Tijdschr. Geneeskd.,** 1986, 130, 292–296.
38. Lamberts, H, Brouwer, H, Groen, A S M, and Huisman, H. Het Transitiemodel in de Huisartspraktijk. **Huisarts Wetensch.,** 1987, 30, 105–113.
39. Lamberts, H. Morbidity in General Practice. Diagnosis-Related Information from the Monitoring Project. Utrecht, Huisartsenpers BV, 1984.
40. Lamberts, H. The use and relevance of the International Classification of Primary Care (ICPC) in structuring patient information. In: Present Status of Computer Support in Ambulatory Care. Eds. Reichertz, P L, Engelbrecht, R, and Piccolo, U. Berlin, Heidelberg, Springer-Verlag, 1987.
41. Lamberts, H, Meads, S, and Wood, M. Classification of reasons why persons seek primary care: pilot study of a new system. **Public Health Rep.,** 1984, 99, 597–605.
42. Lamberts, H, Meads, S, and Wood, M. International classification of primary care: a multi-purpose classification. Presentation at the International Epidemiological Association Meeting, Vancouver, September 1984.
43. Lamberts, H, Meads, S, and Wood, M. Results of the international field trial with the Reason for Encounter classification (RFEC). **Med. Sociale Preventive,** 1985, 30, 80–87.
44. Lamberts, H, Meads, S, and Wood, M. Results of the international field trial with the Reason for Encounter classification (RFEC). In: Role of Informatics in Health Data Coding and Classification Systems. Eds. Cote', R A, Protti, A J, and Scherner, J R. Amsterdam, Elsevier Sci. Publ./JFIP-JMIA, 1985.
45. Lamberts, H, Meads, S, and Wood, M. Reason for Encounter classification for use in primary care. A pilot study in The Netherlands. MEDINFO-83, Eds. van Bemmel/Ball/Wigertz. IFIP-IMIA; North-Holland, 1983.
46. Last, M J, Ed. A Dictionary of Epidemiology. A Handbook Sponsored by the International Epidemiological Association. Oxford, Oxford University Press, 1983.
47. Lipkin, M and Kupka, K, Eds. Psycho-social Factors Affecting Health. New York, Praeger, 1982.
48. Meads, S. The WHO Reason for Encounter classification. **WHO Chronicle,** 1983, 37 (5), 159–162.
49. Meijer, J S, Brouwer, H, and Lamberts, H. De ICPC als diagnostische classificatie I + II. **Huisarts Wetensch.,** 1987, 30, 13–19 and 44–48.
50. Nylenna, M. Why do our patients see us? A study of reasons for encounter in general practice. **Scand. J. Prim. Health Care,** 1985, 3,155–162.
51. Nelson, E, Conger, V, Douglass, R *et al.* Functional health status levels of primary care patients. **J. Am. Med. Ass.,** 1983, 249, 3331–3338.
52. Ovesen, L. Reason for encounter in general practice. **Scand. J. Prim. Health Care,** 1985, 3, 1292–1300.
53. Patients' reasons for visiting physicians: National Ambulatory Medical Care

Survey, United States, 1977–1978. Data from the National Health Survey. Hyattsville, MD: Series 13, 56, 1981 (DHS Publications 82-1717).

54. Psychological factors affecting health assessment, classification and utilization. Report of the World Health Organization on the Bellagio Conference, WHO, Geneva, 1980.

55. Report of the International Conference on Primary Care, Alma Ata, USSR,6–12, September 1978; WHO/Alma Ata/78.10.

56. Report: to develop a classification of the 'Reasons for Contact with Primary Health Care Services'. Report by the Working Party to the ICD Unit of the World Health Organization, Geneva, Switzerland, 1981.

57. Salkever, D S, Skinner, E A, Steinwachs, D M, and Katz, H. Episode-based efficiency comparisons for physicians and nurse practitioners. **Med. Care,** 1982, 20, 143–53.

58. Stevens, J L. Quality of care in general practice: can it be assessed? **J. R. Coll. Gen. Pract.,** 1977, 27, 456–466.

59. Stewart, A L, Ware, J E, and Brook, R H. Advances in the measurement of functional status: construction of aggregate indexes. **Med. Care,** 1981, 19 (Special issue), No. 5.

60. Variations in medical practice. **Health Affairs,** 1984 (Special issue), **3,** 34-148.

61. Weed, L. Medical Records, Medical Education and Patient Care. The Problem-Oriented Record as a Basic Tool. Cleveland (Ohio), Case Western Reserve University Press, 1969.

62. White, K L. Evaluation and medicine, 1982. In: Evaluation in Health Care. Ed. Holland, W. Oxford, Oxford University Press.

63. White, K L. Information for health care: an epidemiological perspective. **Inquiry,** 1980, 17, 296–312.

64. White, K L. Restructuring the international classification of diseases: need for a new paradigm. **J. Fam. Pract.,** 1985, 21, 17–20.

65. Wood, M. Evaluation of Primary Care Classifications and the Potential Impact of the Reason for Encounter Classification; International Conference on Health Statistics for the Year 2000, 1984. Bellagio, Italy, September 27 to October 1, l982. WHO, Statistical Publishing House, Budapest, l984.

66. Wood, M. Family medicine classification systems in evolution. **J. Fam. Pract.,** 1981, 12, 199–200.

67. Wood, M, Mayo, F, and Marsland, D. Practice-based recording as an epidemiological tool. **Am. Rev. Public Health,** 1986, 7, 357–89.

9 Glossary of terms and definitions

Age. The age of the patient at his/her last birthday should be recorded.

Age groups. Standard age groups: Less than 1; 1 to 4; 5 to 14; 15 to 24; 25 to 44; 45 to 64; 65 and greater. These groups may be subdivided into smaller cohorts (for example, 5–9 years and 10–14 years) provided the standard division points are retained.

Age–sex register. The list of all patients by age and sex. The primary purpose of this register is to provide a defined population against which rates of observed occurrence of phenomena in a practice may be calculated. It can also be used to monitor programs, identify groups at special risk, monitor practice size, plan physician education priorities, and for other purposes.

Ancillary staff. Non-medical personnel working in a practice, including nurse or practice sister, health visitor, medical social worker, secretary, practice aide, receptionist, administrator, business manager, bookkeeper, and others. The ancillary staff differs from practice to practice, and from country to country.

Axis. The direction or reference within a classification system. The ICPC Classification is bi-axial, with its primary axis representing body systems (chapters) and the other axis representing components.

Case. A person in the population or study group identified as having the particular disease, health disorder, or condition under investigation.

Chart. The medical dossier or record of a patient.

Chapters. The main divisions within the ICPC. There are 17 chapters primarily representing the body systems.

Classification. A classification system is an arrangement of elements of a subject into groups according to established criteria. In the ICPC the elements are symptoms, signs, complaints, interventions, diseases and injuries, which are grouped together into chapters, components, and rubrics.

    Family of classifications—a group of classifications which describe different aspects of health care problems such as diseases, injuries, external causes, signs and symptoms, operative procedures, and diagnostic tests. There may be a common method for linkage.

Cohort. A defined group of people who are followed up over time so that their experiences and characteristics can be ascertained as they enter successive time and age periods.

Compatibility. The ability to exist together in harmony. In the area of classifications, the ability to interrelate in an established consistent manner.

Comparability. The quality or state of being equivalent or similar. One classification may be a subset of a larger system and would be equivalent at some level; for example, the diagnosis/disease component 7 of the ICPC is comparable with the ICD-9 and ICHPPC-2.

Complaint. A symptom or disorder expressed by the patient when seeking care. (*See* Problem.)

Component. A constituent part of a classification. Components sum to a total by means of a common linkage method.

Consultant. A physician with special competence in a particular area of medicine who provides services related to this area at the request of another health care provider.

Consultation. In the United Kingdom, Australia, and New Zealand a consultation is an occasion on which a patient receives professional advice, help, or treatment, usually on the doctor's premises. A domiciliary consultation (usually called home visit or house call) occurs when the doctor and a consultant meet at the patient's house to assess the patient. In North America a consultation is an exchange of information between doctors about a patient. The consultation may be informal (corridor consultation) or may involve the examination of the patient by the consultant in a more formal fashion, either in the presence or absence of the primary care physician, with a later exchange of information by verbal or written communication.

Contact. See Encounter.

Core. The basic essential part of an entity or class. A core group of people.

Denominator. The population at risk in the calculation of a rate or ratio.

Demand. The way in which perceived need is translated into a 'request(s) for health care' by a primary care provider. Demand can be classified in the form of the 'reason for encounter'.

Descriptive studies. A form of observational study which does not test a specific hypothesis. Usually, it takes the form of an analysis of routine statistics and does not identify individual subjects.

Diagnosis. A formal statement of the provider's understanding of the patient's problems.

1. *Principal diagnosis* (main diagnosis) — the most important problem, as determined by the health care provider.

2. *Associated diagnosis* (concurrent diagnosis) — another diagnosis made at the same time as the principal diagnosis. Normally, any ongoing condition which is presently under control and of which the patient does not complain will not be recorded.

Diagnostic criteria. Those signs, symptoms, and investigative findings that are essential to making a diagnosis.

Diagnostic index. A system in which the disease, illness, and social problems in a patient population are recorded by diagnosis, or problem, date of presentation, patient name (or number), age, and sex. This index helps in retrieval of the medical records for cohorts of patients with similar health problems, and may be used to facilitate follow-up.

Disability. Any restriction or lack (resulting from an impairment) of ability to perform an activity in the manner or within the range considered normal for a human being.

Disease. The failure of the physiological or psychological adaptive mechanisms of an organism to counteract adequately, the stimuli or stresses to which it is subject, resulting in a disturbance in the function or structure of any part, organ, or system of that body.
1. *Acute disease* (short-term disease) — an episode of disease with a duration of four weeks or less.
2. *Subacute disease* — an episode of disease with a duration of between four weeks and six months.
3. *Chronic disease* (long-term disease) — an episode lasting six months or more.

Effectiveness. The extent to which a specific intervention, procedure, regimen, or service, when deployed in the field, does what it is intended to do for a defined population.

Efficacy. The extent to which a specific intervention, procedure, regimen or service produces a beneficial result under ideal conditions. Ideally, the determination of efficacy is based on the results of a randomized controlled trial.

Efficiency. The effects or end-results achieved in relation to the effort expended in terms of money, resources, and time. The extent to which the resources used to provide a specific intervention, procedure, regimen, or service of known efficacy and effectiveness are minimized. A measure of the economy (or cost in resources) with which a procedure of known efficacy and effectiveness is carried out.

Encounter. Any professional interchange between a patient and one or more members of a health care team. One or more problems or diagnoses may be identified at each encounter. Analyses of encounter data should distinguish encounters from problems.
1. *Direct encounter* (face-to-face meeting) — an encounter in which

there is face-to-face meeting of patient and professional. This can be further divided into:

(a) *Office encounter* (surgery encounter, consultation in the U.K. and South Africa) — a direct encounter in the provider's office or surgery.

(b) *Home encounter* (housecall, visit in the U.K. and Australia, home visit or housecall in South Africa) — a direct encounter occurring at the patient's residence (this includes home or a friend's home where a patient is visiting, hotel, room, etc).

(c) *Hospital encounter* — a direct encounter in the hospital setting. One encounter is counted for each patient visit. Hospital encounters are further subdivided:

  (i) *Inpatient encounter* — a direct encounter with an inpatient.

  (ii) *Outpatient encounter* — a direct encounter with an outpatient in either the emergency room or the outpatient clinic.

(d) *Problem contact* — a patient–provider transaction with regard to one problem. There may be several problem contacts during each encounter.

2. *Indirect encounter* — an encounter in which there is no physical or face-to-face meeting between the patient and the professional. These encounters may be subdivided by the mode of communication, e.g., telephone encounter, written encounter, or encounter by message or through a third party.

Episode. For the practical use of ICPC an operational definition of an episode is required. 'An episode of illness is a health problem or illness occurring during the time from the moment of its first presentation to a health care provider until the completion of the last encounter for that same health problem or illness.' This definition is illustrated in Figs 2, 7, and 8.

Examination. Culture-specific — unique to each country.

1. *Complete* — the term 'complete examination' refers to an examination which contains those elements of professional assessment which by consensus of a group of local professionals reflects the 'usual standard of care'. This examination will be complete with regard to either the body system (e.g. eye, ear, etc.) or as a complete general examination (Chapter A).

2. *Partial* — The term 'partial examination' refers to an examination directed to a specific organ (or system) or function or to the general chapter but which is limited and incomplete. Most encounters will include a 'partial examination' to evaluate acute and simple illnesses or return visits for chronic illnesses.

Family. A group of persons sharing a common household. A relationship (including, but not necessarily limited by, blood or marriage ties) is implied. For purposes of this definition, persons who temporarily reside away from the household are included.

Family physician/general practitioner. A physician who provides and coordinates personal, primary, and continuing comprehensive health care to individuals and families. He/she provides care for both sexes of all ages, for physical, behavioural, and social problems.

Function.
1. *Functional index* — a numerical indication of a specific function of a given population derived from a specified composite formula.
2. *Function indicator* — a variable, susceptible to direct measurement, which reflects the level of function of persons in a community (these measures may be used as components in the calculation of a function index).
3. *Function status index* — a measure designed to describe the level of function of members of a population, which assesses physical function, emotional well-being, activities of daily living, feelings, etc.

Handicap. A disadvantage for a given individual resulting from an impairment or a disability that limits or prevents the fulfillment of a role that is normal (depending on age, sex, and social and cultural factors) for that individual.

Health care. Assessment, health maintenance, therapy, education, promotion of health, prevention of illness, and related activities (provided by qualified professionals) to improve or maintain health status.

Health care provider. A qualified person who renders health care services. Besides the primary physician, other health care providers include qualified graduates (professionals and paraprofessionals) of disciplines other than medicine who also render health care. These include, for example, dentist, pharmacist, physician associate, medex, physiotherapist, nurse practitioner — graduate nurse, public health nurse, psychologist, social worker, minister of religion, and others.

Health care system. The organizational structure through which health care is provided.

Hierarchical. The characteristic of entities being arranged in a graded series. The ICPC is organized on the basis of three digit rubrics which are further defined. These more precisely defined elements of their respective three-digit categories can be collapsed back to the three-digit level.

Hogben number. A unique personal identifying number constructed by using a sequence of digits for birth date, sex, birth place, and other identifiers.

Illness. A condition marked by pronounced deviation from the normal health state. (The subjective state of the person who feels aware of not being well).

Illness behaviour. The conduct of persons in response to abnormal body signals. Such behavior influences the manner in which a person monitors, defines, and interprets bodily symptoms, takes remedial actions, and uses the health care systems.

Impairment. Any reduction of functional, psychological, physiological, and anatomical capacity to participate in activities of daily life.

Incidence. The number of new cases of a given disease arising within a defined population during a defined period of time (usually one year).

Information system. A combination of vital and health statistical data drawn from multiple sources, used to derive information about the health needs and demands, health resources, costs, use of health services and outcomes of use, by the population of a specified jurisdiction.

Intervention. That which is being done by a medical care provider and which is based on explicit professional considerations.

Linkage. In a classification system, the linkage is the manner in which parts of separate classifications can be united.

Mode. One of the several ways in which a certain tool or instrument can be used.

Module. Part of the whole; a section or separate unit. In the 'family of classifications' concept, modules have been described as 'separate classifications which may be united through a common linkage system'.

Morbidity. Any departure, subjective or objective, from a state of physiological or psychological well being. In this sense, sickness, illness, and morbid conditions are synonymous.

NEC. Not elsewhere classified. Code to a ICPC rubric containing this abbreviation only when the ICPC term is not included in another rubric.

Nomenclature. A systematically arranged set of names, as of anatomical structures, organisms, diseases, etc. A list of all approved terms for describing and recording observations.

NOS. Not otherwise specified. Coding to a rubric containing this abbreviation means that the term to be coded is expressed in vague terms which cannot be classified to a more specific rubric.

Nosology. The classification of ill persons into groups by whatever criteria, based on agreement as to the boundaries of the groups.

Numerator. The upper portion of a fraction used to calculate a rate or a ratio.

NYD. Not yet diagnosed. This follows a diagnosis in which the diagnostic tests are incomplete and more specificity of the type (cause, organism or site) cannot yet be determined.

Observational study. A study in which nature is allowed to take its course and changes or differences in one characteristic are studied in relation to changes or differences in another characteristic, without the intervention of the investigator(s).

Open-ended. The ability of a classification to be organized in such a manner as to allow for contingencies and permit additional codes.

Patient. A person who receives or contracts for professional advice or services from a health care provider.

1. *Registered patient* — a patient who receives ongoing health care from a practice (excludes former, temporary, transient patients).
2. *Visiting patient* — a registered patient who has received services from the practice at least once in the last two years. This includes attending patients.
3. *Attending patient* — a registered patient who has personally received services from the practice in the past year.
4. *Non-visiting patient* — a registered patient who has received no services from the practice within the last two years.
5. *Temporary or transient patient* — a patient who receives one or more services from a practice, but who usually receives health care elsewhere.
6. *Formerly registered patient* — a patient (excluding temporary or transient patients) who has previously been registered, but who is no longer considered (by the practice or by personal determination) to be part of the practice population, and is removed from the register.
7. For practices registered by families:
    (a) *Active registered patient* — a registered patient who has received services from a practice at least once and belongs to a family, one member of which has received services within the last two years.
    (b) *Inactive registered patient* — a registered patient who has received services from the practice at least once, but neither he nor any member of his family has received services within the last two years.

Patients at risk. Patients from the practice population considered to be at greater risk for a disease than other individuals in the same population.

Perceived need. A felt need. It usually refers to need for health care that is felt by the person or community concerned, but which may not be perceived by health professionals.

Person-time. A unit of measurement comprising persons and time, used as denominator in instantaneous incidence rates. It is the sum of individual units of time over which the persons in the study population have been exposed to the condition of interest.

Physician of first contact. The first physician seen by a patient during an episode of illness or injury, or for preventive and/or health education matters.

Population at risk. A population of persons, within a geographically defined area, a random sample or a group selected by specific criteria from the greater population, may be used. At times the registered patient population may be considered the population at risk.

1. *Practice population* — the total number of active registered patients in a practice.
2. *Study population* — All patients included in a study during the period of a project.
3. *Registered population* — The total number of active registered patients in a practice, taken at the mid-point of a study. It is often difficult to count this population. It may be possible to calculate the population from encounter data; if this is done, the method used should be specified.

Precursor. An early stage in the course of a disease or a condition or the state preceding pathological onset of a disease; sometimes detectable by screening.

Prevalence. The number of cases of a given disease present in a defined population at one point in time (point prevalence) or during a defined period of time (period prevalence).

Primary care (primary health care). 'Primary health care is essential health care made universally accessible to individuals and families in the community by means acceptable to them, through their full participation and at a cost that the community and country can afford. It forms an integral part of the country's health system, of which it is the nucleus, and of the overall social economic development of the community' (WHO — Alma Ata, 1978). With regards to the work of general practitioners/family physicians this emphasizes responsibility for the patient, beginning at the time of the first encounter and continuing thereafter. This includes overall management and coordination of health care, such as appropriate use of consultants, specialists, and other medical/health care resources. In addition, maintenance of continuity on a long-term basis, including coordination of secondary and tertiary care is required.

Primary physician (primary care physician). A family physician, general practitioner or other specialist who practices primary care.

Problem. A provider-determined assessment of anything that concerns a patient, the provider (in relation to the health or the patient), or both. Problems should be recorded at the highest level of specificity determined at the time of that particular visit.

1. *New problem* — the first presentation of a problem, including the first presentation of a recurrence of a previously resolved problem, but excluding the presentation of a previously assessed problem to a different provider.
2. *Continuing problem* — a previously assessed problem which

requires ongoing care. It includes follow-up for a problem or an initial presentation to a provider of a problem previously assessed by another provider.

Problem-oriented medical record (POMR). A medical record in which the patient's history, physical findings, laboratory results, etc. are organized to give a cumulative record of problems rather than disease. The record includes subjective, objective, and significant negative information, discussions and conclusions, and diagnostic and treatment plans with respect to each problem.

Process. That which is done in the course of the management of a reason for encounter, problem or disease identified by a provider in a health care system.

Provider. A person to whom a patient has access when contacting the care system. In the majority of instances, this will be a professional such as a general practitioner, a nurse, a midwife, a physician assistant, a medical social worker, a physical therapist, or other allied health personnel. In some cultures, the provider may be a lay person with limited or no medical training.

Reason for encounter. The agreed statement of the reason(s) why a person enters the health care system, representing the demand for care by that person. The terms written down and later classified by the provider, clarify the reason for encounter and consequently the patient's demand for care, without interpreting it in the form of a diagnosis. The reason for encounter should be recognized by the patient as an acceptable description of that person's demand for care.

Recorder. The person who records or supervises the recording of information under study.

Record (medical). A file of information relating to transaction in personal health care, comprising data on health status together with personal identifying data, and often incorporating administrative and economic data.

Record linkage. Any process of linking different items of information (e.g. a record) on the same individual.

Referral. A referral is made when resources outside any health care provider's command (whether in or outside the practice) are requested on the patient's behalf. Patients may be referred for a specific service, a general opinion, or for other desirable reasons.

Reliability. The extent to which the same measure will provide the same results under the same conditions. The study of reliability corresponds to the *inter* and *intra*-observer variability.

Sickness. A state of social dysfunction, i.e., a role that the individual assumes when ill (the sickness role).

Stratification. Separating a sample into several sub-samples according to specified criteria, such as age groups, socio-economic status, etc.

Supplemental classifications. Supplemental classifications are separate, additional classifications which exist without standard linkage capability. They are used in combination with other more basic classification systems. The ICD is a basic classification of disease while a classification of morphology is a supplemental classification.

Symptom. Any subjective evidence of disease or of a patient's condition, i.e., such evidence as perceived by the patient. Cough, pain, and bleeding are symptoms.

Syndrome. A symptom complex in which the symptoms/signs coexist more frequently than would be expected by chance on the assumption of independence.

Taxonomy. A systematic classification into related groups.

Thesaurus. A 'storehouse' of knowledge such as an exhaustive encyclopedia or dictionary.

Terminology. The vocabulary of a science. In the context of morbidity classification systems the words relating to the diseases, symptoms, problems, etc., are the terminology of that system.

Transition. The transition of a health problem or illness is the process of change which occurs during the episode of illness as it passes through the different elements of health care, including all the changes in the status or phase of that problem or illness.

Validity. The extent to which a particular measure reflects what it is supposed to measure.

Variable. Any quantity which varies.

Visit. *See* Encounter.

Want. Individual's own recognition of his/her desire for health care services.

10 International Classification of Primary Care: tabular list

Standard Process Components of ICPC

The dash (—) shown in first position must be replaced with the appropriate alpha code for each chapter.

Component 2 — DIAGNOSTIC AND PREVENTIVE PROCEDURES
—30 Medical examination/health evaluation — complete
—31 Medical examination/health evaluation — partial
—32 Sensitivity test
—33 Microbiological/immunological test
—34 Blood test
—35 Urine test
—36 Feces test
—37 Histological/exfoliative cytology
—38 Other laboratory test NEC
—39 Physical function test
—40 Diagnostic endoscopy
—41 Diagnostic radiology/imaging
—42 Electrical tracings
—43 Other diagnostic procedures
—44 Preventive immunizations/medications
—45 Observation/health education/advice/diet
—46 Consultation with primary care provider
—47 Consultation with specialist
—48 Clarification/discussion of patient's RFE/demand
—49 Other preventive procedures

Component 3 — MEDICATION, TREATMENT, THERAPEUTIC PROCEDURES
—50 Medication–prescription/request/renewal/injection
—51 Incision/drainage/flushing/aspiration/removal body fluid (*excl.* catheterization — 53)
—52 Excision/removal tissue/biopsy/destruction/debridement/cauterization
—53 Instrumentation/catheterization/intubation/dilation
—54 Repair/fixation–suture/cast/prosthetic device (apply/remove)
—55 Local injection/infiltration
—56 Dressing/pressure/compression/tamponade

—57   Physical medicine/rehabilitation
—58   Therapeutic counselling/listening
—59   Other therapeutic procedures/minor surgery, NEC

Component 4 — RESULTS

—60   Results tests/procedures
—61   Results examination/test/record/letter from other provider

Component 5 — ADMINISTRATIVE

—62   Administrative procedure

Component 6 — REFERRALS AND OTHER REASONS FOR ENCOUNTER

—63   Follow-up encounter unspecified
—64   Encounter/problem initiated by provider
—65   Encounter/problem initiated by other than patient/provider
—66   Referral to other provider/nurse/therapist/social worker (*excl.* M.D.)
—67   Referral to physician/specialist/clinic/hospital
—68   Other referrals NEC
—69   Other reason for encounter NEC

A General and unspecified

Component 1 — Symptoms and complaints

A01 PAIN: GENERALIZED/UNSPECIFIED
A02 CHILLS
A03 FEVER
A04 GENERAL WEAKNESS/TIREDNESS/ILL-FEELING (*excl.* PSYCHOL.)
A05 GENERAL DETERIORATION (*excl.* PSYCHOL.)
A06 FAINTING (SYNCOPE), LOSS OF CONSCIOUSNESS
A07 COMA
A08 SWELLING (*excl.* EDEMA K07)
A09 SWEATING PROBLEMS
A10 BLEEDING, SITE NOS
A12 ALLERGY/ALLERGIC REACTION NOS
A13 CONCERN ABOUT DRUG REACTION
A14 INFANTILE COLIC
A15 EXCESSIVE CRYING INFANT
A16 IRRITABLE/FIDGETY INFANT
A17 OTHER GENERAL SYMPT. OF INFANTS NEC
A20 EUTHANASIA REQUEST/DISCUSSION
A25 FEAR OF DEATH
A26 FEAR OF CANCER, NOS, NEC
A27 FEAR OF OTHER DISEASE NOS, NEC
A28 DISABILITY/IMPAIRMENT NOS
A29 OTHER GENERAL SYMPT./COMPLT.

Component 2 — Diagnostic and preventive procedures
A30–A49

Component 3 — Medication, treatment and therapeutic procedures
A50–A59

Component 4 — Results
A60–A61

Component 5 — Administrative
A62

Component 6 — Referrals and Other Reasons for Encounter
A63–A69

Component 7 — Diagnosis/Diseases
A70 TUBERCULOSIS, GENERALIZED (*excl.* RESPIRATORY R70)
A71 MEASLES
A72 CHICKENPOX
A73 MALARIA

A74 RUBELLA
A75 INFECTIOUS MONONUCLEOSIS
A76 OTHER VIRAL DISEASES WITH EXANTHEMS
A77 OTHER VIRAL DISEASES, NOS
A78 OTHER INFECTIOUS DISEASES NOS

A79 CARCINOMATOSIS (UNKNOWN PRIMARY SITE)

A80 ACCIDENT/INJURY NOS
A81 MULTIPLE TRAUMA/INTERNAL INJURIES CHEST, PELVIS, ABDOMEN
A82 LATE EFFECTS OF TRAUMA
A84 POISONING BY MEDICAL AGENT
A85 ADVERSE EFFECT MEDICAL AGENT PROPER DOSE
A86 TOXIC EFFECT OTHER SUBSTANCES
A87 COMPLICATION SURGERY/MEDICAL TREATMENT, X-RAY
A88 ADVERSE EFFECTS PHYSICAL FACTORS NEC (*excl.* H85)
A89 EFFECTS (LATE) PROSTHETIC DEVICE/APPLIANCE NEC

A90 MULTIPLE CONGENITAL SYNDROMES/CONGENITAL ANOMALIES

A91 INVESTIGATION WITH ABNORMAL RESULTS, NOS (*excl.* B84, B85, B86, X86, U98)
A92 TOXOPLASMOSIS INCL. CONGENITAL
A93 PREMATURE/IMMATURE LIVEBORN INFANT*
A94 ALL PERINATAL MORBIDITY
A95 PERINATAL MORTALITY
A96 DEATH (*excl.* PERINATAL)
A97 NO DISEASE
A99 OTHER GENERALIZED DISEASES/MULTIPLE SYNDROMES

*Liveborn infant weighing less than 2500 g at birth.

B   Blood, blood-forming organs, lymphatics, spleen

Component 1 — Symptoms and complaints
B02   ENLARGED LYMPH GLAND(S)
B03   OTHER SYMPT. LYMPHATIC GLANDS
B04   SYMPT.BLOOD/BLOOD-FORMING ORGANS
B25   FEAR OF AIDS
B26   FEAR OF CANCER OF BLOOD/BLOOD-FORMING ORGANS/
       LYMPHATICS/SPLEEN
B27   FEAR OF OTHER BLOOD/LYMPH DISEASE
B28   DISABILITY/IMPAIRMENT
B29   OTHER SYMPT./COMPLT.BLOOD/BLOOD-FORMING ORGANS/
       SPLEEN NOS

Component 2 — Diagnostic and preventive procedures
B30–B49

Component 3 — Medication, treatment, and therapeutic procedures
B50–B59

Component 4 — Results
B60–B61

Component 5 — Administrative
B62

Component 6 — Referrals and other reasons for encounter
B63–B69

Component 7 — Diagnosis/diseases
B70   ACUTE LYMPHADENITIS
B71   CHRONIC/NON—SPECIFIC LYMPHADENITIS/MESENTERIC

B72   HODGKIN'S DISEASE
B73   LEUKEMIA
B74   OTHER MALIGNANT NEOPLASMS
B75   BENIGN NEOPLASMS

B76   RUPTURED SPLEEN
B77   OTHER INJURIES

B78   HEREDITARY HEMOLYTIC ANEMIAS
B79   OTHER CONGENITAL ANOMALIES

B80   IRON DEFICIENCY ANEMIA
B81   PERNICIOUS/FOLATE DEFICIENCY ANEMIA
B82   ANEMIA OTHER/UNSPECIFIED

B83 PURPURA/COAGULATION DEFECTS/ABNORMAL
PLATELETS
B84 ABNORMAL WHITE CELLS
B85 ABNORMAL UNEXPLAINED BLOOD TEST
B86 OTHER HEMATOLOGICAL ABNORMALITY
B87 SPLENOMEGALY
B90 HIV—INFECTION (*incl.* AIDS/ARS)
B99 OTHER DISORDERS OF BLOOD/LYMPH/SPLEEN

D Digestive

Component 1 — Symptoms and complaints
D01 GENERALIZED ABDOMINAL PAIN/CRAMPS
D02 STOMACH ACHE/STOMACH PAIN
D03 HEARTBURN
D04 RECTAL/ANAL PAIN
D05 PERIANAL ITCHING
D06 OTHER LOCALIZED ABDOMINAL PAIN
D08 FLATULENCE, GAS PAIN, BELCHING, WINDY
D09 NAUSEA
D10 VOMITING (*excl.* BLOOD D14/PREGNANCY W06)
D11 DIARRHEA
D12 CONSTIPATION
D13 JAUNDICE
D14 HEMATEMESIS/VOMIT BLOOD
D15 MELENA/BLACK, TARRY STOOLS
D16 RECTAL BLEEDING
D17 INCONTINENCE OF BOWEL (FECAL)
D18 CHANGE IN FECES/BOWEL MOVEMENTS
D19 SYMPT./COMPLT.TEETH, GUMS
D20 SYMPT./COMPLT.MOUTH, TONGUE, LIPS
D21 SWALLOWING PROBLEMS
D22 WORMS/PINWORMS/OTHER PARASITES
D24 ABDOMINAL MASS NOS
D25 CHANGE IN ABDOMINAL SIZE/DISTENSION
D26 FEAR OF CANCER OF DIGESTIVE SYSTEM/ORGAN
D27 FEAR OF OTHER DIGESTIVE DISEASE
D28 DISABILITY/IMPAIRMENT
D29 OTHER SYMPT./COMPLT.DIGEST.

Component 2 — Diagnostic and preventive procedures
D30–D49

Component 3 — Medication, treatment, and therapeutic procedures
D50–D59

Component 4 — Results
D60–D61

Component 5 — Administrative
D62

Component 6 — Referrals and other reasons for encounter
D63–D69

Component 7 — Diagnosis/diseases

D70 INFECTIOUS DIARRHEA, DYSENTERY
D71 MUMPS
D72 INFECTIOUS HEPATITIS
D73 OTHER PRESUMED INFECTIONS OF DIGESTIVE SYSTEM

D74 MALIGN. NEOPL. STOMACH
D75 MALIGN. NEOPL. COLON, RECTUM
D76 MALIGN. NEOPL. PANCREAS
D77 MALIGN. NEOPL. OTHER AND UNSPECIFIED SITES
D78 BENIGN NEOPLASMS

D79 FOREIGN BODY THROUGH ORIFICE
D80 OTHER INJURIES

D81 CONGENITAL ANOMALIES DIGESTIVE SYSTEM
D82 DISEASE OF TEETH/GUMS
D83 DISEASE OF MOUTH/TONGUE/LIPS
D84 DISEASE OF ESOPHAGUS
D85 DUODENAL ULCER
D86 OTHER PEPTIC ULCERS
D87 DISORDERS OF STOMACH FUNCTION/GASTRITIS
D88 APPENDICITIS
D89 INGUINAL HERNIA
D90 HIATUS (DIAPHRAGM) HERNIA
D91 OTHER ABDOMINAL HERNIA
D92 DIVERTICULAR DISEASE INTESTINES
D93 IRRITABLE BOWEL SYNDROME
D94 CHRONIC ENTERITIS/ULCERATIVE COLITIS
D95 ANAL FISSURE/PERIANAL ABSCESS (*excl.* PILONIDAL CYST S85)
D96 HEPATOMEGALY
D97 CIRRHOSIS/OTHER LIVER DISEASE
D98 CHOLECYSTITIS/CHOLELITHIASIS
D99 OTHER DISEASE DIGESTIVE SYST. (*excl.* HEMORRHOIDS K96)

F Eye

Component 1 — Symptoms and complaints

F01 EYE PAIN
F02 RED EYE
F03 DISCHARGE FROM EYE
F04 FLOATERS/SPOTS
F05 OTHER PROBLEMS WITH VISION (*excl.* BLINDNESS F94)
F13 ABNORMAL SENSATIONS OF EYE
F14 ABNORMAL EYE MOVEMENTS
F15 ABNORMAL APPEARANCE OF EYES
F16 SYMPT. OF EYELIDS
F17 SYMPT./COMPLT. GLASSES
F18 SYMPT./COMPLT. CONTACT LENS
F27 FEAR OF EYE DISEASE
F28 DISABILITY/IMPAIRMENT
F29 OTHER SYMPT./COMPLT. OF EYE

Component 2 — Diagnostic and preventive procedures

F30–F49

Component 3 — Medication, treatment, and therapeutic procedures

F50–F59

Component 4 — Results

F60–F61

Component 5 — Administrative

F62

Component 6 — Referrals and other reasons for encounter

F63–F69

Component 7 — Diagnosis/diseases

F70 INFECTIOUS CONJUNCTIVITIS (VIRAL/BACTERIAL)
F71 ALLERGIC CONJUNCTIVITIS
F72 BLEPHARITIS/STYE/CHALAZION
F73 OTHER INFECTIONS OF EYE (*excl.* HERPES, TRACHOMA)

F74 NEOPLASMS OF EYE/ADNEXA

F75 CONTUSION/ABRASIONS/BLACKEYE
F76 FOREIGN BODY IN EYE
F79 OTHER INJURIES

F80 BLOCKED LACRIMAL DUCT OF INFANT
F81 OTHER CONGENITAL ANOMALIES EYE

F82 DETACHED RETINA
F83 RETINOPATHY, DIABETIC AND HYPERTENSIVE
F84 MACULAR DEGENERATION
F85 CORNEAL ULCER (*incl.* HERPETIC)
F86 TRACHOMA
F91 REFRACTIVE ERRORS
F92 CATARACT
F93 GLAUCOMA
F94 BLINDNESS, ALL TYPES
F95 STRABISMUS
F99 OTHER DISEASES EYE/ADNEXA

H Ear

Component 1 — Symptoms and complaints
H01   EAR PAIN/EARACHE
H02   HEARING COMPLAINTS (*excl.* DEAFNESS H84)
H03   RINGING/BUZZING/TINNITUS
H04   DISCHARGE FROM EAR (*excl.* BLOOD H05)
H05   BLOOD IN/FROM EAR
H13   PLUGGED FEELING
H15   CONCERN WITH APPEARANCE OF EARS
H27   FEAR OF EAR DISEASE
H28   DISABILITY/IMPAIRMENT
H29   OTHER SYMPT./COMPLT.OF EAR

Component 2 — Diagnostic and preventive procedures
H30–H49

Component 3 — Medication, treatment, and therapeutic procedures
H50–H59

Component 4 — Results
H60–H61

Component 5 — Administrative
H62

Component 6 — Referrals and other reasons for encounter
H63–H69

Component 7 — Diagnosis/diseases
H70   OTITIS EXTERNA
H71   ACUTE OTITIS MEDIA/MYRINGITIS
H72   SEROUS OTITIS MEDIA, GLUE EAR
H73   EUSTACHIAN SALPINGITIS
H74   CHRONIC OTITIS MEDIA, OTHER INFECTIONS OF EAR

H75   NEOPLASMS OF EAR

H76   FOREIGN BODY IN EAR
H77   PERFORATION TYMPANIC MEMBRANE (*excl.* INFECTION H71)
H78   SUPERFICIAL INJURY OF EAR
H79   OTHER INJURIES

H80   CONGENTAL ANOMALIES OF EAR

H81   EAR WAX (EXCESSIVE)

H82 VERTIGINOUS SYNDROME/LABYRINTHITIS/VESTIBULITIS
(*excl.* VERTIGO N17)
H83 OTOSCLEROSIS
H84 PRESBYACUSIS
H85 ACUSTIC TRAUMA, NOISE INDUCED DEAFNESS
H86 DEAFNESS/PARTIAL OR COMPLETE NEC
H99 OTHER DISEASES OF EAR/MASTOID

K Circulatory

Component 1 — Symptoms and complaints

K01   PAIN ATTRIBUTED TO HEART
K02   PRESSURE, TIGHTNESS, HEAVINESS ATTRIBUTED TO
      HEART (*excl.* R02)
K03   OTHER PAIN ATTRIBUTED TO CIRCULATORY SYSTEM
K04   PALPITATIONS/AWARENESS OF HEARTBEATS
K05   OTHER ABNORMAL/IRREGULAR HEARTBEAT/PULSE
K06   PROMINENT VEINS
K07   SWOLLEN ANKLES/EDEMA
K24   FEAR OF HEART ATTACK
K25   FEAR OF HYPERTENSION (*excl.* KNOWN HYPERTENSION)
K27   FEAR OF OTHER DISEASE CIRCULATORY SYSTEM
K28   DISABILITY/IMPAIRMENT
K29   OTHER SYMPT./COMPLT.HEART/CIRC.SYSTEM (*excl.* FLUID
      IN CHEST R93)

Component 2 — Diagnostic and preventive procedures

K30–K49

Component 3 — Medication, treatment, and therapeutic procedures

K50–K59

Component 4 — Results

K60–K61

Component 5 — Administrative

K62

Component 6 — Referrals and other reasons for encounter

K63–K69

Component 7 — Diagnosis/diseases

K70   INFECTIOUS DISEASE CIRCULATORY SYSTEM
K71   ACUTE RHEUMATIC FEVER/CHRONIC RHEUM.HEART
      DISEASE

K72   NEOPLASM CIRC.SYSTEM

K73   CONGENITAL ANOMALIES HEART/CIRC.SYSTEM

K74   ANGINA PECTORIS
K75   ACUTE MYOCARDIAL INFARCTION
K76   OTHER AND CHRONIC ISCHEMIC HEART DISEASE
K77   HEART FAILURE
K78   ATRIAL FIBRILLATION/FLUTTER

K79 PAROXYSMAL TACHYCARDIA
K80 ECTOPIC BEATS, ALL TYPES
K81 HEART MURMUR, NOS
K82 PULMONARY HEART DISEASE
K83 HEART VALVE DISEASE, NOS, NON-RHEUMATIC
K84 OTHER DISEASE OF HEART
K85 ELEVATED BLOODPRESSURE WITHOUT HYPERTENSION
K86 UNCOMPLICATED HYPERTENSION
K87 HYPERTENSION WITH INVOLVEMENT TARGET ORGANS
K88 POSTURAL HYPOTENSION (LOW BLOOD PRESSURE)
K89 TRANSIENT CEREBRAL ISCHEMIA
K90 STROKE/CEREBROVASCULAR ACCIDENT
K91 ATHEROSCLEROSIS (*excl.* HEART/BRAIN)
K92 OTHER ARTERIAL OBSTRUCTION/PERIPH.VASCULAR
     DISEASE
K93 PULMONARY EMBOLISM
K94 PHLEBITIS AND THROMBOPHLEBITIS
K95 VARICOSE VEINS OF LEG (*excl.* ULCER S97)
K96 HEMORRHOIDS
K99 OTHER DISEASE OF CIRCULATORY SYSTEM

L   Musculoskeletal

Component 1 — Symptoms and complaints
L01   NECK SYMPTOMS/COMPLAINTS (*excl.* HEADACHE)
L02   BACK SYMPTOMS/COMPLAINTS
L03   LOW BACK SYMPTOMS/COMPLAINTS WITHOUT RADIATION
(*excl.* DISC L86)
L04   CHEST SYMPTOMS/COMPLAINTS
L05   FLANK SYMPTOMS/COMPLAINTS
L06   AXILLA SYMPTOMS/COMPLAINTS
L07   JAW SYMPTOMS/COMPLAINTS
L08   SHOULDER SYMPTOMS/COMPLAINTS
L09   ARM SYMPTOMS/COMPLAINTS
L10   ELBOW SYMPTOMS/COMPLAINTS
L11   WRIST SYMPTOMS/COMPLAINTS
L12   HAND & FINGER SYMPTOMS/COMPLAINTS
L13   HIP SYMPTOMS/COMPLAINTS
L14   LEG/THIGH SYMPTOMS/COMPLAINTS
L15   KNEE SYMPTOMS/COMPLAINTS
L16   ANKLE SYMPTOMS/COMPLAINTS
L17   FOOT & TOE SYMPTOMS/COMPLAINTS
L18   MUSCLE PAIN, MYALGIA, FIBROSITIS
L19   OTHER SYMPT./COMPLT. MULTIPLE/UNSPEC.MUSCLES
L20   SYMPT./COMPLT.MULTIPLE JOINTS
L26   FEAR OF CANCER OF MUSCULOSKELETAL SYSTEM
L27   FEAR OF OTHER MUSCULOSKELETAL DISEASE
L28   DISABILITY/IMPAIRMENT
L29   OTHER SYMPT./COMPLT. MUSCULOSKELETAL SYSTEM

Component 2 — Diagnostic and preventive procedures
L30–L49

Component 3 — Medication, treatment, and therapeutic procedures
L50–L59

Component 4 — Results
L60–L61

Component 5 — Administrative
L62

Component 6 — Referrals and other reasons for encounter
L63–L69

Component 7 — Diagnosis/diseases
L70   INFECTIONS

L71 NEOPLASMS

L72 FRACTURE: RADIUS/ULNA
L73 FRACTURE: TIBIA/FIBULA
L74 FRACTURE: CARPAL/METACARPAL/TARSAL/METATARSAL/
PHALANGES
L75 FRACTURE: FEMUR
L76 FRACTURE: OTHER
L77 SPRAINS & STRAINS OF ANKLE(S)
L78 SPRAINS & STRAINS OF KNEE(S)
L79 SPRAINS & STRAINS OF OTHER JOINTS
L80 DISLOCATIONS
L81 OTHER INJURY MUSCULOSKELETAL SYSTEM

L82 CONGENITAL ANOMALIES

L83 SYNDROMES RELATED TO CERVICAL SPINE
L84 OSTEOARTHRITIS OF SPINE (ANY REGION) (*excl.*DISC
SYNDROME L83/L86)
L85 ACQUIRED DEFORMITIES OF SPINE/SCOLIOSIS/KYPHOSIS
L86 LUMBAR DISC LESION, BACK PAIN WITH RADIATING
SYMPTOMS
L87 GANGLION JOINT/TENDON
L88 RHEUMATOID ARTHRITIS AND ALLIED CONDITIONS
L89 OSTEOARTHRITIS OF HIP
L90 OSTEOARTHRITIS OF KNEE
L91 OTHER OSTEOARTHRITIS AND ALLIED CONDITIONS (*excl.*
L84/L89/L90)
L92 SHOULDER SYNDROME
L93 TENNIS ELBOW, LATERAL EPICONDYLITIS
L94 OSGOOD/SCHLATTER, OTHER OSTEOCHONDROSES
L95 OSTEOPOROSIS
L96 ACUTE DAMAGE MENISCUS/LIGAMENT OF KNEE
L97 CHRONIC INTERNAL KNEE DERANGEMENT
L98 ACQUIRED DEFORMITIES OF LIMBS
L99 OTHER DISEASE MUSCULOSKELETAL SYSTEM/CONNECTIVE
TISSUE

N Neurological

Component 1 — Symptoms and complaints

N01 HEADACHE (*excl.* SINUS PAIN R09, MIGRAINE N89)
N02 TENSION HEADACHE
N03 PAIN, FACE
N04 RESTLESS LEGS SYNDROME
N05 TINGLING FINGERS/FEET/TOES
N06 OTHER SENSATION DISTURBANCES AND ABN.
     INVOLUNTARY MOVEMENTS
N07 CONVULSIONS/SEIZURES
N16 OTHER DISTURBANCE SENSE/SMELL/TASTE
N17 VERTIGO/DIZZINESS (*excl.* H82)
N18 PARALYSIS/WEAKNESS (*excl.* GENERAL WEAKNESS A04)
N19 DISORDER OF SPEECH
N26 FEAR OF CANCER OF NEUROLOGICAL SYSTEM
N27 FEAR OF OTHER NEUROLOGICAL DISEASE
N28 DISABILITY/IMPAIRMENT
N29 OTHER SYMPT./COMPLT.NEUROLOGICAL SYSTEM

Component 2 — Diagnostic and preventive procedures

N30–N49

Component 3 — Medication, treatment, and therapeutic procedures

N50–N59

Component 4 — Results

N60–N61

Component 5 — Administrative

N62

Component 6 — Referrals and other reasons for encounter

N63–N69

Component 7 — Diagnosis/diseases

N70 POLIOMYELITIS/OTHER ENTEROVIRUS
N71 MENINGITIS/ENCEPHALITIS
N72 TETANUS
N73 OTHER INFECTION NEUROLOGICAL SYSTEM

N74 MALIGNANT NEOPLASMS
N75 BENIGN NEOPLASMS
N76 UNSPECIFIED NEOPLASMS

N79 CONCUSSION
N80 OTHER HEAD INJURY WITHOUT SKULL FRACTURE

N81   OTHER INJURIES

N85   CONGENITAL ANOMALIES

N86   MULTIPLE SCLEROSIS
N87   PARKINSONISM/PARALYSIS AGITANS
N88   EPILEPSY, ALL TYPES
N89   MIGRAINE
N90   CLUSTER HEADACHE
N91   FACIAL PARALYSIS, BELL'S PALSY
N92   TRIGEMINUS NEURALGIA
N93   CARPAL TUNNEL SYNDROME
N94   OTHER PERIPHERAL NEURITIS/NEUROPATHIA
N99   OTHER DISEASES OF NEUROLOGICAL SYSTEM

P   Psychological

Component 1 — Symptoms and complaints

P01   FEELING ANXIOUS/NERVOUS/TENSE//INADEQUATE
P02   ACUTE STRESS/TRANSIENT SITUATIONAL DISTURBANCE
P03   FEELING DEPRESSED
P04   FEELING/BEHAVING IRRITABLE/ANGRY
P05   FEELING/BEHAVING OLD, SENILE/CONCERN WITH AGING
P06   DISTURBANCES OF SLEEP/INSOMNIA
P07   INHIBITION/LOSS/LACK OF SEXUAL DESIRE/EXCITEMENT
P08   INHIBITION/LOSS/LACK OF SEXUAL FULFILMENT
P09   CONCERN WITH SEXUAL PREFERENCE
P10   STAMMERING, STUTTERING, TICS
P11   EATING PROBLEMS IN CHILDREN
P12   BEDWETTING, ENURESIS (*excl.* U04)
P13   ENCOPRESIS, OTHER PROBLEM WITH BOWEL TRAINING
P15   CHRONIC ALCOHOL ABUSE
P16   ACUTE ALCOHOL ABUSE
P17   TOBACCO ABUSE
P18   MEDICINAL ABUSE
P19   DRUG ABUSE
P20   DISTURBANCES OF MEMORY/CONCENTRATION/
       ORIENTATION
P21   OVERACTIVE CHILD, HYPERKINETIC
P22   OTHER CONCERN WITH BEHAVIOR OF CHILD
P23   OTHER SYMPT./COMPLT. CONCERNING BEHAVIOR OF
       ADOLESCENT
P24   SPECIFIC LEARNING PROBLEMS/DELAY IN DEVELOPMENT:
       CHILD/ADOLESCENT
P25   PHASE OF LIFE PROBLEM ADULT
P27   FEAR OF MENTAL DISORDER
P28   DISABILITY/IMPAIRMENT
P29   OTHER PSYCHOLOGICAL SYMPTOMS AND COMPLAINTS

Component 2 — Diagnostic and preventive procedures
P30–P49

Component 3 — Medication, treatment, and therapeutic procedures
P50–P59

Component 4 — Results
P60–P61

Component 5 — Administrative
P62

Component 6 — Referrals and other reasons for encounter
P63–P69

Component 7 — Diagnosis/diseases
P70 DEMENTIA (INCL. SENILE, ALZHEIMER)
P71 OTHER ORGANIC PSYCHOSIS
P72 SCHIZOPHRENIA, ALL TYPES
P73 AFFECTIVE PSYCHOSIS
P74 ANXIETY DISORDER/ANXIETY STATE
P75 HYSTERICAL/HYPOCHRONDRIACAL DISORDER
P76 DEPRESSIVE DISORDER
P77 SUICIDE ATTEMPT
P78 NEURASTHENIA, SURMENAGE
P79 OTHER NEUROTIC DISORDER
P80 PERSONALITY DISORDER
P85 MENTAL RETARDATION
P98 OTHER /UNSPECIFIED PSYCHOSES
P99 OTHER MENTAL/PSYCHOLOGICAL DISORDER

R Respiratory

Component 1 — Symptoms and complaints

R01   PAIN: ATTRIBUTED TO RESPIRATORY SYSTEM (*excl.* SINUS PAIN R09)
R02   SHORTNESS OF BREATH, DYSPNEA
R03   WHEEZING
R04   OTHER BREATHING PROBLEMS
R05   COUGH
R06   NOSE BLEED/EPISTAXIS
R07   SNEEZING/NASAL CONGESTION/RUNNY NOSE
R08   OTHER SYMPTOMS/COMPLAINTS OF NOSE
R09   SYMPT./COMPLT.SINUS (*incl.* PAIN)
R21   SYMPT./COMPLT.THROAT
R22   SYMPT./COMPLT.TONSILS
R23   VOICE SYMPTOMS/COMPLAINTS
R24   HEMOPTYSIS
R25   ABNORMAL SPUTUM/PHLEGM
R26   FEAR OF CANCER OF RESPIRATORY SYSTEM
R27   FEAR OF OTHER RESPIRATORY DISEASE
R28   DISABILITY/IMPAIRMENT
R29   OTHER SYMPT./COMPLT.RESPIRIRATORY SYSTEM NEC

Component 2 — Diagnostic and preventive procedures

R30–R49

Component 3 — Medication, treatment, and therapeutic procedures

R50–R59

Component 4 — Results

R60–R61

Component 5 — Administrative

R62

Component 6 — Referrals and other reasons for encounter

R63–R69

Component 7 — Diagnosis/diseases

R70   TUBERCULOSIS (*excl.* A70 TB GENERAL)
R71   WHOOPING COUGH
R72   STREP-THROAT/SCARLET FEVER
R73   BOIL/ABSCESS NOSE
R74   URI (HEAD COLD)
R75   SINUSITIS ACUTE/CHRONIC
R76   TONSILLITIS ACUTE
R77   ACUTE LARYNGITIS/TRACHEITIS/CROUP

R78   ACUTE BRONCHITIS/BRONCHIOLITIS
R80   INFLUENZA (PROVEN) WITHOUT PNEUMONIA
R81   PNEUMONIA
R82   PLEURISY, ALL TYPES (*excl.* TB R70)
R83   OTHER INFECTIONS RESPIRATORY SYSTEM

R84   MALIGN.NEOPL.TRACHEA/BRONCHUS/LUNG
R85   OTHER MALIGN. NEOPLASMS
R86   BENIGN NEOPLASMS

R87   FOREIGN BODY IN NOSE/LARYNX/BRONCHUS
R88   OTHER INJURIES

R89   CONGENITAL ANOMALIES OF RESPIRATORY SYSTEM

R90   HYPERTROPHY/CHRONIC INFECTION TONSILS/ADENOIDS
R91   CHRONIC BRONCHITIS/BRONCHIECTASIS
R93   PLEURAL EFFUSION NOS
R95   EMPHYSEMA/CHRONIC OBSTRUCTIVE PULMONARY
        DISEASE
R96   ASTHMA
R97   HAYFEVER, ALLERGIC RHINITIS
R98   HYPERVENTILATION
R99   OTHER DISEASE RESPIRATORY SYSTEM

S   Skin

Component 1 — Symptoms and complaints

S01 PAIN, TENDERNESS OF SKIN
S02 PRURITIS, SKIN ITCHING (*excl.* ANOGENITAL D05)
S03 WARTS
S04 LOCALIZED SWELLING/PAPULES/LUMP/MASS/SKIN/SUBCUT. TISSUE
S05 GENERALIZED MULTIPLE SWELLING/PAPULES/LUMPS/SKIN/ SUBCUT.TISSUE
S06 LOCALIZED REDNESS/ERYTHEMA/RASH OF SKIN
S07 GENERALIZED/MULTIPLE REDNESS/ERYTHEMA/RASH OF SKIN
S08 OTHER CHANGES IN SKIN COLOR
S09 INFECTED FINGER/TOE; PARONYCHIA
S10 BOIL/CARBUNCLE/CELLULITIS LOCALIZED
S11 OTHER LOCALIZED SKIN INFECTION
S12 INSECT BITE
S13 ANIMAL/HUMAN BITE
S14 BURNS/SCALDS
S15 FOREIGN BODY IN SKIN
S16 BRUISE/CONTUSION/CRUSHING WITH INTACT SKIN SURFACE
S17 ABRASION/SCRATCH/BLISTER
S18 LACERATION/CUT
S19 OTHER INJURY TO SKIN AND SUBCUTANEOUS TISSUE
S20 CORNS/CALOSITIES
S21 SYMPTOMS/COMPLAINTS OF SKIN TEXTURE
S22 SYMPTOMS/COMPLTAINTS NAILS
S23 BALDNESS, LOSING HAIR (*incl.* ALOPECIA)
S24 OTHER SYMPT./COMPLT. HAIR & SCALP
S26 FEAR OF CANCER OF SKIN
S27 FEAR OF HAVING OTHER SKIN DISEASE
S28 DISABILITY/IMPAIRMENT
S29 OTHER SYMPT./COMPLT. SKIN/SUBCUTANEOUS TISSUE

Component 2 — Diagnostic and preventive procedures
S30–S49

Component 3 — Medication, treatment, and therapeutic procedures
S50–S59

Component 4 — Results
S60–S61

Component 5 — Administrative
S62

Component 6 — Referrals and other reasons for encounter
S63–S69

Component 7 — Diagnosis/diseases
S70 HERPES ZOSTER
S71 HERPES SIMPLEX (*excl.* EYE F85; GENITAL X90, Y72)
S72 SCABIES AND OTHER ACARIASES
S73 PEDICULOSIS AND OTHER SKIN INFESTATIONS
S74 DERMATOPHYTOSIS
S75 MONILIASIS/MONILIA INFECTION/CANDIDIASIS (*excl.* UROGEN.)
S76 OTHER INFECTIOUS SKIN DIS.NEC/ERYSIPELAS

S77 MALIGN. NEOPLASMS OF SKIN
S78 LIPOMA OF SKIN
S79 OTHER BENIGN NEOPLASMS OF SKIN
S80 OTHER UNSPECIFIED NEOPLASM SKIN

S81 HEMANGIOMA/LYMPHANGIOMA
S82 NEVUS/MOLE
S83 OTHER CONGENITAL LESIONS

S84 IMPETIGO
S85 PILONIDAL CYST/FISTULA
S86 SEBORRHOIC DERMATITIS/OTHER ERYTHEMATOUS DERMATOSES
S87 ATOPIC DERMATITIS/ECZEMA
S88 CONTACT DERMATITIS/OTHER ECZEMA
S89 DIAPER RASH
S90 PITYRIASIS ROSEA
S91 PSORIASIS W/WO ARTHROPATHY
S92 POMPHOLYX/OTHER DIS. SWEAT GLANDS
S93 SEBACEOUS CYST
S94 INGROWN TOENAIL/OTHER DISEASE OF NAIL
S95 MOLLUSCA CONTAGIOSA
S96 ACNE
S97 CHR.ULCER SKIN/BEDSORE (*incl.* VARICOSE ULCER)
S98 URTICARIA
S99 OTHER DISEASE SKIN/SUBCUTANEOUS TISSUE

T   Endocrine, metabolic and nutritional

Component 1 — Symptoms and complaints
T01   EXCESSIVE THIRST
T02   EXCESSIVE APPETITE
T03   LOSS OF APPETITE (*excl.* T06)
T04   FEEDING PROBLEM OF INFANT/CHILD (*excl.* PSYCHOL. P11)
T05   FEEDING PROBLEM OF ADULT (*excl.* T06)
T06   ANOREXIA NERVOSA W/WO BULEMIA
T07   WEIGHT GAIN
T08   WEIGHT LOSS (*excl.* T06)
T10   LACK OF EXPECTED PHYSIOLOGICAL DEVELOPMENT/
        DELAY/FAILURE TO THRIVE
T11   DEHYDRATION
T15   THYROID LUMP, MASS (*excl.*NODULE T81)
T26   FEAR OF CANCER OF ENDOCRINE SYSTEM
T27   FEAR OF OTHER ENDOCR.METAB.NUTR.DIS.
T28   DISABILITY/IMPAIRMENT
T29   OTHER SYMPT./COMPLT.ENDO.METAB.NUTRI.

Component 2 — Diagnostic and preventive procedures
T30–T49

Component 3 — Medication, treatment, and therapeutic procedures
T50–T59

Component 4 — Results
T60–T61

Component 5 — Administrative
T62

Component 6 — Referrals and other reasons for encounter
T63–T69

Component 7 — Diagnosis/diseases
T70   INFECTIOUS DISEASE

T71   MALIGN, NEOPLASM THYROID
T72   BENIGN NEOPLASM THYROID
T73   OTHER/UNSPEC. NEOPLASMS

T78   THYROGLOSSAL DUCT(CYST)
T80   OTHER CONGENITAL ANOMALIES

T81   GOITER, THYROID NODULE WO THYROTOXICOSIS
T82   OBESITY (BMI > 30)

T83 OVERWEIGHT (BMI < 30)
T85 HYPERTHYROIDISM/THYROTOXICOSIS
T86 HYPOTHYROIDISM/MYXEDEMA
T87 HYPOGLYCEMIA
T88 RENAL GLUCOSURIA
T90 DIABETES MELLITUS
T91 VITAMIN DEFICIENCY/OTHER NUTRITIONAL DISORDER
T92 GOUT
T93 LIPID METABOLISM DISORDER
T99 OTHER ENDOCR.METAB.NUTR.DISEASE

U   Urology

Component 1   — Symptoms and complaints
U01 PAINFUL URINATION
U02 FREQUENT/URGENT URINATION
U04 INCONTINENCE, URINE (*excl.* PSYCH. P12)
U05 OTHER URINATION PROBLEMS
U06 BLOOD IN URINE
U07 OTHER COMPLAINTS OF URINE
U13 OTHER SYMPT./COMPLT.BLADDER
U14 SYMPT./COMPLT.KIDNEY
U26 FEAR OF CANCER OF URINARY SYSTEM
U27 FEAR OF OTHER URINARY DISEASE
U28 DISABILITY/IMPAIRMENT
U29 OTHER SYMPT./COMPLT.URINARY SYSTEM

Component 2 — Diagnostic and preventive procedures
U30–U49

Component 3 — Medication, treatment, and therapeutic procedures
U50–U59

Component 4 — Results
U60–U61

Component 5 — Administrative
U62

Component 6 — Referrals and other reasons for encounter
U63–U69

Component 7 — Diagnosis/diseases
U70 PYELONEPHRITIS/PYELITIS, ACUTE
U71 CYSTITIS/OTHER URINARY INFECT.NON—VENEREAL
U72 URETHRITIS, NON—SPECIFIC/NON—VENEREAL

U75 MALIGN. NEOPLASM, KIDNEY
U76 MALIGN. NEOPLASM, BLADDER
U77 OTHER MALIGN. NEOPLASM
U78 BENIGN NEOPLASM URINARY TRACT.
U79 OTHER UNSPEC.NEOPLASM URINARY TRACT

U80 INJURIES

U85 CONGENITAL ANOMALIES URINARY TRACT

U88 GLOMERULONEPHRITIS/NEPHROSIS

U90 ORTHOSTATIC ALBUMINURIA/PROTEINURIA
U95 URINARY CALCULUS ALL TYPES/SITES
U98 ABNORMAL URINE TEST FINDING, NOS
U99 OTHER DISEASE URINARY SYSTEM

W   Pregnancy, childbearing, family planning

Component 1 — Symptoms and complaints

W01   QUESTION OF PREGNANCY (*excl.* FEAR OF BEING
      PREGNANT)
W02   FEAR OF BEING PREGNANT
W03   ANTEPARTUM BLEEDING
W05   VOMITING /NAUSEA OF PREGNANCY
W10   MORNING AFTER PILL, POSTCOITAL CONTRACEPTION
W11   FAMILY PLANNING/ORAL CONTRACEPTIVE
W12   FAMILY PLANNING/IUD
W13   FAMILY PLANNING/STERILIZATION/REFERRAL FOR
W14   FAMILY PLANNING/OTHER
W15   COMPLAINTS OF INFERTILITY
W17   HEAVY POST-PARTUM BLEEDING
W18   OTHER COMPLAINTS OF POST-PARTUM PERIOD
W19   SYMPTOMS/COMPLAINTS OF LACTATION
W20   OTHER SYMPTOMS/COMPLAINTS OF BREAST (DURING
      PREGNANCY)
W27   FEAR OF COMPLICATIOS OF PREG./DELIVERY (*incl.* FEAR
      OF LOSING PREGNANCY)
W28   DISABILITY/IMPAIRMENT
W29   OTHER SYMPTOMS/COMPLAINTS OF PREGNANCY/
      CHILDBEARING/FAMILY PLANNING

Component 2 — Diagnostic and preventive procedures
W30–W49

Component 3 — Medication, treatment, and therapeutic procedures
W50–W59

Component 4 — Results
W60–W61

Component 5 — Administrative
W62

Component 6 — Referral and other reasons for encounter
W63–W69

Component 7 — Diagnoses

W70   PUERPERAL INFECTION, ENDOMETRITIS, SEPSIS
W71   OTHER INFECTIOUS CONDITIONS† COEXISTING WITH
      PREGNANCY/PUERPERIUM

W72   MALIGNANT NEOPLASM† COEXISTING WITH PREGNANCY
W73   BENIGN NEOPLASM† COEXISTING WITH PREGNANCY

W75   INJURIES† COMPLICATING PREGNANCY

W76   CONGENITAL ANOMALIES† OF MOTHER COMPLICATING
PREGNANCY

W77   OTHER NON-OBSTETRICAL CONDITIONS/DISEASES†
AFFECTING PREGNANCY, CHILDBIRTH AND PUERPERIUM
W78   PREGNANCY: CONFIRMED
W79   UNWANTED PREGNANCY: CONFIRMED
W80   ECTOPIC PREGNANCY
W81   TOXEMIA, (PRE)ECLAMPSIA
W82   ABORTION, SPONTANEOUS
W83   ABORTION, INDUCED
W84   PREGNANCY REQUIRING SPECIAL CARE (HIGH RISK)
W90   NORMAL DELIVERY LIVEBORN(S)
W91   NORMAL DELIVERY DEADBORN(S)
W92   COMPLICATED DELIVERY LIVEBORN(S)
W93   COMPLICATED DELIVERY DEADBORN(S)
W94   MASTITIS PUERPERALIS
W95   OTHER DISORDERS OF BREAST IN PUERPERIUM/
DISORDERS OF LACTATION
W96   OTHER COMPLICATIONS OF PUERPERIUM (POSTNATAL)
W99   OTHER DISORDERS OF PREGNANCY, DELIVERY AND
PUERPERIUM

†Double coding required

X   Female genital system (including breast)

Component 1 — Symptoms and complaints

X01   GENITAL PAIN (*excl.* MENSTRUAL PAIN X02)
X02   MENSTRUAL PAIN
X03   INTERMENSTRUAL PAIN
X04   PAINFUL/DIFFICULT INTERCOURSE
X05   MENSTRUATION ABSENT/SCANTY (*excl.* QUESTION OF
        PREGNANCY W02)
X06   MENSTRUATION EXCESSIVE
X07   MENSTRUATION IRREGULAR/FREQUENT
X08   INTERMENSTRUAL BLEEDING AND OTHER DISORDERS OF
        MENSTRUAL CYCLE
X09   PREMENSTRUAL SYMPTOMS
X10   POSTPONEMENT (SELECTED) OF MENSTRUATION
X11   MENOPAUSAL SYMPT./COMPLT.
X12   POSTMENOPAUSAL BLEEDING
X13   POSTCOITAL BLEEDING
X14   VAGINAL DISCHARGE   (*excl.* BLEEDING)
X15   OTHER SYMPT./COMPLT.VAGINA
X16   SYMPT./COMPLT.VULVA
X17   SYMPT./COMPLT.PELVIS
X18   BREAST PAIN
X19   LUMP/MASS BREAST
X20   SYMPT./COMPLT.NIPPLE
X21   OTHER SYMPT./COMPLT.BREAST
X23   FEAR OF VENEREAL DISEASE
X24   FEAR OF SEXUAL DYSFUNCTION
X25   FEAR OF GENITAL CANCER
X26   FEAR OF BREAST CANCER
X27   FEAR OTHER GENITAL/BREAST DISEASE
X28   DISABILITY/IMPAIRMENT
X29   OTHER SYMPT./COMPLT.GENITAL SYSTEM

Component 2 — Diagnostic and preventive procedures
X30–X49

Component 3 — Medication, treatment, and therapeutic procedures
X50–X59

Component 4 — Results
X60–X61

Component 5 — Administrative
X62

Component 6 — Referrals and other reasons for encounter

X63–X69

Component 7 — Diagnosis/diseases

X70 SYPHILIS, FEMALE GENITAL & NOS
X71 GONORRHOEA, FEMALE GENITAL & NOS
X72 UROGENITAL CANDIDIASIS, PROVEN
X73 UROGENITAL TRICHOMONIASIS, PROVEN
X74 PELVIC INFLAMMATORY DISEASE

X75 MALIGN. NEOPLASM CERVIX
X76 MALIGN. NEOPLASM BREAST
X77 OTHER MALIGNANT NEOPLASM
X78 FIBROID/MYOMA (UTERUS/CERVIX)
X79 BENIGN NEOPL.BREAST (*excl.* CYSTIC X88)
X80 OTHER BENIGN NEOPLASM FEM.GENIT.
X81 OTHER UNSPEC.NEOPLASM FEM.GENIT.

X82 INJURIES

X83 CONGENITAL ANOMALIES FEMALE GENITAL

X84 VAGINITIS/VULVITIS, NON-VENEREAL NOS
X85 CERVICITIS/CERV.EROSION/OTHER CERVICAL DISEASE
X86 ABNORMAL PAP SMEAR
X87 UTEROVAGINAL PROLAPSE
X88 CHRONIC CYSTIC DISEASE BREAST
X89 PREMENSTRUAL TENSION SYNDROME
X90 HERPES GENITALIS
X91 CONDYLOMATA ACUMINATA
X99 OTHER DISEASES FEMALE GENITAL SYSTEM

Y   Male genital system

Component 1 — Symptoms and complaints
Y01   PAIN IN PENIS
Y02   PAIN IN TESTIS/SCROTUM
Y03   DISCHARGE FROM PENIS/URETHRA
Y04   OTHER SYMPT./COMPLT.OF PENIS
Y05   SYMPT./COMPLT.SCROTUM AND TESTIS
Y06   SYMPT./COMPLT. PROSTATE
Y07   SYMPT./COMPLT. POTENCY (*excl.* P07,P08)
Y08   OTHER SYMPT./COMPLT.SEXUAL FUNCTION (*excl.* P07,P08)
Y10   INFERTILITY/SUBFERTILITY
Y13   FAMILY PLANNING/STERILIZATION
Y14   FAMILY PLANNING/OTHER
Y16   SYMPT./COMPLT. MALE BREAST
Y24   FEAR OF SEXUAL DYSFUNCTION
Y25   FEAR OF VENERAL DISEASE (*excl.* B25)
Y26   FEAR OF CANCER OF MALE GENITAL ORGANS
Y27   FEAR OF OTHER GENITAL DISEASE
Y28   DISABILITY/IMPAIRMENT
Y29   OTHER SYMPT./COMPLT.MALE REPROD.SYST.

Component 2 — Diagnostic and preventive procedures
Y30–Y49

Component 3 — Medication, treatment, and therapeutic procedures
Y50–Y59

Component 4 — Results
Y60–Y61

Component 5 — Administrative
Y62

Component 6 — Referrals and other reasons for encounter
Y63–Y69

Component 7 — Diagnosis/diseases
Y70   SYPHILIS MALE GENITAL & NOS
Y71   GONORRHOEA MALE GENITAL & NOS
Y72   GENITAL HERPES
Y73   PROSTATITIS/SEMINAL VESICULITIS
Y74   ORCHITIS/EPIDIDYMITIS
Y75   BALANITIS
Y76   CONDYLOMATA ACUMINATA

Y77   MALIGN. NEOPLASM PROSTATE

Y78 OTHER MALIGN. NEOPLASM MALE GENITAL
Y79 BENIGN NEOPLASM MALE GENITAL

Y80 INJURIES

Y81 PHIMOSIS/REDUNDANT PREPUCE
Y82 HYPOSPADIA
Y83 UNDESCENDED TESTICLE/CRYPTORCHISM
Y84 OTHER CONGENITAL ANOMALIES

Y85 BENIGN PROSTATIC HYPERTROPHY
Y86 HYDROCELE
Y99 OTHER DISEASE MALE GENITAL INCL. BREAST

Z Social problems

Component 1 — Symptoms and complaints

Z01 POVERTY/FINANCIAL PROBLEMS
Z02 PROBLEMS FOOD AND WATER
Z03 PROBLEMS HOUSING/NEIGHBORHOOD CONDITIONS
Z04 PROBLEMS SOCIAL, CULTURAL SYSTEM/MIGRATION
Z05 PROBLEMS WITH WORKING CONDITIONS, OCCUPATIONAL PROBLEMS
Z06 PROBLEMS WITH BEING UNEMPLOYED
Z07 PROBLEMS WITH EDUCATION
Z08 PROBLEMS WITH SOCIAL INSURANCE/WELFARE
Z09 PROBLEMS LEGAL/POLICE
Z10 PROBLEMS HEALTH CARE SYSTEM/ACCESS/AVAILABILITY
Z11 PROBLEMS WITH BEING ILL
Z12 RELATIONSHIP PROBLEMS BETWEEN PARTNERS
Z13 PROBLEMS WITH BEHAVIOR OF PARTNER
Z14 PROBLEMS WITH PARTNER BEING ILL
Z15 LOSS OR DEATH OF PARTNER
Z16 RELATIONSHIP PROBLEMS WITH CHILD
Z18 PROBLEMS WITH CHILD BEING ILL
Z19 LOSS OR DEATH OF CHILD
Z20 RELATIONSHIP PROBLEMS WITH PARENT/OTHER FAMILY MEMBER
Z21 PROBLEMS WITH BEHAVIOR PARENT/OTHER FAMILY MEMBER
Z22 PROBLEMS WITH PARENT/OTHER FAMILY MEMBER BEING ILL
Z23 LOSS OR DEATH OF PARENT/OTHER FAMILY MEMBER
Z24 PROBLEMS IN RELATIONSHIPS WITH FRIENDS
Z25 PROBLEMS RESULTING FROM ASSAULTS/HARMFUL EVENTS
Z27 FEAR OF HAVING A SOCIAL PROBLEM
Z28 SOCIAL HANDICAP
Z29 OTHER SOCIAL PROBLEMS/NEC

Component 2 — Diagnostic and preventive procedures

Z30–Z49

Component 3 — Medication, treatment, and therapeutic procedures

Z50–Z51

Component 4 — Results

Z60–Z61

Component 5 — Administrative

Z62

Component 6 — Referrals and other reasons for encounter

Z63–Z69

11 The relationship between ICPC and other diagnostic classifications

ICPC as a diagnostic classification system has relations both with ICD-9 and with other ICD-9 derived systems being used in primary care. In order to understand the compatibility and comparability of ICPC with other systems, the codes of the rubrics in the first and the seventh component of ICPC have been converted to three other classification systems. The conversion is presented in the listing with the short titles of ICPC, to be used for computer input. All rubrics of the first and the seventh component of ICPC, including their synonyms, as they can be found in the index, have been converted to the corresponding rubrics of three other diagnostic classification systems[49]:

1. The International Classification of Health Problems in Primary Care (ICHPPC-2)[25]. An asterisk added to the ICHPPC position number indicates those ICHPPC-2 rubrics which are defined with the help of inclusion criteria.
2. The Classification of Diseases, Problems and Procedures 1984, Royal College of General Practitioners (RCC)[10].
3. The International Classification of Diseases, 9th revision (ICD-9)[27].

The conversion is illustrated in Table 8, where a few rubrics from the seventh component of Chapter D have been converted to the three other systems.

The conversion is in one direction: from ICPC to the other systems. As a consequence, only the conversion from ICPC to ICHPPC-2 covers all rubrics of the latter. The conversions to RCC and to ICD-9 for this reason do not cover all rubrics of these two classification systems. Several signs in the list indicate the degree of compatibility between the several codes.

If the corresponding code does not carry a sign at all, conversion is possible on a one-to-one basis: the corresponding rubric is similar, the systems are completely compatible for this rubric. If possible, the three-digit main ICD-9 rubrics are represented. A four-digit ICD code is used only when necessary. As a consequence, all four-digit ICD codes are more specific than the three-digit main ICD-9 rubric. No sign is added to a consecutive series of ICD rubrics, because it is evident that a series of

Table 8. Conversion of several ICPC rubrics to three other classifications

ICPC code	Main title	Corresponding codes		
		ICHPPC-2	RCC	ICD-9
D84	Disease of esophagus	150	−2655 −2660 −2665 −2670	530
D85	Duodenal ulcer	151*	−2685 −2690	532
D86	Other peptic ulcers	152*	−2675 −2680 −2695	−531, −533, −534
D87	Disord. stomach function	153*	−2700 −2705 −2310	535, −537

separate codes always has more specificity than the corresponding ICPC rubric.

A + sign added to the conversion code indicates that the content of this rubric is less specific than that of the corresponding ICPC rubric. The ICPC thus is more specific.

A − sign indicates the reverse situation. The corresponding rubric is more specific than the ICPC rubric. Three-digit main ICD-9 rubrics are very often more specific than the ICPC rubric, even if they don't carry a − sign.

Sometimes an S sign is added to the conversion to ICD-9, indicating that a collection of different ICD-9 codes together correspond to an ICPC code. This happens with 'rag bag' or 'grab all' rubrics of ICPC.

When an ICPC rubric is incompatible with the other classification this is indicated by a blank position. This does not necessarily mean that conversion is absolutely impossible. All classifications have 'grab all' or 'rag bag' rubrics, which can absorb a variety of codes. It does mean, however, that this ICPC rubric can not be satisfactorily and logically converted to the other classification system. Most of the time it also means that it cannot be found in the alphabetical index of ICD-9.

In Table 9 the consequences of the conversion of the first and the seventh component of ICPC to the two primary care classifications — ICHPPC-2 and RCC — are summarized.

It is evident that ICPC as a diagnostic classification differs considerably from both. The rubrics of component 1 (322 different symptoms and complaints) are relatively seldom replicated on a one-to-one basis: 14 per cent in ICHPPC-2 and 16 per cent in RCC. More than a third of the

Table 9. Compatability of ICPC with ICHPPC-2 and RCC (percentages)

		1–1	+	–	+/–	0
Component 1 (*n*=322)	ICHPPC-2	14	45	0	1	40
	RCC	16	33	4	7	39
Component 7 (*n*=363)	ICHPPC-2	46	48	2	3	1
	RCC	40	24	22	13	1
Total (*n*=685)	ICHPPC-2	31	47	1	1	20
	RCC	29	28	14	10	19

symptoms and complaints cannot be found at all in ICHPPC-2 or in RCC. Many rubrics in component 1 are more specific than the corresponding rubrics in ICHPPC-2 (45 per cent) or RCC (33 per cent).

The 363 diagnostic rubrics in component 7 of ICPC correspond quite well with ICHPPC-2, as can be expected. 48 per cent of the ICPC rubrics in component 7 are, however, more specific than the corresponding ICHPPC-2 rubrics.

The specificity of the Royal College Code in component 7 is slightly higher than that of ICPC but different. The percentage of rubrics with a mixed compatibility is considerable (13 per cent). The overall conclusion from Table 9 is that the compatibility — and consequently the comparability — of ICPC with ICHPPC-2 is good.

Table 10 illustrates that, compared with ICHPPC-2, the distribution of the etiological diagnoses over the seventh component of the chapters of ICPC is responsible for most of its specificity. However, etiological diagnoses in ICPC can readily be lumped together to the corresponding ICHPPC-2 rubrics. The inclusion criteria of ICHPPC-2-Defined can be used in both systems which makes their data highly comparable.

The Royal College Code does not rely on inclusion criteria for the use of its rubrics, which diminishes its comparability with ICPC and ICH-PPC-2. The comparability and the compatibility of diagnostic information, collected and analyzed with ICPC and with RCC is also limited, because the relatively strong orientation of the latter to specific morphological diagnoses.

Table 10. Distribution of etiological and morphological diagnoses from the seventh component of ICPC, compared with ICHPPC-2 and RCC.

	ICPC	ICHPPC-2	RCC
Total	363	235	506
Infectious diseases	72	29	52
Neoplasms	44	15	37
Injuries	40	34	55
Congenital anomalies	23	5	17
Specific morphological diseases	184	152	345

ICD-9 can still be recognized in the structure of ICPC and especially in its nomenclature. However, when patient oriented information from primary care settings is collected and analysed, ICPC and ICD-9 are practically incompatible.

12 ICPC short titles with conversion codes and references to ICHPPC-2-Defined

Symbols used in table

+   Content of this rubric is less specific than corresponding ICPC rubric.
−   Corresponding rubric is more specific than corresponding ICPC rubric(s).
S   (ICD-9 codes only). A collection of ICD-9 codes together corresponds with an ICPC rubric.
*   Refers to an ICHPPC-2 rubric which has inclusion criteria listed in ICHPPC-2-Defined
†   Double coding required.

See Chapter 11 for further information.

Abbreviations used in this table

abdom.	abdomen	irreg.	irregular
abn.	abnormal	medic.	medication
arter.	arterial	menstr.	menstrual
attrib.	attributed	metab.	metabolism
B/P	blood pressure	movmt.	movement
behav.	behaviour	neuro.	neurological
bronch.	bronchus	nutr.	nutrition
cerv.	cervical	obstet.	obstetrical
circ.	circulatory	obstr.	obstructive
coag.	coagulation	paras.	parasite
complicat.	complication	pernic.	pernicious
complt.	complaint	preg.	pregnancy
cond.	condition	prob.	problem
def.	deficiency	psychol.	psychological
depress.	depression	pt.	part of
destruct.	destruction	redund.	redundant
diaph.	diaphragm	relat.	relation
dis.	disease	reprod.	reproductive
disturb.	disturbed	respir.	respiratory
endocr.	endocrine	situat.	situational
esoph.	esophagus	spec.	specific
exam.	example	stom.	stomatitis
excl.	excluding	subcut.	subcutaneous
fem.	female	sympt.	symptom
freq.	frequent	syst.	system
FX.	function	T & A	tonsils and
gen.	genital		adenoid
hyperkin.	hyperkinetic	trach.	trachea
hypertro.	hypertrophy	tymp.	tympanic
incl.	including	undesc.	undescended
infect.	infection	unspec.	unspecific
infest.	infestation	urin.	urinary
inj.	injection	vagin.	vaginal
intest.	intestine	w	with
investig.	investigation	wo	without
involv.	involvement		

ICPC code	Main title	Corresponding codes		
		ICHPPC-2	RCC	ICD-9

A— General and unspecified

A01	PAIN:GENERALIZED/UNSPECIFIED	+300	+4720	+780.9
A02	CHILLS	+300	+4720	+780.9
A03	FEVER	291*	4520	780.6
A04	GENERAL WEAKNESS/TIREDNESS	295*	−4525 +4915	−780.7,−799.3
A05	GENERAL DETERIORATION	+300	+4915	+799.8
A06	FAINTING(SYNCOPE)	264*	4500	780.2
A07	COMA	+300	+4720	780.0
A08	SWELLING (*excl.* EDEMA K07)	+296	+4720	+782.2
A09	SWEATING PROBLEMS	290*	· 4530	780.8
A10	BLEEDING, SITE NOS			
A12	ALLERGY/ALLERGIC REACTION NOS	378	5260	−995.0,.1,.3,.4
A13	CONCERN ABOUT DRUG REACTION			
A14	INFANTILE COLIC	+297	+4700	+789.0
A15	EXCESSIVE CRYING INFANT			
A16	IRRITABLE INFANT			
A17	OTHER GEN. SYMPT. INFANTS NEC			
A20	EUTHANASIA REQUEST/DISCUSSION			
A25	FEAR OF DEATH			
A26	FEAR OF CANCER, NOS, NEC			
A27	FEAR OF OTHER DISEASE,UNSPEC.			
A28	DISABILITY/IMPAIRMENT NOS			
A29	OTHER GENERAL SYMPT./COMPLT.	+300	+4720	+780.9
A70	TUBERCULOSIS, GENERAL. (*excl.*R70)	+4*	+0020 +0290	−010.0,.8,.9, 013−018, −137.1,.2,.3,.4
A71	MEASLES (*excl.* RUBELLA A74)	12*	0105	055
A72	CHICKENPOX	9*	0075	052
A73	MALARIA	21*	0190	084
A74	RUBELLA	13*	0110	056
A75	INFECTIOUS MONONUCLEOSIS	17*	0155	075
A76	OTHER VIRAL DIS. WITH EXANTHEMS	14	0115	−050,−051, −057
A77	OTHER VIRAL DISEASES, NOS	+20 +31	−0120 −0135 −0145 +0150 +0180	−060,−061, −065,−066, −071,−073 −074,+079.9
A78	OTHER INFECTIOUS DISEASES, NOS	+31	−0025 −0030 +0060 +0185 +0210 −0250 +0280	020−031, 038−041, 080−083, 086−088, −100,114−118, −136
A79	CARCINOMATOSIS(UNKN PRIM.SITE)	+39*	−0520 +0590	−199,−234
A80	ACCIDENT/INJURY, NOS	+333	+5230 −5280	−959.S,−E81.9
A81	MULT. TRAUMA/INTERNAL INJ.	+333	+5165	−862,−867,−868, −869
A82	LATE EFFECTS OF TRAUMA	+332	+5180	909.S
A84	POISONING BY MEDICAL AGENT	334	5290	960−979
A85	ADV.EFFECT MED.AGENT PROPER DOSE	377*	−5265	995.2
A86	TOXIC EFFECT OTHER SUBSTANCES	335*	5295	980−989
A87	COMPLICAT.SURG/MED.TREATMENT	336	−5275 +5300	996−999

ICPC code	Main title	Corresponding codes		
		ICHPPC-2	RCC	ICD-9
A88	ADVERSE EFFECTS PHYS.FACTORS	337	−5235	990−994
			−5240	
			−5245	
			−5250	
			−5255	
			+5300	
			−5345	
A89	EFFECTS PROSTHETIC DEVICE			
A90	MULT.SYNDROMES/CONG.ANOMALIES	+22	+0195	−0.90,
		+252	−4285	−758,−759
			−4290	
			+4295	
A91	INVESTIG. ABNORMAL RESULTS, NEC	299*	+4830	792−796,
				ex.795.0,
				ex.796.2
A92	TOXOPLASMOSIS	+31	+0280	−130
		+253	+4450	−771.2
A93	PREMAT/IMMATURE LIVEBORN INFANT	+253	4410	765
A94	ALL PERINATAL MORBIDITY	+253	−4400	760−764,
			−4405	766−779
			−4415	
			−4420	
			−4425	
			−4445	
			+4450	
			−4460	
			−4465	
			+4470	
A95	PERINATAL MORTALITY	+253	+4470	799.9
A96	DEATH (*excl.* PERINATAL)	+300	−4905	+798
			+4915	+799
A97	NO DISEASE			
A99	OTHER GENERALIZED DISEASES			

B— Blood

B02	ENLARGED LYMPH GLAND(S)	266*	4615	785.6
B03	OTHER SYMPT. LYMPHATIC GLANDS			
B04	SYMPT. BLOOD/BLOOD FORM ORGANS			
B25	FEAR OF AIDS			
B26	FEAR OF CANCER OF BLOOD/BLOOD ORG.			
B27	FEAR OF OTHER BLOOD/LYMPH.DISEASE			
B28	DISABILITY/IMPAIRMENT			
B29	OTHER SYMPT.BLOOD/SPLEEN NOS			
B70	ACUTE LYMPHADENITIS	209*	3620	683
B71	CHRON./NON-SPEC.LYMPHADENITIS	63*	+0935	−289.1,.2,.3
B72	HODGKIN'S DISEASE	+38*	0530	200−202
B73	LEUKEMIA	+38*	0540	204−208
B74	OTHER MALIGNANT NEOPLASMS	+46	−0535	−203,+235.5,
			+0590	−238.4,.6,.7
B75	BENIGN NEOPLASMS	+45	+0575	−211.9,−229.0
B76	RUPTURED SPLEEN	+333	+5165	+865
B77	OTHER INJURIES	+333	+5230	+959.S
B78	HEREDITARY HEMOLYTIC ANEMIAS	60*	0915	282
B79	OTHER CONGENITAL ANOMALIES	+61	+0920	284.0
B80	IRON DEFICIENCY ANEMIA	58*	0900	280
B81	PERNIC./FOLATE DEFICIENCY ANEMIA	59*	−0905	−281.0,.1,
			+0910	.2,.3

ICPC code	Main title	Corresponding codes ICHPPC-2	RCC	ICD-9
B82	ANEMIA OTHER/UNSPECIFIED	+61	+0910	−281.4,.8,.9
			+0920	−283,−284,
				−285
B83	PURPURA/COAG.DEFECTS ABN.PLATE	62	−0925	−286
			−0926	−287
B84	ABNORMAL WHITE CELLS	64*	0930	288
B85	ABNORMAL UNEXPLAINED BLOOD TEST	51*	−4805	−790.2,.3,.4,.5
			−4810	
B86	OTHER HEMATOLOGICAL ABNORMALITY	375*	4800	−790.0,.1
B87	SPLENOMEGALY	+277*	+4705	789.2
B90	HIV-INFECTION (AIDS, ARS)	+20	+0180	+079.9
B99	OTHER DIS/BLOOD/LYMPH/SPLEEN	+65	+0935	−289.0,.4,
				.5,.9

D— Digestive

D01	GENERALIZED ABD. PAIN/CRAMPS	+279*	+4700	+789.0
D02	STOMACH ACHE/STOMACH PAIN	+153	+2705	+536
D03	HEARTBURN	275*	4660	+787.1
D04	RECTAL/ANAL PAIN	+163	+2780	+569.4
D05	PERIANAL ITCHING	+218	3710	698.0
D06	OTHER LOCALIZED ABDOMINAL PAIN	+279*	+4700	+789.0
D08	FLATULENCE/GAS PAIN/BELCHING	+278*	−1160	−306.4
			+4665	+787.3
D09	NAUSEA	+274*	+4655	+787.0
D10	VOMITING (*excl.* PREG W06)	+274*	+4655	+787.0
D11	DIARRHEA			
D12	CONSTIPATION	161*	2765	564.0
D13	JAUNDICE	+300	4560	782.4
D14	HEMATEMESIS/VOMIT BLOOD	+276*	+2830	578.0
D15	MELENA/BLACK, TARRY STOOLS	+276*	+2830	578.1
D16	RECTAL BLEEDING	164*	2795	569.3
D17	INCONTINENCE OF BOWEL (FECAL)	+300	4670	787.6
D18	CHANGE IN FECES/BOWEL MOVEMENTS	+300	+4720	787.7
D19	SYMPT./COMPLT.TEETH,GUMS			
D20	SYMPT./COMPLT.MOUTH,TONGUE,LIP	+149	+2650	−529.3,.6,.8,
		+300	+4720	−781.1,+784.9
D21	SWALLOWING PROBLEMS	+300	+4720	787.2
D22	WORMS/PARASITES	28*	−0255	120−129
			−0260	
D24	ADBOMINAL MASS, NOS	+296*	4710	+789.3
D25	CHANGE IN ABD.SIZE/DISTENSION	+278	+4665	+787.3,+789.3
		+296	+4710	
D26	FEAR OF CANCER OF DIGEST. SYSTEM			
D27	FEAR OF OTHER DIGESTIVE DISEASE			
D28	DISABILITY/IMPAIRMENT			
D29	OTHER SYMPT./COMPLT.DIGEST.	+300	+4915	+799.8
D70	INFECTIOUS DIARRHEA, DYSENTERY	1*	0005	001−008
D71	MUMPS	16*	0140	072
D72	INFECTIOUS HEPATITIS	15*	0130	070
D73	OTHER PRESUMED INFECTIONS	2	0015	009
D74	MALIG.NEOPL.STOMACH	+32*	0410	151
D75	MALIG.NEOPL.COLON,RECTUM	+32*	−0415	−153,−154
			−0420	
D76	MALIG.NEOPL.PANCREAS	+39*	0430	157
D77	MALIG.NEOPL.OTHER/UNSPEC.	+39*	−0400	140−150
			−0405	−152,−155,−156
			−0425	−158,−159,−230

ICPC code	Main title	Corresponding codes		
		ICHPPC-2	RCC	ICD-9
			+0515	−235.0,.1,.2,
			+0590	.3,.4
D78	BENIGN NEOPLASMS	+45	+0575	−210,−211
D79	FOREIGN BODY THROUGH ORIFICE	+331	+5215	938.S
D80	OTHER INJURIES	+323	+5165	−863,−864,
		+333	+5170	−873.6
D81	CONGENITAL ANOMAL.DIGEST.SYSTEM	+252	−4230	749−751
			−4235	
			−4295	
D82	DISEASE OF TEETH/GUMS	148	−2600	520−526
			−2605	
			−2610	
			−2615	
D83	DISEASE OF MOUTH/TONGUE/LIPS	+149	−2620	527−529
			−2625	(ex.529.3,.6,
			−2630	.8)
			−2635	
			−2640	
			−2645	
			+2650	
D84	DISEASE OF ESOPHAGUS	150	−2655	530
			−2660	
			−2665	
			−2670	
D85	DUODENAL ULCER	151*	−2685	532
			−2690	
D86	OTHER PEPTIC ULCERS	152*	−2675	−531,−533,−534
			−2680	
			−2695	
D87	DISORD.STOMACH FUNCTION	+153*	−2700	−535,+536,−537
			+2705	
			−2710	
D88	APPENDICITIS	154*	+2715	540−542
D89	INGUINAL HERNIA	155*	2720	550
D90	HIATUS (DIAPHR.) HERNIA	156*	2730	551.3,552,3
				553.3
D91	OTHER ABDOMINAL HERNIAS	157	−2725	551−553,
			−2735	(ex. 551.3,
				552.3,553.3)
D92	DIVERTICULAR DIS.INTESTINES	158*	2760	562
D93	IRRITABLE BOWEL SYNDROME	−159*	−2770	−564.1,.5,.6
		−163	+2780	
D94	CHR. ENTERITIS/ULCERAT. COLITIS	160*	−2740	−555,−556
			−2745	
D95	ANAL FISSURE/PERIANAL ABSCESS	162*	2785	−565,−566
D96	HEPATOMEGALY	+277*	+4705	789.1
D97	CIRRHOSIS/OTHER LIVER DISEASE	165*	−2810	570−573
			+2840	
D98	CHOLECYSTITIS/CHOLELITHIASIS	166*	−2815	574−576
			−2820	
D99	OTHER DIS.DIGESTIVE SYST.	167	+2715	−543
			−2750	557−561
			−2755	−564.2,.7,.8
			−2775	567−569
			−2790	−577,−579
			−2800	
			−2825	
			−2835	
			+2840	

ICPC code	Main title	Corresponding codes		
		ICHPPC-2	RCC	ICD-9

F— Eye

F01	EYE PAIN	+99	+1630	379.8
F02	RED EYE	+99	+1630	+379.9
F03	DISCHARGE FROM EYE	+99	+1630	−375.2,+379.9
F04	FLOATERS/SPOTS	+99	1620	379.2
F05	OTHER PROBLEMS WITH VISION	+99	+1630	−368.2,.8,.9
F13	ABN.SENSATIONS OF EYE			
F14	ABN.EYE MOVEMENTS			
F15	ABN.APPEARANCE OF EYES			
F16	SYMPT./COMPLT. OF EYELIDS			
F17	SYMPT./COMPLT.GLASSES			
F18	SYMPT./COMPLT.CONTACT LENS			
F27	FEAR OF EYE DISEASE			
F28	DISABILITY/IMPAIRMENT			
F29	OTHER SYMPT./COMPLT.OF EYE	+99	+1630	368.1
F70	INFECTIOUS CONJUNCTIVITIS	−18*	+0180	−077,−372.0
		+92*	+1570	
F71	ALLERGIC CONJUNCTIVITIS	+92*	+1570	−372.1
F72	BLEPHARITIS/STYE/CHALAZION	93*	−1580	−373.0,.1,.2
			−1585	
F73	OTHER INFECTIONS OF EYE	+99	−1530	−363,−364,
			+1560	−370.2,S,
			−1595	−375.3,
			−1615	+379.9
			+1630	
F74	NEOPLASMS OF EYE/ADNEXA	+39*	+0515	−190,−224
		+45	+0575	−238.8
F75	CONTUSION/ABRASIONS/BLACKEYE	+99	−1575	−372.7
		+326	+5195	−918,−921.0,.9
		+327	+5200	
F76	FOREIGN BODY IN EYE	330	5210	930
F79	OTHER INJURIES	+326	+5195	918,+959
		+333	+5230	
F80	BLOCKED LACR. DUCT OF INFANTS	251*	4215	743.6
F81	OTHER CONGENITAL ANOMALIES EYES	+252	+4295	743 (ex.p.743.6)
F82	DETACHED RETINA	+99	1500	361
F83	RETINOPATHY	+99	−1505	−362.0,−362.1
			−1510	
F84	MACULAR DEGENERATION	+99	1515	362.5
F85	CORNEAL ULCER (HERPETIC)	+11	+1560	−370.0,.1
F86	TRACHOMA	+31	+0180	076
F91	REFRACTIVE ERRORS	94*	1545	367
F92	CATARACT	96*	1540	366
F93	GLAUCOMA	97*	1535	365
F94	BLINDNESS,ALL TYPES	98*	1555	369
F95	STRABISMUS	+99	1610	378
F99	OTHER DISEASES OF EYE	+99	−1520	−360,−362.2S,
			−1550	−368.S,−371,
			−1565	−372.2S,
			−1590	374−377,−379
			−1600	
			−1605	
			−1625	
			+1630	

ICPC code	Main title	Corresponding codes		
		ICHPPC-2	RCC	ICD-9

H— Ear

H01	EAR PAIN/EARACHE	+107	1760	388.7
H02	HEARING COMPLAINTS (*excl.*H84–86)			
H03	RINGING/BUZZING/TINNITUS	+107	1750	388.3
H04	DISCHARGE FROM EAR	+107	1755	388.6
H05	BLOOD IN/FROM EAR			
H13	PLUGGED FEELING			
H15	CONCERN WITH APPEARANCE OF EARS			
H27	FEAR OF EAR DISEASE			
H28	DISABILITY/IMPAIRMENT			
H29	OTHER SYMPT./COMPLT.OF EAR			
H70	OTITIS EXTERNA	100*	1700	−380.1,.2
H71	ACUTE OTITIS MEDIA/MYRINGITIS	101*	−1725	−382.0,.4,.9,
			+1765	−384.0
H72	SEROUS OTITIS MEDIA,GLUE	102*	−1710	−381.0,.1,.2,
			−1715	.3,.4
H73	EUSTACHIAN SALPINGITIS	103*	1720	−381.5,.6
H74	CHRONIC OTITIS, OTHER INFECT.EAR	+107	−1730	−380.0,
			+1765	−382.1,.2,.3,.4
				−383,−384.1,
				−385.3
H75	NEOPLASM OF EAR	+39*	+0515	−173.S,−216.S,
		+45	+0575	−238.S
		+46	+0590	
H76	FOREIGN BODY IN EAR	+331	+5215	931
H77	PERFORATION TYMP.MEMBRANE	+323	+5170	872.6
H78	SUPERFICIAL INJURY OF EAR	+326	+5195	−910
H79	OTHER INJURIES	+333	+5230	+959.0
H80	CONGENITAL ANOMALIES OF EAR	+252	−4220	−744.0,.1,.2,.3
			+4265	
H81	EAR WAX (EXCESSIVE)	106*	1705	380.4
H82	VERTIGINOUS SYNDROMES	104*	1735	386
H83	OTOSCLEROSIS	+105	1740	387
H84	PRESBYACUSIS	+107	1745	388.0
H85	ACUSTIC TRAUMA	+107	+1765	388.1
H86	DEAFNESS/PARTIAL OR COMPLETE	+105*	+1765	−388.2,.5
		+107	+1765	−389
			−1770	
			−1775	
			−1780	
H99	OTHER DISEASES OF EAR/MASTOID	+107	+1765	−380.3,.5,.8,.9
				−381.7,.8,.9,
				−384.2,.8,.9
				−385 (excl.
				385,3,.4)
				−386.4,.5,.8,.9
				−388.4,.8,.9

K— Circulatory

K01	PAIN ATTRIBUTED TO HEART	+262*	+4640	+786.5
K02	PRESSURE,TIGHTNESS, ATTRIB.TO HEART			
K03	OTHER PAIN ATTRIB. TO CIRCULATION			
K04	PALPITATIONS/AWARE OF HEARTBEAT	263*	4600	−785.0,.1
K05	OTHER ABN./IRREG.HEARTBEAT/PULSE			
K06	PROMINENT VEINS			

ICPC code	Main title	Corresponding codes		
		ICHPPC-2	RCC	ICD-9
K07	SWOLLEN ANKLES/EDEMA	265*	4555	782.3
K24	FEAR OF HEART ATTACK			
K25	FEAR OF HYPERTENSION			
K27	FEAR/OTHER DIS. CIRC. SYSTEM			
K28	DISABILITY/IMPAIRMENT			
K29	OTHER SYMPT. HEART/CIRC.SYSTEM			
K70	INFECTIOUS DIS.CIRC.SYSTEM	+118 +132	−1965 +2315	−420,−421,−422, +459.9
K71	RHEUMATIC FEVER/HEART DISEASE	108*	−1900 −1905	390−398
K72	NEOPLASM CIRC.SYSTEM	+39* +45 +46	+0515 +0575 +0590	−164,−212.7, −238.8
K73	CONG ANOMALIES HEART/CIRC.SYST.	247	4225	745−747
K74	ANGINA PECTORIS	+110*	1950	413
K75	ACUTE MYOCARDIAL INFARCTION	109*	1940	−410,−411
K76	OTH AND CHRON ISCHEMIC HEART DIS.	+110*	1945	−412,−414
K77	HEART FAILURE	112*	−2005 −2010 −2015	428
K78	ATRIAL FIBRILLATION/FLUTTER	113*	1990	427.3
K79	PAROXYSMAL TACHYCARDIA	114*	−1985 +2000	−427.0,.1,.2
K80	ECTOPIC BEATS, ALL TYPES	115*	1995	427.6
K81	HEART MURMUR, NOS	116*	4605	785.2 pt.785.9
K82	PULMONARY HEART DISEASE	117*	1960	416
K83	HEART VALVE DIS. NOS,NON−RHEUM	111*	1970	+396,−424
K84	OTHER DISEASE OF HEART	+118	−1975 −1980 +2000 −2020	−417,−423,−425, −426, −427.4,.5,.8, .9,−429
K85	ELEVATED B/P W/O HYPERTENSION	119*	4860	796.2
K86	UNCOMPLICATED HYPERTENSION	120*	−1910 −1930	−401 +405
K87	HYPERT.WITH INVOLV.TARG ORGANS	121*	−1915 −1920 −1925 −1935	402−404, +405 −437.2
K88	POSTURAL HYPOTENSION (LOW B/P)	131*	2310	458
K89	TRANSIENT CEREBRAL ISCHEMIA	123*	2110	435
K90	STROKE/CEREBROVASC. ACC.	+124*	−2100 +2105 −2115	−430,−431, −432,−434 −436,−438
K91	ATHEROSCLEROSIS *excl.*HEART/BRAIN	125*	2200	440
K92	OTHER ARTER. OBSTR./PERIPH.VASC.DIS.	+124* −126*	+2105 −2210 −2215 −2220 −2225 −2230	−433,−437 (ex. 437.2) −443 −444
K93	PULMONARY EMBOLISM	127*	1955	415.1
K94	PHLEBITIS AND THROMBOPHLEBITIS	128*	−2245 +2315	−451,−452, −453
K95	VARICOSE VEINS OF LEGS (*excl.*S97)	+129*	−2260 −2265 −2275	−454.1,.9
K96	HEMORRHOIDS	130*	−2280 −2285 −2290	455

ICPC code	Main title	Corresponding codes		
		ICHPPC-2	RCC	ICD-9
K99	OTHER DIS. CIRCULATORY SYSTEM	+132	−2205 −2235 −2240 −2295 −2300 −2305 +2315	−441,−442, −446,−447, −448,−456, −457,−459

L— Musculoskeletal

L01	NECK SYMPT./COMPLT.(*excl.*HEADACHE)			
L02	BACK SYMPTOMS/COMPLAINTS	+238	+4020	724.5,.7
L03	LOW BACK COMPLT. W/O RADIATION	+238	+4020	724.2
L04	CHEST SYMPTOMS/COMPLAINTS	+262	+4640	+786.5
L05	FLANK SYMPTOMS/COMPLAINTS			
L06	AXILLA SYMPTOMS/COMPLAINTS			
L07	JAW SYMPTOMS/COMPLAINTS			
L08	SHOULDER SYMPTOMS/COMPLAINTS			
L09	ARM SYMPTOMS/COMPLAINTS			
L10	ELBOW SYMPTOMS/COMPLAINTS			
L11	WRIST SYMPTOMS/COMPLAINTS			
L12	HAND & FINGER SYMPTOMS/COMPLT.			
L13	HIP SYMPTOMS/COMPLAINTS			
L14	LEG/THIGH SYMPTOMS/COMPLAINTS			
L15	KNEE SYMPTOMS/COMPLAINTS			
L16	ANKLE SYMPTOMS/COMPLAINTS			
L17	FOOT & TOE SYMPTOMS/COMPLAINTS			
L18	MUSCLE PAIN/FIBROSITIS	+234 −286	+4075 +4090	−729.0,.1,.3, .4,.8
L19	OTHER SYMPT. MULT./UNSPEC. MUSCLES	+234	+4150	+728.2,+729.9
L20	SYMPT.MULTIPLE/UNSPEC.JOINTS	+246 −288* −289*	−3975 −3980 +4150	−719.0,.4,.5,.6 .9
L26	FEAR OF CANCER			
L27	FEAR OF OTHER MUSCULOSKELETAL DIS.			
L28	DISABILITY/IMPAIRMENT			
L29	OTHER & MULT. MUSCULOSKEL. SYMPT.	+246 +286 +300	−4080 +4115 +4150 +4540 +4720	+719.7,−729.5 −733.9,+781.2, −781.9
L70	INFECTIONS	+31 +246	+0150 −4095 +4150	−074.1,−728.0, −730.0,.1,.2, .3,.9
L71	NEOPLASMS	+39* +45 +46	−0445 +0515 +0575 +0590	−170,−171, −213,−215, −238.0,.1,
L72	FRACTURE: RADIUS/ULNA	306*	5035	813
L73	FRACTURE: TIBIA/FIBULA	310*	5060	823,824
L74	FRACTURE: HAND/FOOT BONES	−307* −308*	−5040 −5045 −5065	814−816, −825,−826
L75	FRACTURE: FEMUR	309*	−5050 −5055	−820,−821
L76	FRACTURE: OTHER	−301* −302* −303*	−5000 −5005 −5010	800−812, 817−819,−822, 827−829

ICPC code	Main title	Corresponding codes		
		ICHPPC-2	RCC	ICD-9
		−304*	−5015	
		−305*	−5020	
		−311*	−5025	
			−5030	
			−5056	
			−5075	
L77	SPRAINS & STRAINS OF ANKLE(S)	317	5130	845.0
L78	SPRAINS & STRAINS OF KNEE(S)	316*	5125	844
L79	SPRAINS & STRAINS OF OTH JOINTS	−314*	−5110	840–843,
		−315*	−5115	−845.1
		−318*	−5120	846–848
		−319*	−5135	
		−320*	−5140	
		−321*	−5145	
			−5150	
			−5155	
L80	DISLOCATIONS	313	−5080	830–835,
			−5085	836.3,.4,.5,.6
			−5090	837–839
			−5095	
			−5100	
			+5105	
L81	OTHER INJURY	+323	−5175	860–869,
		+332	+5180	−897.S,
		+333	+5230	900−909
				958, 959
L82	CONGENITAL ANOMALIES	−248*	−4260	754–756
		+252	−4265	
L83	SYNDROMES OF CERVICAL SPINE	−235	−3990	−721.0,.1,
		+237*	−4000	−722.0,.4,
			−4010	−723
L84	OSTEOARTHRITIS OF SPINE	+237*	−3995	−721.2,.5,.6,
			+4150	.7,.8,.9
L85	ACQUIRED DEFORMITIES OF SPINE	240	4145	737
L86	LUMBAR DISC,LESION,RADIATION	239*	4005	−722.1,.5,.9
				−724.3,.4
L87	GANGLION JOINT/TENDON	241*	4060	727.4
L88	RHEUMATOID ARTHRITIS/ALLIED COND.	228*	−3905	−714
			−3910	−720.0,.2
			−3985	
L89	OSTEOARTHRITIS OF HIP	+229*	3935	+715
L90	OSTEOARTHRITIS OF KNEE	+229*	3940	+715
L91	OTHER OSTEOARTHRITIS	+229*	−3915	+715
			−3920	
			−3925	
			−3930	
			−3945	
			−3950	
			−3955	
L92	SHOULDER SYNDROME	232*	4030	−726.0,.1,.2
L93	TENNIS ELBOW	+233	4035	726.3
L94	OSGOOD–SCHLATTER, OSTEOCHONDROS	242*	4105	732
L95	OSTEOPOROSIS	243*	4110	733.0
L96	ACUTE MENISCUS/LIGAMENT KNEE	312*	+5105	−836.0,.1,.2
L97	CHRONIC INTERNAL KNEE DERANGEMENT	244*	3965	717
L98	ACQUIRED DEFORMITIES OF LIMBS	+245*	−4125	734–736
			−4130	
			−4140	
L99	OTHER DIS.MUSCULOSKELETAL SYSTEM	−230*	−3900	710–713
		−231*	−3960	(ex. 712.0),

ICPC code	Main title	Corresponding codes		
		ICHPPC-2	RCC	ICD-9
		+233	−3965	−716,−718,
		+245*	−3970	−719,−725,
		+246	−4025	−726.4,.5,.6,
			−4040	.7,.8,.9
			−4045	−727
			−4050	(ex. 727.4),
			−4055	−728,−731,
			−4070	−733
			−4100	(ex. 733.0)
			+4115	−738.1,.2,.3,
			−4120	.4,.5,.6
			+4150	

N— Neurological

ICPC code	Main title	ICHPPC-2	RCC	ICD-9
N01	HEADACHE (*excl.*R09,N89)	+258*	+4585	+784.0
N02	TENSION HEADACHE	+76*	+1190	+307.8
N03	PAIN, FACE	+258*	+4585	+784.0
N04	RESTLESS LEGS SYNDROME	+91	+1325	+333.9
N05	TINGLING FINGERS/FEET/TOES	+259	+4545	+782.0
N06	OTHER SENSA. DISTURB./AB. INVOL MOV	+91	+1325	−333.3,−781.0,
		−255*	+4545	+782.0
		+259*	+4720	
N07	CONVULSIONS/SEIZURES	254*	4505	780.3
N16	OTHER DISTURB.SENSE/SMELL/TASTE	+259	+4545	−781.1,
		+300	+4720	+782.0
N17	VERTIGO/DIZZINESS (*excl.*H82)	256*	4510	780.4
N18	PARALYSIS/WEAKNESS (*excl.*A04)	+300	+4720	−781.4
N19	DISORDER SPEECH	+257*	+4590	−784.3,.5
			+4720	
N26	FEAR OF CANCER OF NEURO.SYSTEM			
N27	FEAR OF OTHER NEURO.DISEASE			
N28	DISABILITY/IMPAIRMENT			
N29	OTHER SYMPT/COMPLT.NEURO.SYSTEM	+300	+4540	−781.3,.9
			+4720	
N70	POLIOMYELITIS/OTH ENTEROVIRUS	+8	−0065	−045,−046,
			−0070	−048,−138
			+0290	
N71	MENINGITIS/ENCEPHALITIS	+8	−0055	−036,−047,
		+31	+0120	−049,−062,−063,
		+91	−1305	−064,
				320−323
N72	TETANUS	+31	+0060	037
N73	OTHER INFECT.NEURO.SYSTEM	+91	+1385	324−326
N74	MALIGNANT NEOPLASMS	+39*	−0510	−191,−192,
			+0515	
N75	BENIGN NEOPLASMS	+45	+0575	−225
N76	UNSPEC. NEOPLASMS	+46	+0590	−237.5,.6,.7,.9
N79	CONCUSSION	+322*	+5160	850
N80	OTHER HEAD INJ.WO SKULL FX.	+322*	+5160	−851,−852,−853,
				−854
N81	OTHER INJURIES	+333	5225	−950.0,−952.9,
				−957.9,.S
N85	CONGENITAL ANOMALIES	+252	−4200	−740,−741,
			−4205	−742
			−4210	
			+4295	
N86	MULTIPLE SCLEROSIS	87*	1335	340

ICPC code	Main title	Corresponding codes		
		ICHPPC-2	RCC	ICD-9
N87	PARKINSONISM	88*	−1315	332
			−1320	
N88	EPILEPSY, ALL TYPES	89*	−1365	−345
			−1370	
			−1375	
N89	MIGRAINE	+90*	+1380	−346.0,.1,.8,.9
N90	CLUSTER HEADACHE	+90*	+1380	346.2
N91	FACIAL PARALYSIS, BELL'S PALSY	+91	1395	351
N92	TRIGEMINUS NEURALGIA	+91	1390	350
N93	CARPAL TUNNEL SYNDROME	+91	1400	354.0
N94	OTHER PERIPHERAL NEURITIS	+91	−1405	−353,−354.1,.2,
			−1410	.3,.4,.5,.8,.9,
			−1415	−355,−356,−357
N99	OTHER DIS. OF NEUR. SYSTEM.	+91	+1310	−330,−331.3,.4,
			+1325	.5,.6,.9,
			−1330	−333−337
			−1340	341−344,
			−1345	347−349,−352,
			−1350	−358,−359,
			−1355	
			−1360	
			+1385	
			−1420	
			−1425	

P— Psychological

P01	FEELING ANXIOUS/NERVOUS/TENSE			
P02	ACUTE STRESS/TRAN. SITUAT. DISTUR.	77*	1200	−308,
				−309
P03	FEELING DEPRESSED			
P04	FEELING/BEHAVING IRRITABLE			
P05	FEELING/BEHAVING OLD/SENILE	297*		797
P06	DISTURBANCES OF SLEEP/INSOMNIA	75*	1175	307.4
P07	INHIB./LOSS SEXUAL DESIRE	+79*	+1095	+302.7
			−1165	−306.5
P08	INHIB./LOSS SEXUAL FULFILMENT	+79*	+1095	+302.7
P09	CONCERN SEXUAL PREFERENCE	+86	+1090	+302.1,.2,
				.3,.4,.5,.6,
				.8,.9
P10	STAMMERING,STUTTERING,TICS	+86	+1225	+307.0,.2,.3
P11	EATING PROBLEMS CHILD	+86	+1180	+307.5
P12	BEDWETTING,ENURESIS (excl.U04)	+86	1185	307.6
P13	ENCOPRESIS	+86	+1225	307.7
P15	CHRONIC ALCOHOL ABUSE	80*	−1005	−291
			−1100	−303
P16	ACUTE ALCOHOL ABUSE	81	1115	305.0
P17	TOBACCO ABUSE	82*	1140	305.1
P18	MEDICINAL ABUSE	+83	+1110	+304,
			+1225	−305.4,.8,+305.9
P19	DRUG ABUSE	+83	1010	−292,−304,
			+1110	−305.2,.3,.5,
			+1225	.6,.7,.8,.9,+305.9
P20	DISTURB.MEMORY/CONCENTRATION	+300	+4720	−780.1,.9
P21	OVERACTIVE CHILD, HYPERKIN.	+78	+1210	314
P22	OTHER CONCERN BEHAV.CHILD	+78	+1210	+312,+313
P23	OTHER S/C BEHAVIOR ADOLESCENT	+78	+1210	+312,+313
P24	SPECIFIC LEARNING PROBLEMS	74	1215	315

ICPC code	Main title	Corresponding codes		
		ICHPPC-2	RCC	ICD-9
P25	PHASE OF LIFE PROBLEM ADULT	368	6900	+V62.8
P27	FEAR OF MENTAL DISORDER			
P28	DISABILITY/IMPAIRMENT			
P29	OTHER PSYCHOLOGICAL SYMPTOMS	+86	+1225	+307.9
P70	DEMENTIA/SENILE,ALZHEIMERS	+66*	−1000	−290,
		+91	+1310	−331.0,.1,.2
P71	OTHER ORGANIC PSYCHOSIS	+66*	−1015	−293,−294,
		+86	−1205	−310
P72	SCHIZOPHRENIA, ALL TYPES	67*	−1020	−295,−297,
			−1030	−298.3,.4
			+1035	
P73	AFFECTIVE PSYCHOSIS	68*	−1025	296,−298.0
			+1035	
P74	ANXIETY DISORDER/ANXIETY STATE	70*	1040	300.0
P75	HYSTERICAL/HYPOCHONDRIACAL DIS.	+71*	−1045	−300.1,.7,
			−1070	−306.2
			−1155	
P76	DEPRESSIVE DISORDER	72*	1060	−300.4,−311
			+1225	
P77	SUICIDE ATTEMPT	+73	5330	
P78	NEURASTHENIA,SURMENAGE	+73	1065	300.5
P79	OTHER NEUROTIC DISORDER	+73	−1050	−300.2,.3
			−1055	−300.6,.8,.9
			−1075	
P80	PERSONALITY DISORDER	84*	−1080	301
P85	MENTAL RETARDATION	85*	1220	317−319
P98	OTHER/UNSPEC. PSYCHOSIS	69	+1035	−298.2,.8,.9,
				−299
P99	OTH MENTAL/PSYCHOL. DISORDERS	+78	+1210	+312,

R— Respiratory

R01	PAIN:ATTRIB TO RESPIR. SYSTEM	+262*	+4640	+786.5
R02	SHORTNESS OF BREATH, DYSPNEA	+269*	+4620	+786.0
R03	WHEEZING	+269*	+4620	+786.0
R04	OTHER BREATHING PROBLEMS	+269*	+4650	−786.7,
		+300	+4720	+786.9
R05	COUGH	270*	4630	786.2
R06	NOSE BLEED/EPISTAXIS	267*	4595	784.7
R07	SNEEZING/NASAL CONGESTION	+300	+4720	+784.9
R08	OTHER SYMPTOMS OF NOSE			
R09	SYMPT/COMPLT SINUS (*incl.*PAIN)			
R21	SYMPT/COMPLT THROAT			
R22	SYMPT/COMPLT TONSILS			
R23	VOICE SYMPT./COMPLT.	+257	+4590	784.4
R24	HEMOPTYSIS	268*	4635	786.3
R25	ABNORMAL SPUTUM/PHLEGM	+300	+4720	786.4
R26	FEAR OF CANCER OF RESPIR.SYSTEM			
R27	FEAR OF OTHER RESPIR.DISEASE			
R28	DISABILITY/IMPAIRMENT			
R29	OTH SYMPT. RESPIR. SYSTEM NEC	+300	−4645	−786.8,
			+4650	+786.9
R70	TUBERCULOSIS RESPIR. (*excl.*A70)	+4*	+0020	−010.1,−011,
			+0290	−012,+137.0
R71	WHOOPING COUGH	6*	0040	033
R72	STREP.THROAT/SCARLET FEVER	+7*	0045	034
R73	BOIL/ABSCESS NOSE	146	2470	+478.1

ICPC code	Main title	Corresponding codes		
		ICHPPC-2	RCC	ICD-9
R74	URI (HEAD COLD)	133*	2400	−460,−462, −465
R75	SINUSITIS ACUTE/CHRON.	134*	−2405 −2445	−461−473
R76	TONSILLITIS ACUTE	135*	−2410 −2455	−463,−475
R77	ACUTE LARYNGIT./TRACHEIT./CROUP	137*	2415	464
R78	ACUTE BRONCHITIS/BRONCHIOLITIS	138*	−2420 +2535	−466,−490
R80	INFLUENZA (PROVEN)WO PNEUMONIA	139*	2485	−487.1,.8
R81	PNEUMONIA	140*	2475	480–486, 487.0
R82	PLEURISY ALL(*excl.*R70)	141*	2520	511
R83	OTHER INFEC. RESPIR. SYSTEM	+31 +147	−0035 +0210 −0285 −2440 −2480 +2535	−032,−101, −135,−472, −476,−510
R84	MALIGN. NEOPL. BRONCHUS/LUNG	+33*	0440	162
R85	OTHER MALIGN. NEOPL.	+33*	−0435 +0515	−160,−161,−163 −165
R86	BENIGN NEOPLASM	+45	+0575	−212
R87	FOREIGN BODY NOSE/LARYNX/BRONC.	+331	+5215	−932,−933,−934
R88	OTHER INJURIES	+333	+5230	874
R89	CONG ANOMAL OF RESPIR. SYSTEM	+252	+4295	748
R90	HYPERTR./CHR. INFECT. T & A	136*	2450	474
R91	CHRONIC BRONCHITIS/BRONCHIECTASIS	142*	+2490 −2505	−491 −494
R93	PLEURAL EFFUSION NOS	5	2525	−511.1,.8,.9
R95	EMPHYSEMA/COPD	143*	+2490 −2495	−492,−496
R96	ASTHMA	144*	2500	493
R97	HAY FEVER,ALLERGIC RHINITIS	145*	−2460 −2465	477
R98	HYPERVENTILATION	+71	1150	306.1
R99	OTHER DISEASE RESPIR. SYSTEM	+147	−2430 −2435 −2510 −2515 −2530 +2535	−470,−471, −478,−495, 500–508, 512–519

S— Skin

S01	PAIN, TENDERNESS OF SKIN	+259	+4545	782.0
S02	PRURITUS, SKIN ITCHING	+218	3720	698 (ex.698.0)
S03	WARTS	+19*	+0165 −0170	+078.1
S04	LOCAL SWELLING/PAPUL./LUMP/MASS	+296	+4720	782.2
S05	GEN.SWELLING/PAPUL./LUMP/MASS			
S06	LOCAL REDNESS/ERYTHEMA/RASH	+292*	+4550	+782.1
S07	GEN.REDNESS/ERYTHEMA/RASH	+292*	+4550	+782.1
S08	OTHER CHANGES IN SKIN COLOR	+227 +300	+3780 +4720	+709.0,−782.6, .9
S09	INFECTED FINGER/TOE/PARONYCHIA	+207*	−3605 −3610 +3615	−681

ICPC code	Main title	Corresponding codes		
		ICHPPC-2	RCC	ICD-9
S10	BOIL/CARBUNCLE/CELLULITIS LOCAL	+207*	−3600 +3615	−680,−682
S11	OTHER LOCALIZED SKIN INFECTION	+211 +222	+3635 +3745	+686.9,−704.8
S12	INSECT BITE	325	5190	919.4
S13	ANIMAL/HUMAN BITE	+323	+5170	+879.8
S14	BURNS/SCALDS	328	5220	940–949
S15	FOREIGN BODY IN SKIN	329	+5195	pt. 910–919
S16	BRUISE/CONTUSION INTACT SKIN	+327	+5200 −5205	920–929
S17	ABRASION/SCRATCH/BLISTER	+326	+5195	pt. 910–919
S18	LACERATION/CUT	+323	+5170 +5175	873–897
S19	OTHER INJURY TO SKIN	+333	+5230	959.8
S20	CORNS, CALLOSITIES	219*	3725	700
S21	SYMPT/COMPL.OF SKIN TEXTURE	+300	+4720	782.8
S22	SYMPT./COMPLT. NAILS			
S23	BALDNESS/LOSING HAIR	+222	+3745	−704.0,.9
S24	OTHER SYMPT./COMPLT. HAIR & SCALP	+222	+3745	−704.1,.2,.3
S26	FEAR OF CANCER OF SKIN			
S27	FEAR OF HAVING OTHER SKIN DIS.			
S28	DISABILITY/IMPAIRMENT			
S29	OTHER SYMPT./COMPLT. SKIN	+227	−3730 +3780	−701.3,+709
S70	HERPES ZOSTER	10*	0090	053
S71	HERPES SIMPLEX (*excl.*F85,X90,Y72)	+11*	0100	−054.0,.2,.5,.6,.7,.8,.9
S72	SCABIES AND OTHER ACARIASES	30*	0275	133
S73	PEDICULOSIS/OTHER SKIN INFEST.	29*	0270	−132 −134
S74	DERMATOPHYTOSIS	24*	−0215 −0220	−110 −111
S75	MONILIASIS/CANDIDIASIS(*excl.*GU)	25*	−0225 −0240	−112.0,.3, 5,.9
S76	OTHER INFECTIOUS SKIN DIS.	+7* +31 +211	−0050 +0185 +0210 −3635	−035,−085, −102,−103, +686
S77	MALIGN. NEOPLASMS OF SKIN	34*	−0450 −0455	−172,−173
S78	LIPOMA OF SKIN	40*	0545	214
S79	OTHER BENIGN NEOPLASM OF SKIN	41*	0550	216
S80	OTHER/UNSPEC. NEOPLASM SKIN	+46	+0590	238.2
S81	HEMANGIOMA/LYMPHANGIOMA	44*	0570	−228.0,.1
S82	NEVUS/MOLE	+252	4270	757.3
S83	OTHER CONGENITAL LESIONS	+252	−4280 −4295	757 (ex.p.757.3)
S84	IMPETIGO	210*	3625	684
S85	PILONIDAL CYST/FISTULA	+211	3630	685
S86	SEBORRHEIC DERMATITIS	212*	3645	690
S87	ATOPIC DERMATITIS/ECZEMA	213*	3655	691.8
S88	CONTACT DERMATITIS/OTHER ECZEMA	214*	−3660 −3665	−692,−693
S89	DIAPER RASH	215*	3650	691.0
S90	PITYRIASIS ROSEA	216*	3700	696.3
S91	PSORIASIS W/WO ARTHROPATHY	217*	−3690 −3695	−696.0,.1
S92	POMPHOLYX/ DIS. SWEAT GLANDS	223	−3750 −3755	705
S93	SEBACEOUS CYST	220*	3765	706.2
S94	INGROWN TOENAIL/OTHER DIS. OF NAIL	221	3740	703

ICPC code	Main title	Corresponding codes		
		ICHPPC-2	RCC	ICD-9
S95	MOLLUSCA CONTAGIOSA	+31	0160	078.0
S96	ACNE	224*	3760	−706.0,.1
S97	CHR ULCER SKIN/INCL. VARICOSE	+129	−3770	−707
		−225	−2255	−454.0
S98	URTICARIA	226*	3775	708
S99	OTHER DIS. SKIN/SUBCUT. TISSUE	+227	−3670	694–695,
			−3675	−697,−701
			−3680	(ex.701.3),
			−3685	−702,+709
			−3705	
			−3735	
			+3780	
			+3785	
			−4295	

T— Endocrine & metabolic

T01	EXCESSIVE THIRST	+300	+4720	783.5
T02	EXCESSIVE APPETITE	+300	+4720	783.6
T03	LOSS OF APPETITE	273*	4565	783.0
T04	FEEDING PROBLEM INFANT (*excl.*P11)	+53*	+4575	+783.3
T05	FEEDING PROBLEM ADULT (*excl.*T06)	+53*	+4575	+783.3
T06	ANOREXIA NERVOSA	+86	−1170	−307.1
			+1180	+307.5
T07	WEIGHT GAIN	+300	+4720	783.1
T08	WEIGHT LOSS (*excl.*T06)	293*	−4570	−783.2
			−4910	−799.4
T10	FAILURE TO THRIVE	294*	4580	783.4
T11	DEHYDRATION			
T15	THYROID LUMP, MASS			
T26	FEAR OF CANCER OF ENDOCR. SYSTEM			
T27	FEAR OF OTHER ENDOCR.NUTR. DIS.			
T28	DISABILITY/IMPAIRMENT			
T29	OTHER SYMPT./COMPLT. ENDOCR. NUTR.	+300	+4720	783.9
T70	INFECT. DIS. ENDOCR. METAB. NUTR.	+31	+0280	+136.9
T71	MALIGN. NEOPLASM THYROID	+39*	+0515	193
T72	BENIGN NEOPLASM THYROID	+45	+0575	226
T73	OTHER/UNSPEC.NEOPLASMS	+39*	+0515	−194,−227,
		+45	+0575	−237.4
		+46	+0590	
T78	THYROGLOSSAL DUCT(CYST)	+252	+4295	+759.2
T80	OTHER CONGENITAL ANOMALIES	+252	+4295	+759.2
T81	GOITER/NODULE W/O THYROTOX.	47*	0700	−240,−241
T82	OBESITY (BMI > 30)	+55	+0785	+278.0
T83	OVERWEIGHT (BMI < 30)	+55	+0785	+278.0
T85	HYPERTHYROIDISM/THYREOTOX.	48*	0705	242
T86	HYPOTHYROIDISM/MYXEDEMA	49*	0710	−243,−244
T87	HYPOGLYCEMIA	+57	0725	251.0,..1,..2
T88	RENAL GLUCOSURIA	+57	0755	271.4
T90	DIABETES MELLITUS	50*	0720	250
T91	VITAMIN DEFIC/OTHER NUTR. DIS	52	0750	260–269
				(excl.266.2)
T92	GOUT	54*	0770	274
T93	LIPID METABOLISM DISORDER	56	0765	272
T99	OTH ENDO. METAB. NUTR. DISEASE	+57	−0715	−245,−246,
			−0730	251–259,270,
			−0735	271,273,275,
			−0740	276,277,279
			−0745	

ICPC code	Main title	Corresponding codes		
		ICHPPC-2	RCC	ICD-9
			−0760	
			−0775	
			−0780	

U— Urology

U01	PAINFUL URINATION	280*	4680	788.1
U02	FREQUENT/URGENT URINATION	283*	4695	788.4
U04	INCONTINENCE,(*excl.*P12)	281*	4690	788.3
U05	OTHER URINATION PROBLEMS	+300	−4685	−788.2,.5,.6
			+4720	
U06	BLOOD IN URINE	373*	2950	599.7
U07	OTHER COMPLAINTS OF URINE			
U13	OTHER SYMPT./COMPLT. BLADDER	+300	+4720	+788.9
U14	SYMPT./COMPLT. KIDNEY	+300	−4675	−788.0,+788.9
			+4720	
U26	FEAR OF CANCER OF URINARY SYST.			
U27	FEAR OF OTHER URINARY DISEASE			
U28	DISABILITY/IMPAIRMENT			
U29	OTHER SYMPT. URINARY SYSTEM	+300	+4720	+788.9
U70	PYELONEPHRITIS/PYELITIS,ACUTE	169*	2910	−590.1,.3,.8,.9
U71	CYSTITIS/OTHER URIN. INFECT. NEC	−170*	−2935	−595,−599.0,
		−198*	−3350	−646.5,.6
U72	URETHRITIS, NON SPECIFIC	−172*	−0205	−099.4,
		−372*	−2940	−597
U75	MALIGN. NEOPL. KIDNEY	+37*	+0505	189
U76	MALIGN. NEOPL. BLADDER	+37*	0500	188
U77	OTHER MALIGN. NEOPL. URINARY TRACT	+37*	+0505	−189.2,.3,.9
U78	BENIGN NEOPL.URINARY TRACT	+45	+0575	223
U79	OTHER UNSPEC.NEOPL.URINARY TRACT	+46	+0585	−233.9,−236.7,
			+0590	.9
U80	INJURIES	+333	+5165	+867.S
U85	CONG ANOMALIES URIN. TRACT	+252	+4250	753
U88	GLOMERULONEPHRITIS/NEPHROSIS	168*	2900	580–583
U90	ORTHOSTATIC ALBUMINURIA	173*	2925	593.6
U95	URIN. CALCULUS ALL TYPES/SITES	171*	−2920	−592,
			−2930	−594
U98	ABN. URINE TEST FINDING, NOS	298*	−4820	−791.0,.9
			+4830	
U99	OTHER DISEASE URINARY SYSTEM	174	−2905	584–589,
			−2915	−590.0,.2,
			−2926	−591,−593
				(ex.593.6)
			−2945	−596,−598,
			−2955	−599 (ex. 599.7)

W— Pregnancy & family planning

W01	QUESTION OF PREGNANCY (*excl.* W02)			
W02	FEAR OF BEING PREGNANT			
W03	ANTE-PARTUM BLEEDING	+197	−3320	−640,
			+3325	−641
W05	VOMITING/NAUSEA OF PREGNANCY	+202	3335	643.0,−9
W10	MORNING AFTER PILL	+346	+6400	+V25.8

ICPC code	Main title	ICHPPC-2	RCC	ICD-9
W11	FAMILY PLAN./ORAL CONTRACEPTIVE	344*	−6355 −6360	+V25.0,4
W12	FAMILY PLAN./IUD	345*	6370	−V25.1,+V25.4
W13	FAMILY PLAN./STERILIZATION	+343* +347*	6340	V25.2
W14	FAMILY PLANNING/OTHER	+346* +347*	−6350 +6400	+V25.0,+V25.8
W15	COMPLAINTS OF INFERTILITY	+195*	3155	628
W17	HEAVY POST-PARTUM BLEEDING	+204	3420	666
W18	OTHER COMPLT. POST-PARTUM PERIOD			
W19	SYMPT./COMPLT. LACTATION			
W20	OTHER S/C BREAST(IN PREG.)	+205	3475	676.2
W27	FEAR OF COMPLICATIONS OF PREG.			
W28	DISABILITY/IMPAIRMENT			
W29	OTH SYMPT.PREG/FAMILY PLANNING	+202	+3355	+646.1,−646.2
W70	PUERPERAL INFECTION, SEPSIS	+206	−3450 +3490	−670,−672
W71	OTHER INFECTIOUS CONDITIONS†	+202	+3360	647
W72	MALIGNANT NEOPLASM†	+39*	+0515	181
W73	BENIGN NEOPLASM†	+45 +202	+0575 +3200	−219.8,−630
W75	INJURIES COMPLICATING PREG.†	+202	+3355	
W76	CONG.ANOMALIES OF MOTHER†	+204	+3381	654.9
W77	OTHER NON-OB CONDITIONS†	+202 +204	+3360 +3380	−648.9,−653, −654.6
W78	PREGNANCY: CONFIRMED	+350*	+6285	+V22
W79	UNWANTED PREGNANCY: CONFIRMED	+350*	+6285	+V22
W80	ECTOPIC PREGNANCY	196*	3305	633
W81	TOXEMIA, (PRE)ECLAMPSIA	199*	−3330	642
W82	ABORTION, SPONTANEOUS	201*	−3300 −3310 +3355	−632,−634, −637,+648.9
W83	ABORTION, INDUCED	200*	3315 −636	−635
W84	PREGNANCY HIGH RISK	+202 +204	−3340 −3345 +3355 −3370 −3375 +3380 +3445	644–646 (ex.646.5,.6) −648,−651.0,.9, −652.9,−654.2, .5,−659.5,.9
W90	NORMAL DELIVERY LIVEBORN(S)	+203*	3365	650
W91	NORMAL DELIVERY DEADBORN(S)	+203*	+3385	+656.4
W92	COMPLICATED DELIVERY LIVEBORN	+204	+3390 +3395 +3400 +3405 +3410 +3415 +3425 +3430 +3435 +3440 +3445	+(651–669) ex.666
W93	COMPLICATED DELIVERY DEADBORN		+3385 +3390 +3395 +3400 +3405	+(651–669) ex.666

ICPC code	Main title	Corresponding codes		
		ICHPPC-2	RCC	ICD-9
			+3410	
			+3415	
			+3425	
			+3430	
			+3435	
			+3440	
			+3445	
W94	MASTITIS PUERPERALIS	+205*	3460	675
W95	OTHER DISORDERS OF BREAST	+205*	−3465	676
			−3470	(ex.676.2)
			−3480	
			−3485	
			+3490	
W96	OTHER COMPLIC. PUERPERIUM	+206	+3490	−674.9
W99	OTHER DIS. PREG. DELIV. PUERPERIUM	+197	−3315	−638,−639
		+204	+3325	−641
			+3345	−645

X— Female genital system

X01	GENITAL PAIN			
X02	MENSTRUAL PAIN	+191*	+3100	625.3
X03	INTERMENSTRUAL PAIN	+191*	+3100	625.2
X04	PAINFUL INTERCOURSE	374*	3090	−625.0,.1
X05	MENSTRUATION ABSENT/SCANTY	189	−3115	−626.0,.1
			−3120	
X06	MENSTRUATION EXCESSIVE	+190	3130	+626.2,.3
				−627.0
X07	MENSTRUATION IRREGULAR/FREQ.	+190	−3125	+626.2
			+3135	−626.4,
X08	INTERMENSTRUAL BLEEDING	+193	+3135	−626.5,.6,.9
X09	PREMENSTRUAL SYMPTOMS			
X10	POSTPONEMENT OF MENSTR.			
X11	MENOPAUSAL SYMPT./COMPLT.	+187*	−3145	−627.2,.3.4,
			−3150	.8,.9
X12	POSTMENOPAUSAL BLEEDING	+187*	3140	627.1
X13	POSTCOITAL BLEEDING	+193	+3135	626.7
X14	VAGINAL DISCHARGE	+194	3085	623.5
X15	OTHER SYMPT./COMPLT. VAGINA			
X16	SYMPT./COMPLT. VULVA	+194	+3095	−624.9,
		+218	−3715	−698.1
X17	SYMPT./COMPLT. PELVIS	+296	+4710	+789.3
X18	BREAST PAIN	+182	+3030	+611.7
X19	LUMP/MASS BREAST	+182	+3030	+611.7
X20	SYMPT./COMPLT. NIPPLE	+182	+3030	−611.0,.2
				+611.7
X21	OTHER SYMPT./COMPLT. BREAST	+182	+3030	+611.1,.7
X23	FEAR OF VENEREAL DISEASE			
X24	FEAR OF SEXUAL DYSFUNCTION			
X25	FEAR OF GENITAL CANCER			
X26	FEAR OF BREAST CANCER			
X27	FEAR OTHER GENITAL/BREAST DISEASE			
X28	DISABILITY/IMPAIRMENT			
X29	OTH.SYMPT/GENITAL SYSTEM.	+300	+4720	+788.7
X70	SYPHILIS, FEM.(GENIT.& NOS)	+22*	+0195	+091–097
X71	GONORRHOEA,FEM.(GENIT.& NOS)	+23*	+0200	+098
X72	UROGENITAL CANDIDIASIS, PROVEN	+26*	0230	112.1
X73	UROGENITAL TRICHOMONIASIS, PROV.	+27*	+0265	+131.0,

ICPC code	Main title	Corresponding codes		
		ICHPPC-2	RCC	ICD-9
X74	PELVIC INFLAMMATORY DISEASE	183*	3035	−614,−615
X75	MALIGN. NEOPL. CERVIX	+36*	−0470	−180,−233.1
			−0580	
X76	MALIGN. NEOPL. BREAST	+35*	+0465	−174,−233.0
		+39*	+0590	
X77	OTHER MALIGN. NEOPL.	+36*	−0475	−179,−182,
		+39*	−0480	−183,−184,
			−0495	−233.2
			+0515	
			+0590	
X78	FIBROID/MYOMA (UTERUS/CERVIX)	43*	−0560	−218,−219
			+0575	
X79	BENIGN NEOPL. BREAST (*excl.*X88)	+42*	+0555	+217
X80	OTH BENIGN NEOPL. FEM. GENIT.	+45	−0565	−220,−221
			+0575	
X81	OTH/UNSPEC. NEOPL. FEM. GENIT.	+46	+0590	−236.3,+238.3
X82	INJURIES	+323	+5165	−867.6,+878.8
		+333	+5170	
X83	CONGENITAL ANOMALIES FEM. GENIT.	+252	+4250	−752.0,.1,.2,.3,.4,.7,.8,.9
X84	VAGINITIS/VULVITIS,NOS	185*	3045	616.1
X85	CERVICITIS/OTHER CERV. DISEASE	184*	−3040	−616.0
			−3075	−622
			−3080	
			+3095	
X86	ABNORMAL PAP SMEAR	376*	−4845	795.0
			−4850	
			−4855	
X87	UTEROVAGINAL PROLAPSE	186*	−3060	−618
			−3110	−625.6
X88	CHRONIC CYSTIC DIS. BREAST	181*	3020	610
X89	PREMENSTRUAL TENSION SYNDROME	188*	3105	625.4
X90	HERPES GENITALIS	+11*	+0095	+054.1
X91	CONDYLOMATA ACUMINATA	+19*	+0165	+078.1
X99	OTHER DIS. FEM. GEN. SYSTEM	+31	+0210	+099,−611.0,
		+182	−3025	−611.9,−616.2,
		+194	+3030	.3,.4,.5,.8,.9
			−3050	−617,−619,
			−3055	−620,−621,−623
			−3065	(ex.623.5)
			+3070	−624,−625.5,
			+3095	−629.9
			−3160	

Y— Male genital system

Y01	PAIN IN PENIS			
Y02	PAIN IN TESTIS/SCROTUM			
Y03	DISCHARGE FROM PENIS/URETHRA			
Y04	OTHER SYMPT./COMPLT. OF PENIS			
Y05	SYMPT./COMPLT.SCROTUM & TESTES			
Y06	SYMPT./COMPLT.PROSTATE			
Y07	SYMPT./COMPLT. POTENCY (*excl.*P07,P08)			
Y08	OTH S/C SEXUAL DYSF. (*excl.*P07,P08)			
Y10	INFERTILITY/SUBFERTILITY	+195*	2990	606
Y13	FAMILY PLANNING/STERILIZATION	+343*	+6340	+V25.2
Y14	FAMILY PLANNING/OTHER	+347*	+6350	+V25.0
Y16	SYMPT./COMPLT. MALE BREAST	+182	+3030	+611.7
Y24	FEAR OF SEXUAL DYSFUNCTION			

ICPC code	Main title	Corresponding codes		
		ICHPPC-2	RCC	ICD-9
Y25	FEAR OF VENEREAL DISEASE			
Y26	FEAR OF CANCER MALE GENITAL			
Y27	FEAR OF OTHER GENITAL DISEASE			
Y28	DISABILITY/IMPAIRMENT			
Y29	OTHER SYMPT. MALE REPROD. SYST.			
Y70	SYPHILIS MALE	+22*	+0195	+091–097
Y71	GONORRHOEA MALE	+23*	+0200	+098
Y72	HERPES GENITALIS	+11*	+0095	+054.1
Y73	PROSTATITIS/SEMINAL VESICULI	176*	−2970	−601,−608.0
			+3015	
Y74	ORCHITIS/EPIDIDYMITIS	178*	2980	604
Y75	BALANITIS	+26*	+0235	+112.2
		+179*	−2995	607.1
Y76	CONDYLOMATA ACUMINATA	+19*	+0165	+078.1
Y77	MALIGN. NEOPL. PROSTATE	+37*	0485	185
Y78	OTHER MALIGN. NEOPL.	+35*	−0490	−175,−186,−187
		+37*	+0495	−236.6
		+46*	+0465	
			+0590	
Y79	BENIGN NEOPL. MALE GENITAL	+42	+0555	+217,−222
		+45	+0575	
Y80	INJURIES	+323	+5170	+878.8,−959.1
		+333	+5230	
Y81	PHIMOSIS/REDUND. PREPUCE	+179*	2985	605
Y82	HYPOSPADIA	+252	+4250	752.6
Y83	UNDESC. TESTICLE/CRYPTORCHISM	249*	4245	752.5
Y84	OTHER CONG.ANOMAL.	+252	+4250	752.7,.8,.9
Y85	BENIGN PROSTATIC HYPERTROPHY	175*	2960	600
Y86	HYDROCELE	177*	2975	603
Y99	OTHER DIS. MALE GEN. INCL. BREAST	+31*	+0210	+099,112.1,.2,
		+26*	+0235	+131,−602,
		+27*	+0265	−607 (ex.607.1)
		+180	−3005	−608 (ex.608.0)
		+182	−3010	+611.1,+611.9
			+3015	
			+3030	

Z— Social problems

Z01	POVERTY/FINANCIAL PROBLEMS	356*	6805	V60.2
Z02	PROBLEM FOOD AND WATER	+369	+6905	+V60.9
Z03	PROBLEM HOUSING/NEIGHBORHOOD	+357*	−6800	V60.0,.1,.3
			−6810	
Z04	PROB. SOCIAL/CULTURAL SYSTEM	−365*	−6850	V61.6,+V62.4
		+366*	+6890	
Z05	PROB. WORKING CONDITIONS	+367*	−6875	V62.1,.2
			−6880	
Z06	PROB. WITH BEING UNEMPLOYED	+367*	6870	V62.0
Z07	PROBLEM WITH EDUCATION	364*	6885	V62.3
Z08	PROB. SOCIAL INSURANCE/WELFARE	+369	+6905	+V62.9
Z09	PROB. LEGAL/POLICE	370*	6895	V62.5
Z10	PROB. HEALTH CARE SYSTEM/ACCESS	+371	+6905	V63
Z11	PROB. WITH BEING ILL	+358*	+6840	+V61.4
Z12	RELATION PROB. PARTNERS	359*	6820	V61.1
Z13	PROB. WITH BEHAV. PARTNER	+358*	+6840	+V61.4
Z14	PROB. WITH PARTNER BEING ILL	+358*	+6840	+V61.4
Z15	LOSS OR DEATH OF PARTNER	+362*	+6815	+V61.0

ICPC code	Main title	Corresponding codes		
		ICHPPC-2	RCC	ICD-9
Z16	RELATION PROBL WITH CHILD	+360*	−6825 −6830	V61.2
Z18	PROB. WITH CHILD BEING ILL	+358*	+6840	+V61.4
Z19	LOSS OR DEATH OF CHILD	+362*	+6815	+V61.0
Z20	RELAT. PROB. PARENT/OTHER FAMILY	+361*	+6835	+V61.3
Z21	PROB. W BEHAV. PARENT/OTH FAMILY	+361*	+6835	+V61.3
Z22	PROB. W PARENT/ FAMILY BEING ILL	+358*	+6840	+V61.4
Z23	LOSS OR DEATH PARENT/FAMILY	+362*	+6815	+V61.0
Z24	PROB. IN RELAT. W FRIENDS	+369	+6905	V62.8
Z25	PROB. ASSAULTS/HARMFUL EVENTS	+369	+6905	+V62.9
Z27	FEAR OF HAVING A SOCIAL PROB.			
Z28	SOCIAL HANDICAP	+366*	+6890	+V62.4
Z29	OTHER SOCIAL PROB./NEC	+366* +369	+6890 +6905	+V60.9,+62.4,9

13 How to use the ICPC alphabetic index

The ICPC alphabetic index provides direction to most of the terms used in primary care. Should the term in question not be available in this ICPC alphabetical index, it is possible that it may be located in the inclusion terms incorporated in the criteria specified for the appropriate defined diagnosis in ICHPPC-2-Defined. It will be necessary for the coder to access ICHPPC-2-Defined, as these inclusion criteria have not been listed in ICPC.

The alphabetical index is provided to assist the user in locating the correct ICPC code in all four modes; namely, (a) Reason for Encounter, (b) Assessment or Diagnosis, (c) Process or Intervention, (d) Comprehensive Use. It must be understood how the index is designed and what can and cannot be found within it, if it is to be used appropriately.

Types of terms

There are many more terms within the index than the rubric titles of the entire ICPC. The tabular list is limited by space and therefore it is impossible to identify all the terms codable to a specific rubric in the tabular list. The alphabetical index should be used frequently, and always when one is in doubt as to the code selection.

Conditions such as 'cough' and 'pain' as well as diseases such as 'diabetes' and 'hepatitis' are indexed under their names. *Always look first for the actual condition rather than the body site or body system.*

Example

'Laceration of left arm' Look in the alphabetical index under the term 'laceration' for the correct ICPC code rather than under the term 'arm'.

Main or Lead terms

These are those terms which are in the first position in the alphabetic index. Many of these main terms are modified and such modifiers are indented under the main term.

Example
> Anemia (main term)
>> Aplastic (modifier)
>>> Congenital (modifier)

ICPC Components 2–6

These components are standard throughout the classification and contain such terms as 'biopsy', 'postoperative visit', and 'results of blood test'. The index will show these rubrics both with and without the chapter assignment (the alpha code). The codes will, therefore, have a dash (–) in place of the alpha code: '–59 Minor Surgery'. The user is expected to add the appropriate alpha code. Minor surgery in the nose would be R59, but repair of laceration of skin would be S54. At no time will a code with a dash in the first place be an acceptable code. Such codes are incomplete and the user must assign the correct alpha code. In some instances modifiers which are indented below the main term contain alpha codes.

Example

—56 Packing
R56 Nasal
X56 Vaginal

Prefixes

Throughout the ICPC the body organs are located within the appropriate body system. Therefore, bronchus, lung, trachea, and larynx are organs which will be coded to the Respiratory System. There may be a reason for encounter in which the body organ involved is not listed in the chapter where the user would expect. To confirm that the correct body system code is being applied, check the term 'prefixes' in the index. Here all the body organs and sites are listed with their appropriate chapter assignment.

Example

Endocardium   K—
Eyelid   F—
Gallbladder   D—
Joint, any   L—

Any reason for encounter which involves the 'endocardium' will be coded to a ICPC code which always begin with the alpha code 'K'. The two dashes (––) indicate the places for the two numeric codes.

General terms

Within the index there are many general terms which contain an alpha code to Chapter A, General and Unspecified. These are only to be used when the coder does not have information which would identify a specific chapter.

Example

Bleeding, blood(y) (in)	A10
Bleeding, post-menopausal	X12
Nonspecific bleeding site	A10
Nonspecific bleeding from female genital tract	X08

Other rules and conventions of the ICPC index

When using the ICPC index there are certain rules or conventions which must be followed in order to code correctly. These are intended to assist in locating the most appropriate code, and are particularly useful when the coder has a choice between several codes. There are three particular ways the index deals with special problems:

1. The term 'NEC'

NEC means 'not elsewhere classified' and is used for those terms which may or may not be modified and assigned to other codes.

Example

Anemia

B82	aplastic
B79	congenital
B81	folate deficiency
B78	hemolytic
B80	iron deficiency
B81	pernicious
B82	unspecified NEC

The various terms indented under 'Anemia' are different types of anemia. As can be seen the categories to which these entries are coded are aplastic, congenital, etc. However, if another specific type of anemia is diagnosed and it cannot be found among those indented, then the Specified NEC code would apply.

2. Parentheses

Throughout the index parentheses function in several ways.

(a) As non-essential modifiers. These show that the coding of a term to a rubric is not affected by the presence or absence of the modifiers in the parentheses.

Example

R78   Bronchiolitis (acute)
This tells the coder that bronchiolitis is to be coded to R78 whether or not the term 'acute' accompanies it. Therefore, both 'bronchiolitis' and 'acute bronchiolitis' will be coded to R78. The term in parentheses tells the coder he need not look below for an indented term to find the correct ICPC code.

(b) As coding direction. These instructions direct the coder elsewhere within the index where the appropriate code can be found.

Example

Hemorrhage (see also Bleeding)
If the diagnosis of 'hemorrhage of the gums' was presented the correct code would be found by following the direction given above since 'gums' is not listed under Hemorrhage. However, the main term 'Bleeding' has an indented term 'gums', which shows the correct code: D19

(c) As additional words which clarify the statements of the condition

Example

Counselling (for) (of)
Because of the additional terms in parentheses, terms indented under the lead term may be read: Counselling *for* abortion (X45); Counselling *of* family (–58).

(d) As guidance in defining the intent and content of rubrics.

Example

Malnutrition (any type)
This clarifies the coding by stating that all types of malnutrition are to be coded to the same code, T91.

3. 'See . . .'

A third convention in the ICPC index is the 'See . . .' references. These direct the user of the ICPC to some other place in the index where the correct codes will be found.

Example

Pain
muscle NEC
    specified site . . . *See* Pain, by site, muscular.
This statement directs the coder to look under the lead term 'pain' then
look for the particular body site (arm, leg, etc.) for the correct code.

Example

Lump . . . *see* Mass
Tumor . . . *see* Neoplasm

Conclusion

It is important that the user of the ICPC become familiar with both the
Tabular List and the Index. The two should be used together in order to
correctly apply the ICPC. While some of the rules mentioned above may
at first seem confusing or complicated, the index was formatted in the
same manner as the ICD and the ICHPPC. Any problems encountered
when using the index should be noted and communicated to:

Henk Lamberts
Professor and Chairman Department of General Practice
University of Amsterdam
Meibergdreef 15
1105 AZ Amsterdam
The Netherlands.

14 ICPC alphabetical index

ABDOMEN, ABDOMINAL
D01 ACUTE
D01 GENERALIZED
D01 COLIC
A14 INFANTILE
CRAMPS
D01 GENERALIZED
D06 LOCALIZED
D01 DISCOMFORT
D24 MASS
D01 PAIN
D01 GENERALIZED
D06 LOCALIZED
SPASMS
D01 GENERALIZED
D06 LOCALIZED

ABNORMAL, ABNORMALITY (OF)
F15 APPEARANCE (OF) EYE(S)
BLOOD TEST (UNEXPLAINED)
B85 BLOOD CHEMISTRY
B85 GLUCOSE TOLERANCE TEST
B85 OTHER NON- SPECIFIC SERUM ENZYME LEVELS
B86 RED BLOOD CELLS
B85 TRANSAMINASE LEVELS
R04 BREATHING NEC
X86 CERVICAL SMEAR
A90 CHROMOSOMAL
COLOR
D20 LIPS
D20 TONGUE
CONGENITAL — *see* CONGENITAL, ANOMALY
EARS
H15 SHAPE
H15 SIZE
H15 STICKING OUT
FORCES OF LABOUR
W93 DEADBORN(S)

W92 LIVEBORN(S)
L29 GAIT
S24 HAIRINESS
K05 HEARTBEAT
B86 HEMATOLOGICAL
B84 LEUCOCYTES
B84 LYMPHOCYTES
N06 MOVEMENT DISORDERS (INVOLUNTARY)
F14 MOVEMENT DISORDERS (INVOLUNTARY) EYE
K05 PALPITATIONS
X86 PAP SMEAR
R25 PHLEGM
B83 PLATELET
K05 PULSE
R03 RESPIRATORY NOISES
SENSATION(S) NEC
H29 EAR
F13 EYE
F05 —VISION
N16 OLFACTORY
N16 SMELL
N16 TASTE
N16 TOUCH
N06 SENSATIONS
R25 SPUTUM
D20 TASTE
U98 URINE TEST FINDINGS NEC
B84 WHITE CELLS

W82 **ABORTION (BY) NEC**
W58 ADVICE ON
W52 D & C OR SUCTION
INDUCED
W83 ILLEGAL
W83 LEGAL
W82 SPONTANEOUS
W03 THREATENED

S17 **ABRASION**
F75 EYE
S17 SKIN

W99 **ABRUPTIO PLACENTA**

ABSCESS

S10	NEC
D95	ANORECTAL
D88	APPENDIX
—51	ASPIRATION
X99	BARTHOLIN
L70	BONE
X99	BREAST (NON-PUERPERAL)
L99	BURSA
D82	DENTAL
Y74	EPIDIDYMIS
S09	FINGER
D98	GALLBLADDER
D82	GUMS
D97	LIVER
R99	LUNG
B70	LYMPH NODE
R73	NOSE
D95	PERIANAL
R76	PERITONSILLAR
S85	PILONIDAL
S10	SKIN
S51	—ASPIRATION
S51	—DRAINAGE
S51	—INCISION
A87	STITCH
L99	TENDON
Y74	TESTIS
S09	TOE

N88	**ABSENCE(S) (COMPLETE) (PARTIAL)**
	CONGENITAL — *see* CONGENITAL, ANOMALY
A97	DISEASE
X05	MENSTRUATION

ABUSE

	ALCOHOL
P16	ACUTE
P15	CHRONIC
Z16	CHILD
	DRUG
P19	DEPENDANT
P19	NONDEPENDANT
P19	GLUE
Z12	HUSBAND
	MEDICINAL
P18	DEPENDANT
P18	NONDEPENDANT
P19	OTHER SUBSTANCE
Z12	PARTNER
P17	TOBACCO
Z12	WIFE

S72	**ACARIASIS**

H80	**ACCESSORY AURICLE**
A80	**ACCIDENT NEC** — *see also* **INJURY**
A80	AUTOMOBILE
K90	CEREBROVASCULAR
—56	**ACE BANDAGE**
D84	**ACHALASIA, ESOPHAGUS**
	ACHE — *see also* **PAIN**
A01	ALL OVER
H01	EAR
N01	HEAD
L99	**ACHILLES TENDONITIS**

ACNE

S96	CONGLOBATA (CYSTIC)
S99	ROSACEA
S96	VULGARIS

H85	**ACOUSTIC TRAUMA**
B90	**ACQUIRED IMMUNO-DEFICIENCY SYNDROME**
T99	**ACROMEGALY**
—57	**ACTIVE EXERCISE**
—59	**ACUPUNCTURE**

ACUTE (AND SUBACUTE)

K70	ENDOCARDITIS
K70	MYOCARDITIS
K70	PERICARDITIS
K77	PULMONARY EDEMA

ADDICTION

P15	ALCOHOL
P17	NICOTINE
P19	SPECIFIED SUBSTANCE NEC

T99	**ADDISON'S DISEASE**
	ADENOMA — *see also* **NEOPLASM, BENIGN**
Y85	PROSTATE
T72	THYROID
D99	**ADHESIONS, ABDOMINAL**

ADJUSTING

L54	BRACE (BACK) (LEG) (NECK)
H54	HEARING AID
L54	ORTHOPEDIC SHOES

ANKLE(S) *contd.*
K07   SWOLLEN

ANOMALY — *see also*
    ABNORMALITY
    CONGENITAL — *see*
        CONGENITAL,
        ANOMALY
F99   PUPILLARY FUNCTION

T06   **ANOREXIA NERVOSA**

D40   **ANOSCOPY**

ANTEPARTUM
W03   BLEEDING
W30   VISIT

—33   **ANTIBODY & AGGLUTINATION
    TITER**

—33   **ANTINUCLEAR ANTIBODY**

—33   **ANTISTREPTOLYSIN TITER**

U05   **ANURIA**

P01   **ANXIETY, ANXIOUS**
P74   DISORDER
P74   STATE

K99   **AORTIC ANEURYSM**

N19   **APHASIA**

R23   **APHONIA**

D83   **APHTHOUS ULCER**

APPENDICITIS
D88   ACUTE
D88   CHRONIC, RECURRENT

APPETITE
T03   DECREASED
T02   EXCESSIVE
T02   INCREASED
T03   LOSS (OF)
T03   POOR

APPLICATION (OF)
L54   CAST
L54   CERVICAL COLLAR
L54   NECK SUPPORT
L54   SPLINT

F99   **ARCUS SENILIS**

ARGUE, ARGUING, ARGUMENT
    ('ALL THE TIME')

Z20   FAMILY NEC
Z24   FRIENDS
Z12   MARITAL
Z16   PARENT–CHILD
Z12   PARTNER

K84   **ARRHYTHMIA**

—51   **ARTERIAL PUNCTURE**

ARTERIOSCLEROSIS — *see*
    ATHEROSCLEROSIS

ARTERITIS
K99   GIANT CELL
K99   TEMPORALIS

L99   **ARTHRITIS NEC**
L99   ACUTE
L99   ALLERGIC
L99   CRYSTAL (*excl.*GOUT)
L91   DEFORMANS
L84   SPINE
L91   DEGENERATIVE
L84   SPINE
L88   INFLAMMATORY
L99   PYOGENIC
L88   RHEUMATOID
L99   TRAUMATIC

L99   **ARTHRODESIS**

L41   **ARTHROGRAM**

**ARTHROPATHY (ASSOCIATED
    WITH)** — *see also*
    ARTHRITIS
L99   BEHCET'S SYNDROME
S91   PSORIATIC
L99   REITER'S DISEASE

L40   **ARTHROSCOPY**

ARTIFICIAL
W59   INSEMINATION
W51   RUPTURE OF MEMBRANES

R99   **ASBESTOSIS**

—51   **ASPIRATION**
U51   BLADDER
—51   BODY ORIFICES
—51   CYST, ABSCESS
H51   EARS
F51   EYES
L51   JOINT, BURSA
R51   NOSE
D51   STOMACH

Z25   **ASSAULT(S)**

BIOPSY *contd.*
X52   ENDOMETRIAL

R99   **BIRD FANCIERS' LUNG**

S83   **BIRTHMARK NEC**
S81   ANGIOMATOUS

BITE
S13   ANIMAL
S13   HUMAN
S12   INSECT

F75   **BLACK EYE (TRAUMATIC)**

S96   **BLACKHEAD**

A06   **BLACKOUTS**

U95   **BLADDER CALCULUS**

A10   **BLEEDING, BLOOD(Y) NEC (IN)**
D16   ANAL
W03   ANTEPARTUM
X21   BREAST
       DISEASE — code to the specific
           disease
H05   EAR
D15   FECES
D15   GASTROINTESTINAL
       GENITAL
X08   FEMALE NEC
W03   —DURING PREGNANCY
X08   —INTERMENSTRUAL
X08   —IRREGULAR
X12   —MENOPAUSAL
X13   —POSTCOITAL
Y03   MALE
         —SPECIFIED SITE — *see*
           SYMPTOMS, BY SITE
D19   GUMS
D15   INTESTINE
D20   LIPS
X12   MENOPAUSAL
D20   MOUTH
X20   NIPPLE
R06   NOSE
       OBSTETRIC:
W03   ANTEPARTUM
W17   POSTPARTUM (HEAVY)
X08   OVULATION
X13   POSTCOITAL
X12   POSTMENOPAUSAL
W17   POSTPARTUM (HEAVY)
W03   PREGNANCY
X06   PUBERTY
D16   RECTAL
B34   TIME
D20   TONGUE
U06   URINATION, URINE

D14   VOMITING

S07   **BLEMISHES**

F72   **BLEPHARITIS**

D99   **BLIND LOOP SYNDROME**

F94   **BLINDNESS**
F99   NIGHT

F14   **BLINKING**

S17   **BLISTER (SKIN)**
S14   DUE TO BURN

D08   **BLOATING**

       BLOCK, BLOCKAGE,
           BLOCKED, BLOCKING
K84   ATRIOVENTRICULAR
K84   BUNDLE BRANCH
H13   EAR
H73   EUSTACHIAN TUBE
K84   HEART
F80   LACRIMAL DUCT, IN
           INFANTS
R07   NOSE
F80   TEAR DUCT

       BLOOD
—34   CHEMISTRY
—34   COUNT (RED, WHITE,
           COMPLETE,
           PLATELET):
—34   DIFFERENTIAL
—33   CULTURE
—34   ELECTROLYTES
B33   GROUPING & TYPING
—34   HGB
—34   MORPHOLOGY:
—34   SICKLE CELL
       PRESSURE:
K85   ELEVATED
K85   HIGH
K88   LOW
K85   PROBLEMS
—34   RETICULOCYTE
—34   SUGAR
—34   TEST (CHEMICAL) NEC:
—33   FOR VD

—33   **BLOOD GROUP**

F02   **BLOODSHOT EYES**

S06   **BLOTCHES (SKIN)**

F05   **BLURRED VISION**

CAN'T *contd.*

U05	STREAM
	STOP:
P15	DRINKING
T06	EATING
P17	SMOKING
D21	SWALLOW
N19	TALK
N16	TASTE
U05	URINATE

A79   **CANCER NEC** — *see also*
 NEOPLASM, MALIGNANT

S75	**CANDIDIASIS**
Y75	MALE
X72	UROGENITAL, PROVEN (FEMALE)

L92   **CAPSULITIS ADHESIVE, SHOULDER**

T99   **CARBOHYDRATE METABOLIC DISORDERS**

S10   **CARBUNCLE**

CARCINOMA — *see also*:

R85	NEOPLASM MALIGNANT *in situ* NEC (OF) RESPIRATORY SYSTEM
	NEOPLASM, MALIGNANT
A79	DISSEMINATED (PRIMARY SITE UNKNOWN)
A79	*in situ* NEC (OF)
X76	—BREAST
X75	—CERVIX
U79	—URINARY SYSTEM
X77	—UTERUS

A79   **CARCINOMATOSIS (PRIMARY SITE UNKNOWN)**

CARDIAC

K84	ARREST
K77	ASTHMA
P75	NEUROSIS

K84   **CARDIOMEGALY**

K84   **CARDIOMYOPATHY**

D84   **CARDIOSPASM**

K71   **CARDITIS** — *see* **MYOCARDITIS RHEUMATIC (CHRONIC**

CARE (OF)

D54	OSTOMY APPLIANCES
K54	PACEMAKER
—54	PROSTHETIC DEVICE

Z05   **CAREER CHOICE PROBLEM**

D82   **CARIES, TEETH**

N93   **CARPAL TUNNEL SYNDROME**

CAST (FOR)

L54	DISLOCATION
L54	FRACTURE
L54	REMOVAL
L54	SPRAIN
L54	STRAIN

—41   **CAT-SCAN**

F92	**CATARACT**
F92	SENILE

—53   **CATHETERIZATION**
U53   BLADDER

N99   **CAUDA EQUINA SYNDROME**

—52   **CAUTERIZATION**

D99   **CELIAC DISEASE**

S10	**CELLULITIS (OF) (LOCALIZED)**
S09	FINGER OR TOE
X74	PELVIS, FEMALE

CEREBRAL

K92	ANEURYSM (UNRUPTURED)
N99	PALSY

CEREBROVASCULAR

K90	ACCIDENT
K92	DISEASE

—62   **CERTIFICATE(S) (BIRTH) (DEATH) (SICK)**

H81   **CERUMEN, EXCESSIVE**

CERVICAL

X85	DYSPLASIA
W84	INCOMPETENCE (SHIRODKAR SUTURE)
X85	LEUKOPLAKIA

L01   **CERVICALGIA**

X85	**CERVICITIS**
X71	GONOCOCCAL

COLIC
D01	BILIARY
D01	DIGESTIVE
A14	INFANTILE
D01	INTESTINAL

COLITIS
	INFECTIOUS
D70	SPECIFIED
D73	UNSPECIFIED
D93	MUCOUS
D94	ULCERATIVE

L99 **COLLAGEN DISEASE**

A06 **COLLAPSE**

L72 **COLLES' FRACTURE**

D93 **COLON, SPASTIC**

D40 **COLONOSCOPY**

COLOR VISION
F99	DEFICIENCIES
F39	TEST

F39 **COLORBLIND TEST**

D99 **COLOSTOMY MALFUNCTION**

X40 **COLPOSCOPY**

A07 **COMA NEC**
T90	DIABETIC
D97	HEPATIC
T87	HYPOGLYCAEMIC
T87	INSULIN
A07	TRAUMATIC

S96 **COMEDO**

R74 **COMMON COLD**

COMPLAINT(S) — *see*
   SYMPTOM(S)

W52 **COMPLICATED DELIVERY**

COMPLICATION (OF) NEC
A87	AMPUTATION STUMP
A87	DEVICES
K29	HEART
A87	IMPLANTS
A87	MEDICAL OR SURGICAL PROCEDURE
A87	POSTOPERATIVE
A87	PROSTHESES
W96	PUERPERIUM (POSTNATAL)

COMPRESSION
—56	ARTERIAL BLEEDING
—56	LYMPHEDEMA

—41 **COMPUTERIZED TOMOGRAPHY**

CONCERN(S) (ABOUT) — *see also*
   FEAR OF
P05	AGING
A13	DRUG REACTION

N79 **CONCUSSION**

CONDYLOMA ACUMINATA
X91	FEMALE
Y76	MALE

P20 **CONFUSION**

CONGENITAL
B79	ANEMIA
	ANOMALY (OF):
B79	BLOOD, BLOOD-FORMING ORGANS NEC
L82	BONE
K73	CIRCULATORY SYSTEM
D81	DIGESTIVE SYSTEM
H80	EAR
T80	ENDOCRINE GLAND NEC
F81	EYE
F80	—BLOCKED LACRIMAL DUCT
	GENITAL SYSTEM NEC
X83	—FEMALE
Y84	—MALE
K73	HEART
W76	MOTHER, COMPLICATING PREGNANCY
A90	MULTIPLE SYNDROMES
L82	MUSCULOSKELETAL SYSTEM
N85	NERVOUS SYSTEM
R89	RESPIRATORY SYSTEM
S83	SKIN
U85	URINARY SYSTEM
Y82	HYPOSPADIAS (MALE)
D81	MEGACOLON
Y81	PHIMOSIS

CONGESTION
R29	CHEST
H13	EAR
R07	NASAL
R09	SINUS

K77 **CONGESTIVE HEART FAILURE**

F71   **CONJUNCTIVITIS NEC**
F71   ALLERGIC
       INFECTIOUS:
F70   CHLAMYDIA
F70   BACTERIAL
F70   VIRAL

D12   **CONSTIPATION**

       CONSULTATION
—46   PRIMARY CARE PROVIDER
—47   SPECIALIST:
        — *see* COUNSELLING

F18   **CONTACT LENS PROBLEM(S)**

       CONTRACTURE
L99   DUPUYTREN'S
L18   MUSCLES NEC

       CONTRAST
—41   RADIOGRAPHY
—41   X-RAY

       CONTUSION
F75   EYE
S16   WITH INTACT SKIN
         SURFACE

       CONVERSION (OF)
K59   CARDIAC RHYTHM
         (EXCEPT PACEMAKER)
K54   PACEMAKER
P75   HYSTERIA

N07   **CONVULSIONS**
W81   IN PREGNANCY

B33   **COOMBS TEST**

R95   **COPD**

K82   **COR PULMONALE**

       CORNEAL
F99   OPACITIES
F85   ULCER

S20   **CORNS**

R74   **CORYZA**

L99   **COSTOCHONDRITIS**

R05   **COUGH, COUGHING (ACUTE,**
       CHRONIC, FEBRILE)
R24   BLOOD
R05   SMOKERS
R05   WITH EXPECTORATION

—45   **COUNSELLING (FOR) (OF)**
       EDUCATION SELF CARE
       THERAPEUTIC

       COUNSELLING (FOR) (OF)
W58   ABORTION (FEMALE)
—45   ALCOHOL CONSUMPTION
—45   BAD HABITS
Z58   CONJUGAL (PARTNER)
—45   DIET
—45   EDUCATION SELF CARE
        PREVENTIVE
—58   EMOTIONAL PROBLEMS
—45   ENVIRONMENTAL RISKS
—45   EXERCISE
        GENETIC:
—45   FEMALE
—45   MALE
—45   HEALTH RISK NEC
—58   MARRIAGE
—45   MEDICINE USE
—45   NUTRITIONAL
—45   OCCUPATIONAL RISK
—45   POSTOPERATIVE
W45   PRENATAL (FEMALE)
—45   PREOPERATIVE
—45   PREVENTIVE:
—45   DIET
—45   DISEASE
—45   FAMILY
—45   GENETIC
—45   MEDICAL
—45   NUTRITIONAL
P58   PSYCHIATRIC
—45   SEATBELTS
—45   SEDENTARY LIFESTYLE
—45   SMOKING
        STERILIZATION:
W13   FEMALE
Y13   MALE
        THERAPEUTIC:
P58   ALCOHOLISM
—58   DISEASE
P58   DRUG ABUSE
—58   FAMILY
—58   MEDICAL
—58   SEXUAL
—45   WEIGHT PROBLEM

A76   **COWPOX**

S73   **CRABS**

       CRACKED
D20   LIPS
W95   NIPPLE

       CRAMP(S), CRAMPING
       ABDOMINAL:
D01   GENERALIZED

CRAMP(S) *contd.*
D06   LOCALIZED
L14   CALF
L17   FOOT
L12   HAND
L14   LEG
X02   MENSTRUAL
L18   MUSCULAR NEC:
          SPECIFIED SITE — *see*
          SYMPTOMS, BY SITE
D02   STOMACH
L14   THIGH

L01   **CRICK, NECK**

F95   **CROSS-EYED**

R77   **CROUP**

S16   **CRUSHING WITH INTACT SKIN
          SURFACE**

CRYING (EXCESSIVE)
P03   ADULT
A15   CHILD/INFANT

—52   **CRYOSURGERY**

—52   **CRYOTHERAPY**

Y83   **CRYPTORCHISM**

L99   **CRYSTAL ARTHRITIS** (*excl.*
          GOUT)

—33   **CULTURE**
—33   FECES
—33   FUNGUS
—33   SKIN
—33   SPUTUM
D33   STOOL
R33   THROAT
U33   URINE:
—33   DIPSLIDE

L85   **CURVATURE OF SPINE**
L82   CONGENITAL

T99   **CUSHING'S SYNDROME**

S18   **CUT**

CYST
—51   ASPIRATION
X99   BARTHOLIN
F72   EYELID
X85   NABOTHIAN (FOLLICLE)
S85   PILONIDAL
S93   SEBACEOUS
S04   SKIN

L87   SYNOVIAL

CYSTIC
X88   BREAST (CHRONIC)
T99   FIBROSIS

U71   **CYSTITIS (NONVENEREAL)**
U71   ACUTE
U71   CHRONIC
U71   PREGNANCY

X87   **CYSTOCELE**

U40   **CYSTOSCOPY**

F73   **DACRYOCYSTITIS**

S86   **DANDRUFF**

H80   **DARWIN'S TUBERCLE**

A96   **DEAD (FOUND)**

H86   **DEAFMUTISM**

**DEAFNESS (COMPLETE)
(PARTIAL)**
H86   CONDUCTIVE
H86   SENSONEURAL
H86   MIXED

DEATH (SUDDEN)
P02   ADJUSTMENT PROBLEM
A96   ADULT
Z19   CHILD
A96   COT
A96   CRIB
Z23   FAMILY MEMBER
A96   INFANT
Z23   PARENT
Z15   PARTNER
P02   REACTION TO

A04   **DEBILITY**

S52   **DEBRIDEMENT OF WOUND**

DECREASE
T03   APPETITE
T08   WEIGHT

DEFECT, DEFECTIVE
B83   COAGULATION
          CONGENITAL — *see*
          CONGENITAL
          ANOMALY
B83   PLATELET
F94   VISION

—41 **DIAGNOSTIC RADIOLOGY**

U59 **DIALYSIS (KIDNEY)**

DIAPHRAGM
W54   INSERTION
W54   REMOVAL

D11 **DIARRHEA**
D70   BACTERIAL
D70   INFECTIOUS

—57 **DIATHERMY**

—45 **DIET**
    COUNSELLING — *see*
      COUNSELLING, DIET
—32   ELIMINATION, FOR
      ALLERGY TEST

**DIFFICULT, DIFFICULTY
(WITH)**
R02   BREATHING
Z20   FAMILY:
Z16   CHILD, CHILDREN
Z20   IN-LAWS
Z20   PARENTS
Z12   PARTNER
Z12   SPOUSE
X04   INTERCOURSE
F05   READING
P20   REMEMBERING
D21   SWALLOWING
U05   URINATION
L28   WALKING

DIFFUSE
X88   CYSTIC MASTOPATHY
L99   DISEASE, CONNECTIVE
      TISSUE

—53 **DILATION**
—53   CERVIX
U53   URETHRAL

R83 **DIPHTHERIA**

F99 **DIPLOPIA**

P15 **DIPSOMANIA**

—30 **DIRECTED HEALTH
    EXAMINATION (BY
    PATIENT, PROVIDER OR
    OTHER) (SPECIFIC BODY
    SYSTEM OR ORGAN)**

A28 **DISABILITY (IMPAIRMENT)
    NEC**
B28   BLOOD, BLOOD-FORMING

      ORGANS, LYMPHATICS,
      SPLEEN
K28   CIRCULATION TRACT
D28   DIGESTIVE SYSTEM
W28   DURING PREGNANCY
T28   ENDOCRINE, METABOLIC
      AND NUTRITIONAL
F28   EYE
X28   FEMALE GENITAL SYSTEM
H28   HEARING
Y28   MALE GENITAL ORGANS
L28   MUSCULOSKELETAL
      SYSTEM
N28   NEUROLOGICAL SYSTEM
W28   PREGNANCY
P28   PSYCHOLOGICAL
R28   RESPIRATORY
S28   SKIN
U28   URINARY SYSTEM

    DISAGREEMENT — *see* **ARGUE**

    DISCHARGE
H04   EAR
F03   EYE
R07   NASAL
X20   NIPPLE
Y03   PENILE
      URETHRA:
X29   FEMALE
Y03   MALE
X14   VAGINAL

A04 **DISCOMFORT** — *see also* **PAIN
    GENERALIZED**

Z04 **DISCRIMINATION (COLOR)
    (RACE) (RELIGION) (SEX)
    NEC**

—58 **DISCUSSION OF SPECIFIC
    PROBLEMS OR DISEASES**
—65   OTHER PERSON
—48   REASON FOR ENCOUNTER

A99 **DISEASE NEC**
A97   ABSENCE OF
R95   AIRWAYS, CHRONIC
      OBSTRUCTIVE
P70   ALZHEIMER'S
K83   AORTIC (VALVE)
      (CHRONIC)
K71   RHEUMATIC
D99   APPENDIX
K99   ARTERIES NEC
K99   ARTERIOLES NEC
A78   ARTHROPOD BORNE
L88   BECHTEREW
B99   BLOOD AND BLOOD-
      FORMING ORGANS NEC

L70	BORNHOLM		MITRAL
X99	BREAST (FEMALE) NEC	K83	(VALVE) (CHRONIC)
Y99	MALE		NONRHEUMATIC
K92	BUERGER'S	K71	VALVE (CHRONIC)
L94	CALVE-PERTHES	D83	MOUTH
K99	CAPILLARIES NEC	L99	MUSCLE NEC
D99	CELIAC	L99	MUSCULOSKELETAL
X85	CERVIX:		SYSTEM NEC
W77	COMPLICATING	A78	MYCOBACTERIAL (OTHER)
	PREGNANCY	S94	NAIL
X71	GONOCOCCAL	N99	NERVOUS SYSTEM NEC
K99	CIRCULATORY SYSTEM	N70	CENTRAL, DUE TO
	NEC		ENTEROVIRUS
K84	CIRCULATION	A97	NONE
	PULMONARY	T91	NUTRITIONAL (ANY)
L99	COLLAGEN	L94	OSGOOD–SCHLATTER
L99	CONNECTIVE TISSUE NEC	L99	PAGET'S (BONE)
	COUNSELLING:	D99	PANCREAS
—45	PREVENTIVE	A78	PARASITIC NEC
—58	THERAPEUTIC	N87	PARKINSON'S
A77	COXSACKIE VIRUS		PELVIC:
D94	CROHN'S	W77	COMPLICATING
L99	DIFFUSE, CONNECTIVE		PREGNANCY
	TISSUE	X74	INFLAMMATORY
D99	DIGESTIVE SYSTEM NEC	X71	—VENEREAL
D92	DIVERTICULAR	K84	PERICARDIUM (OTHER)
	(INTESTINE)	K92	PERIPHERAL VASCULAR
H99	EAR NEC	T99	PITUITARY GLAND
T99	ENDOCRINE NEC	R95	PULMONARY, CHRONIC
D84	ESOPHAGUS		OBSTRUCTIVE
F99	EYE NEC	K92	RAYNAUD'S
D98	GALLBLADDER	R99	RESPIRATORY SYSTEM NEC
A99	GENERALIZED NEC	K71	RHEUMATIC HEART
	GENITAL:		(CHRONIC)
X99	FEMALE	A78	RICKETTSIOSIS
Y99	MALE	D83	SALIVARY GLANDS
D82	GUMS	L94	SCHEUERMANN
S23	HAIR	S99	SKIN NEC
A77	HAND, FOOT, MOUTH	B99	SPLEEN NEC
K84	HEART:	S99	SUBCUTANEOUS TISSUE
K76	ATHEROSCLEROTIC		NEC
K76	ISCHEMIC (CHRONIC)	S92	SWEAT GLANDS NEC
K73	—SUBACUTE	D82	TEETH
K82	PULMONARY	D83	TONGUE
K71	RHEUMATIC (CHRONIC)	R90	TONSILS (AND ADENOIDS)
K84	SPECIFIED NEC		(CHRONIC)
K83	VALVE, NONRHEUMATIC	U99	URINARY NEC
B72	HODGKIN'S		VENEREAL OTHER
A78	INFECTIVE AND PARASITIC	Y99	MALE
	NEC (*see also* INFECTION)	X99	FEMALE
U99	KIDNEY NEC	A77	VIRAL:
D83	LIPS	A76	WITH EXANTHEMS
D97	LIVER		
R95	LUNG, CHRONIC	L80	**DISLOCATION (JOINT)**
	OBSTRUCTIVE	L80	ANKLE
B99	LYMPHATIC SYSTEM NEC	L97	CHRONIC, MENISCUS
H99	MASTOID	L80	ELBOW
H82	MENIERE'S	L80	FINGER
T99	METABOLISM NEC	L80	FOOT
T93	LIPID	L80	HIP

DISLOCATION contd.
KNEE:
L80	COMPOUND
L80	SIMPLE
	PATELLA:
L80	COMPOUND
L80	SIMPLE
L99	RECURRENT
L80	SHOULDER
L80	WRIST
L80	YAW

DISORDER (OF)
BEHAVIOR:
P23	ADOLESCENT
P99	ADULT
P22	CHILD
X99	BREAST NEC:
W95	PUERPERAL, POSTPARTUM
L99	BURSA NEC
T99	ELECTROLYTES
T99	ENDOCRINE NEC
	FEEDING PROBLEM (NON-PSYCHOGENIC)
T05	ADULT
T04	CHILD
T04	INFANT
T99	FLUIDS
K84	HEART RHYTHM NEC
L86	INTERVERTEBRAL DISC:
L83	CERVICAL
D82	JOINT TEMPORO-MANDIBULAR
H82	LABYRINTH
W95	LACTATION
P24	LEARNING
T99	METABOLISM NEC:
T93	LIPID
P79	NEUROTIC NEC
T91	NUTRITIONAL (ANY)
P79	OBSESSIVE–COMPULSIVE
P80	PERSONALITY (ANY TYPE)
P09	PSYCHOSEXUAL IDENTITY
F91	REFRACTION
F99	RETINA (UNSPEC.)
N19	SPEECH
D87	STOMACH FUNCTION
L99	SYNOVIUM NEC
L99	TENDON NEC
H82	VESTIBULAR SYSTEM
R23	VOICE
X16	VULVA

L83	**DISPLACEMENT, INTERVERTEBRAL DISC, CERVICAL**

DISPROPORTION
W93	DEADBORN(S)

W92	LIVEBORN(S)

DISSATISFACTION WITH
Z05	EMPLOYMENT
Z07	SCHOOL ENVIRONMENT

D25	**DISTENSION, ABDOMEN**

DISTURBANCE, DISTURBED
BEHAVIOR
P23	ADOLESCENT
P99	ADULT
P22	CHILD
P21	CHILD VERACTIVE
P20	CONCENTRATION
P21	CONDUCT NEC
P29	EMOTIONAL NEC:
P23	ADOLESCENT
P99	ADULT
P22	CHILD
H02	HEARING
P20	MEMORY
P20	ORIENTATION
P29	PSYCHOLOGICAL NEC
	SENSATION — *see* ABNORMAL, SENSATION
P02	SITUATIONAL TRANSIENT
P06	SLEEP
N19	SPEECH
F05	VISION

D92	**DIVERTICULITIS, DIVERTICULOSIS, DIVERTICULUM**
U99	BLADDER
D84	ESOPHAGUS

Z15	**DIVORCE**

N17	**DIZZINESS**

F99	**DOUBLE VISION**

—51	**DRAINAGE**
—51	FOLLOWING INCISION
R07	NOSE
R09	SINUS

DRESSING
—56	APPLIED
—56	CHANGE

D20	**DRIBBLING (SALIVA)**
U04	URINE

R07	**DRIP, POSTNASAL**

D20	**DROOLING**

K07 **EDEMA**
W84   IN PREGNANCY
K77   PULMONARY (ACUTE)

—45 **EDUCATION, EDUCATIONAL**
    (AS) (FOR) (IN)
    ADVICE — *see*
      COUNSELLING
—45   BABY CARE
Z07   HANDICAP
—45   SELF CARE:
—57   PROSTHETIC DEVICE (*see*
      also TRAINING)

N42 **EEG**

    EFFECT(S)
    ADVERSE NEC
A88   AIR PRESSURE
A88   ALTITUDE
A88   COLD
A88   ELECTRIC SHOCK
A88   ENVIRONMENTAL
    FACTOR
A88   EXPOSURE
A88   HEAT
A88   HUNGER
A88   LIGHTNING
A85   MEDICINAL AGENT,
    PROPER DOSE
A88   PHYSICAL FACTOR
A87   RADIATION (IN MEDICAL
    CARE)
A86   SNAKE BITE VENON
A88   SUBMERSION
A86   VENOM NEC
Z05   WORK ENVIRONMENT
A87   X-RAY
D83   DENTURES
    LATE:
K90   CEREBROVASCULAR
A89   PROSTHETIC DEVICE NEC
A82   TRAUMA
    TOXIC:
A84   MEDICINAL AGENT
    (OVERDOSE) (WRONG
    DRUG)
A86   NONMEDICINAL
    SUBSTANCE
A86   OTHER SUBSTANCES
    (EXCEPT DRUGS)

R93 **EFFUSION, PLEURAL NEC**
R70   TUBERCULOUS

K42 **EKG**

A88 **ELECTRIC SHOCK**

    ELECTRICAL
—57   STIMULATION
—42   TRACING

K42 **ELECTROCARDIOGRAM,**
    EXERCISE, TREADMILL

—52 **ELECTROCAUTERY**

N42 **ELECTROENCEPHALOGRAM**

—42 **ELECTROMYOGRAPHY**

K99 **ELEPHANTIASIS**
    (NONFILARIAL)

B86 **ELEVATION SEDIMENTATION**
    RATE (ESR)

—32 **ELIMINATION DIET**

K92 **EMBOLISM (ARTERIAL)**
K90   CEREBRAL
K75   CORONARY (ARTERY)
K92   PRECEREBRAL
K93   PULMONARY

P01 **EMOTIONAL**

R95 **EMPHYSEMA**

R83 **EMPYEMA**

N71 **ENCEPHALITIS**

P13 **ENCOPRESIS**
D17   ORGANIC ORIGIN

    ENCOUNTER INITIATED BY
—65   OTHER PERSON
—64   PROVIDER

K70 **ENDOCARDITIS (ACUTE)**
    (SUBACUTE)
K71   RHEUMATIC (CHRONIC)

P73 **ENDOGENOUS DEPRESSION**

X52 **ENDOMETRIAL BIOPSY**

X99 **ENDOMETRIOSIS**

X74 **ENDOMETRITIS**

—40 **ENDOSCOPY (DIAGNOSTIC)**
    NEC

W20 **ENGORGED BREAST**
W20   POST-PARTUM

EXCISION REMOVAL *contd.*
S52 ULCER (SKIN)
Y52 VAS DEFERENS
S52 WARTS

—52 **EXCISIONAL BIOPSY**

EXERCISE
—57 ACTIVE
—45 ADVICE:
—45   PREVENTIVE
K42 ECG
—57 PASSIVE

—37 **EXFOLIATIVE CYTOLOGY**

A04 **EXHAUSTION, PHYSICAL**

P09 **EXHIBITIONISM**

F99 **EXOPHTHALMOS**

P31 **EXPLORATION**
    PSYCHOLOGICAL
    PARTIAL

P30 **EXPLORATION**
    PSYCHOLOGICAL
    COMPLETE

K80 **EXTRASYSTOLES**

R83 **EXTRINSIC ALLERGIC**
    ALVEOLITIS

F51 **EYE WASHING**

EYELID(S)
F16 DROOPING
F16 ITCHING
F16 PUFFY
F16 STICKY

F29 **EYESTRAIN**

N91 **FACIAL PALSY**

FAILURE, FAILED
K77 CARDIAC
K77 HEART (CONGESTIVE)
    (LEFT) (RIGHT)
W95 LACTATION
K77 LEFT VENTRICULAR
W92 MECHANICAL INDUCTION
K77 MYOCARDIAL
U99 RENAL
T10 TO THRIVE

A06 **FAINTING**

N17 **FALLING SENSATION**

FAMILY
—58 COUNSELLING
    PLANNING:
W11 CONTRACEPTIVE
    MEDICATION (FEMALE)
W11 —ADVICE (ABOUT)
Y14   MALE
W14 COUNSELLING
W14 FEMALE
W14 GENERAL ADVICE
W12 IUD
Y14 MALE
W10 MORNING AFTER PILL
W11 ORAL CONTRACEPTIVE
W14 OTHER METHODS
W10 POSTCOITAL
    CONTRACEPTION
    STERILIZATION
W13 —FEMALE
Y13 —MALE

R99 **FARMER'S LUNG**

F91 **FARSIGHTEDNESS**

L18 **FASCIITIS NEC (SPECIFIED**
    SITE, *see* **SITE)**

T82 **FAT**

A04 **FATIGUE**

S74 **FAVUS**

FEAR (OF)
B25 AIDS
B27 ANEMIA
    BEING:
P27   CRAZY
W02   PREGNANT
F27 BLINDNESS
X27 BREAST DISEASE
    CANCER:
A26   (OF) NEC
B26   —BLOOD
X26   —BREAST
D26   —DIGESTIVE SYSTEM
T26   —ENDOCRINE SYSTEM
B26   —LYMPHATIC
Y26   —MALE GENITAL
    ORGANS
L26   —MUSCULOSKELETAL
    SYSTEM
N26   —NEUROLOGICAL
    SYSTEM
R26   —RESPIRATORY
S26   —SKIN
U26   —URINARY SYSTEM

FEELS contd.

A04	RUN DOWN
P03	SAD
P77	SELF-DESTRUCTIVE
A04	SICK
P01	TENSE
A04	TERRIBLE
R21	THROAT RAW
K02	TIGHTNESS HEART
A04	TIRED
A04	UNWELL
A04	WEAK
N17	WOOZY
P01	WORRIED

S09	**FELON**

FETAL

W92	AND PLACENTAL PROBLEMS
W84	MALPOSITION
W42	MONITORING

P09	**FETISHISM**
R39	**FEV-1**
A03	**FEVER (FEVERISH)**
A75	GLANDULAR
R97	HAY:
R96	WITH ASTHMA
A77	HEMORRHAGIC ARTHROPOD BORNE
A78	RELAPSING
K71	RHEUMATIC:
K71	ACUTE
R72	SCARLET
A77	YELLOW

FIBRILLATION

K78	ATRIAL
K84	VENTRICULAR

X88	**FIBROADENOSIS BREAST**
X78	**FIBROID (UTERUS)**
L18	**FIBROSITIS NEC**
L92	SHOULDER
A76	**FIFTH DISEASE**

FIGHT — see **ARGUE**

D22	**FILARIASIS**

FISSURE

D95	ANAL
X20	NIPPLE

FISTULA

D95	ANAL
X99	GENITAL TRACT
S85	PILONIDAL
D95	RECTAL
X99	VAGINAL

N07	**FITS**

FITTING, ADJUSTING AND INSERTION (OF)

L54	ARTIFICIAL LIMBS
L54	BACK BRACE
F54	CONTACT LENSES
W54	DIAPHRAGM
F54	GLASSES
H54	HEARING AID
W54	IUD
L54	LEG BRACE
L54	NECK BRACE
L54	ORTHOPEDIC SHOES
X54	VAGINAL PESSARY

—54	**FIXATION (EXTERNAL) OR SUPPORT (OF)**
—54	INTERNAL
L54	JOINT
L54	MUSCLE, SPRAIN, STRAIN IN TENDONS

L98	**FLATFOOT**
D08	**FLATULENCE**
F04	**FLOATERS**
D73	**FLU, GASTRIC**
—51	**FLUSHING**

FLUTTERING (HEART)

K78	ATRIAL
K84	VENTRICULAR

U53	**FOLEY CATHETER INSERTION**
S11	**FOLLICULITIS NEC**
—63	**FOLLOW-UP NEC**
D73	**FOOD POISONING**
D70	*SALMONELLA*

FORCEPS DELIVERY

W93	DEADBORN(S)
W92	LIVEBORN(S)

FOREIGN BODY (IN)

R87	BRONCHUS

K99	**GIANT CELL ARTERITIS**
D70	**GIARDIASIS/LAMBLIASIS**
N17	**GIDDINESS**
D82	**GINGIVITIS**
A78	**GLANDERS**
A75	**GLANDULAR FEVER**
F54	**GLASSES FITTING**
F93	**GLAUCOMA**
F39	TEST
U88	**GLOMERULONEPHRITIS (ACUTE)**
U88	CHRONIC
D83	**GLOSSITIS**
T88	**GLUCOSURIA RENAL**
	GLUE
H72	EAR
P19	SNIFFING (HABITUAL)
D99	**GLUTEN ENTEROPATHY**
T81	**GOITER**
	MULTINODULAR:
T81	NON-TOXIC
T85	TOXIC
T85	WITH HYPERTHYROIDISM, THYROTOXICOSIS
	GONOCOCCAL
—33	CULTURE
	INFECTION:
X71	FEMALE (GENITAL)
Y71	MALE (UROGENITAL)
	GONORRHOEA
X71	FEMALE (GENITAL)
Y71	MALE (UROGENITAL)
T92	**GOUT**
—38	**GRAM STAIN**
N88	**GRAND MAL (STATUS)**
T85	**GRAVE'S DISEASE**
P02	**GRIEF (REACTION)**
D73	**GRIPPE, INTESTINAL**

P58	**GROUP PSYCHOTHERAPY**
	GROWTH — *see also* **NEOPLASM**
T29	EXCESSIVE
T10	LACK OF
T10	SHORT
Y99	**GYNECOMASTIA**
W82	**HABITUAL ABORTION**
	HAIR
S24	FALLING
S24	UNWANTED
S24	**HAIR SUPERFLUOUS**
D20	**HALITOSIS**
P20	**HALLUCINATIONS**
	HALLUX
L98	RIGIDUS
L98	VALGUS
L98	**HAMMER TOE**
D81	**HARELIP**
Z25	**HARMFUL EVENTS**
T99	**HASHIMOTO'S DISEASE**
R97	**HAY FEVER**
F05	**HAZY VISION**
R74	**HEAD COLD**
N01	**HEADACHE NEC**
N90	CLUSTER
N89	MIGRAINE
R09	SINUS
N02	TENSION
—45	**HEALTH PROMOTION**
	HEARING
H02	DIMINISHED
H86	LOSS (OF) (SUDDEN)
H39	TEST
P20	VOICES
	HEART
K31	EXAMINATION
K77	FAILURE
K02	HEAVINESS
K81	MURMUR NEC OR NYD
K01	PAIN
K02	PRESSURE

R23	**HOARSENESS**	K82	PULMONARY (PRIMARY) (IDIOPATHIC)
B72	**HODGKIN'S DISEASE**	K87	RENAL DISEASE
		K86	SECONDARY, BENIGN
	HOLTER	K86	UNCOMPLICATED
K42	MONITOR	K87	WITH LEFT VENTRICULAR
K42	TAPE		HYPERTROPHY
F72	**HORDEOLUM**	T85	**HYPERTHYROIDISM**
—50	**HORMONE(S)**		**HYPERTROPHY, HYPERTROPHIC**
—64	**HOSPITAL VISIT**	R90	ADENOIDS
			BREAST
	HOT		GENITAL:
X11	FLUSHES, FLUSHES	X99	FEMALE
—57	SOAKS	Y99	MALE
		K84	HEART
L99	**HOUSEMAID'S KNEE**	U99	KIDNEY
		Y85	PROSTATE (BENIGN)
W92	**HYDRAMNIOS**	T85	THYROID (THYROTOXIC)
		R90	TONSILS
Y86	**HYDROCELE**		
		R98	**HYPERVENTILATION**
N85	**HYDROCEPHALY**		
		P75	**HYPOCHONDRIASIS**
U99	**HYDRONEPHROSIS**		
		T87	**HYPOGLYCEMIA**
—57	**HYDROTHERAPY**		
		P73	**HYPOMANIA**
—52	**HYFRECATOR**		
		X05	**HYPOMENORRHEA**
W05	**HYPEREMESIS GRAVIDARUM**		
		T99	**HYPOPITUITARISM**
A85	**HYPERGLYCEMIA (DRUG-INDUCED)**	Y82	**HYPOSPADIAS (MALE)**
T87	**HYPERINSULINISM**	K88	**HYPOTENSION (POSTURAL)**
T93	**HYPERLIPIDEMIA**	A88	**HYPOTHERMIA**
X06	**HYPERMENORRHEA**		**HYPOTHYROIDISM**
		T86	ACQUIRED
F91	**HYPERMETROPIA**	T86	CONGENITAL
T99	**HYPERPARATHYROIDISM**	P75	**HYSTERIA**
B99	**HYPERSPLENISM**	—41	**HYSTEROSALPINGOGRAM**
	HYPERTENSION, HYPERTENSIVE	S51	**I & D ABSCESS (SKIN)**
K87	CARDIORENAL	—57	**ICE PACKS**
K86	ESSENTIAL, BENIGN		
K87	HEART DISEASE	S99	**ICHTHYOSIS**
W81	IN PREGNANCY		
K87	INVOLVING TARGET ORGAN	A04	**ILL-FEELING**
K87	MALIGNANT	Z04	**ILLEGITIMACY, ILLEGITIMATE PREGNANCY**
K87	NEPHROPATHY		
W81	PRE-ECLAMPTIC		

INFECTION *contd.*

U70	—KIDNEY NEC
L70	—MUSCULOSKELETAL SYSTEM
S09	—NAIL
N73	—NERVOUS SYSTEM NEC
A87	—POSTOPERATIVE
R83	—RESPIRATORY SYSTEM NEC:
R74	UPPER NEC
D83	—SALIVARY GLAND
R75	—SINUS
S76	—SKIN NEC:
S11	LOCALIZED
R74	—THROAT
S09	—TOE
R90	—TONSILS (AND ADENOIDS), CHRONIC
X73	—TRICHOMONAS (PROVEN)
R74	—UPPER RESPIRATORY NEC
	—URINARY
U71	TRACT
	—GONOCOCCAL
X71	FEMALE
Y71	MALE
	—SYPHILITIC
X70	FEMALE
Y70	MALE
U71	IN PUERPERIUM
X99	—UROGENITAL SYSTEM NEC FEMALE
A77	—VIRAL
B90	INFECTIOUS DISEASE NEC (DUE TO) HIV

| A78 | **INFECTIVE AND PARASITIC DISEASES NEC** |

INFERTILITY

W15	FEMALE
Y10	MALE

INFESTATION (BY)

S73	FLEAS
S73	LARVAE
S73	LICE (BODY) (HEAD) (PUBIC)

INFILTRATION

L55	JOINTS
—55	LOCAL NEC
L55	TENDONS

INFLAMMATION

F73	EYELIDS OTHER
Y04	PENIS
Y05	SCROTUM
D87	STOMACH

Y05	TESTES
R21	THROAT
R22	TONSILS
X84	VAGINA
K94	VEIN
X84	VULVA

R80	**INFLUENZA (PROVEN)**
R44	IMMUNIZATION
R80	WITH OTHER MANIFESTATION
R81	WITH PNEUMONIA
R80	WITH RESPIRATORY MANIFESTATION (OTHER)

| —57 | **INFRARED** |

INFUSION

—53	CATHETER
—53	NEEDLE
—53	TUBATION

| S94 | **INGROWN TOENAIL** |

| —55 | **INJECTION LOCAL NEC** |

—50	**INJECTION(S) (BY) (OF)**
—50	ALLERGY DESENSITIZATION
L55	BURSA
N55	CNS
—50	HORMONES
—44	IMMUNIZATION
—44	INOCULATION
—50	INTRADERMAL
—50	INTRAMUSCULAR
—50	INTRAVENOUS
L55	JOINTS
L55	LOCAL IN JOINT
—50	MEDICATION
N55	NERVE
S55	SKIN LESIONS AND CYSTS
—50	SUBCUTANEOUS
L55	TENDON SHEATH
N55	TRIGGER POINT
—44	VACCINATION
K55	VEINS

A80	**INJURY NEC (TO)**
B77	BLOOD-FORMING ORGAN NEC
W75	COMPLICATING PREGNANCY
D80	DIGESTIVE SYSTEM:
D79	FOREIGN BODY ENTERING THROUGH ORIFICE
H79	EAR NEC:

IRREGULAR *contd.*
X07   FLOW
K05   PULSE

—51   **IRRIGATION**

P04   **IRRITATION, IRRITABLE**
D93   BOWEL SYNDROME
D93   COLON
F13   EYE
P04   PSYCHOLOGICAL
S02   SKIN
X16   VULVA

ISCHEMIA
K89   CEREBRAL, TRANSIENT OR
          INTERMITTENT
K76   MYOCARDIAL (CHRONIC)

ISOLATION
Z29   PERSONAL
Z28   SOCIAL

S02   **ITCH(ING) (Y)**
D05   ANAL
H29   EAR
F13   EYE
S24   HAIR
Y05   JOCK
R08   NOSE
D05   PERIANAL
D05   RECTAL
S02   SCALP
Y05   SCROTUM
S02   SKIN
Y05   TESTES
X15   VAGINA
X16   VULVA

IUD
W12   CHECK UP
W54   INSERTION
W54   REINSERTION
W54   REMOVAL

D13   **JAUNDICE NEC**
D72   INFECTIOUS
A94   NEWBORN

P22   **JEALOUSY**

N06   **JERKING**

JOBST STOCKINGS FOR
K56   LYMPHEDEMA
K56   VARICOSE VEINS

JOCK ITCH

JOINT
L51   ASPIRATION
L54   FIXATION FOR
          JNFLAMMATION
L55   INJECTION
L57   MANIPULATION
L99   MICE (EXCL. KNEE)

S99   **KELOID**

F73   **KERATITIS NOS**

KIDNEY
U59   DIALYSIS
U85   POLYCYSTIC
          (CONGENITAL)

L98   **KNOCK-KNEE (ACQUIRED)**
L82   CONGENITAL

—38   **KOH (CANDIDA, FUNGI)**
          NICROSCOPIC TEST

T91   **KWASHIORKOR**

L85   **KYPHOSIS, KYPHOSCOLIOSIS**
L82   CONGENITAL

K86   **LABILE HYPERTENSION**

LABORATORY TEST
W43   AMNIOTIC FLUID
U43   RENAL CALCULUS
D43   STOMACH CONTENTS

R02   **LABORED BREATHING**

H82   **LABYRINTHITIS**

S18   **LACERATION**
S54   REPAIR (SKIN)

        LACK (OF)
T10   DEVELOPMENT
T10   GROWTH
Z03   HEATING
Z03   HOUSING
P20   MEMORY

F03   **LACRIMATION**

—40   **LAPAROSCOPY**

D22   **LARVA MIGRANS**

R77   **LARYNGITIS (ACUTE)**
R83   CHRONIC

R40   **LARYNGOSCOPY (DIRECT)**

LUMP(S) — *see also* **MASS**
S04	BEHIND EARS
R21	THROAT

R39	**LUNG FUNCTION TEST**

L99	**LUPUS ERYTHEMATOSUS**
L34	CELL PREPARATION

B71	**LYMPHADENITIS (CHRONIC)**
	NEC
B70	ACUTE
B71	MESENTERIC
	(NONSPECIFIC)
B71	UNSPECIFIED

B02	**LYMPHADENOPATHY**

S81	**LYMPHANGIOMA,**
	CONGENITAL

K99	**LYMPHEDEMA**

N71	**LYMPHOCYTIC MENINGITIS**

B72	**LYMPHOMA (MALIGNANT)**
	NEC

B72	**LYMPHOSARCOMA**

F84	**MACULAR DEGENERATION**

A04	**MALAISE**

A73	**MALARIA**
A44	PREVENTION

K87	**MALIGNANT HYPERTENSION**

L98	**MALLET FINGER**

D84	**MALLORY–WEISS SYNDROME**

T91	**MALNUTRITION (ANY TYPE)**

MALPROPORTION
W93	DEADBORN(S)
W92	LIVEBORN(S)

X41	**MAMMOGRAPHY (FEMALE)**

P73	**MANIA NEC**

—57	**MANIPULATION**
L57	JOINT

R32	**MANTOUX**

MANUAL ROTATION
W93	DEADBORN(S)
W92	LIVEBORN(S)

T91	**MARASMUS**

Z12	**MARITAL CONFLICT**

MARK
S82	PORT WINE
S82	RASPBERRY
S82	STRAWBERRY
S29	STRETCH
S29	TATTOO

MARRIAGE
Z15	ABANDONMENT
Z12	CRISIS
Z12	DIFFICULTIES
Z15	DISRUPTION
Z12	PROBLEMS
Z15	SEPARATION

P09	**MASOCHISM**

MASS NEC
D24	ABDOMINAL
X19	BREAST (FEMALE)
Y16	MALE
X17	PELVIS
	SKIN:
S04	LOCALIZED
S05	MULTIPLE
T15	THYROID
X16	VULVA

—57	**MASSAGE**
Y57	PROSTATIC

W94	**MASTITIS PUERPERALIS**

X18	**MASTODYNIA**

H74	**MASTOIDITIS**

A71	**MEASLES**
A74	GERMAN

U72	**MEATITIS**

D81	**MECKEL'S DIVERTICULUM**

—57	**MEDCOLLATOR**

—57	**MEDCOSONOLATOR**

Y85	**MEDIAN BAR (PROSTATE)**

A88	**MOTION SICKNESS**	S22	RIDGED	
		S22	SPLITTING	
N99	**MOTOR NEURONE DISEASE**			
		N99	**NARCOLEPSY**	
D83	**MUCOCELE SALIVARY GLAND**			
			NASAL	
D18	**MUCOUS IN STOOL**	R07	OBSTRUCTION	
		R56	PACKING FOR EPISTAXIS	
	MULTIPLE	—38	SMEAR EOSINOPHILES	
P01	EMOTIONAL FEELINGS			
W84	PREGNANCY	—53	**NASO-GASTRIC TUBE,**	
N86	SCLEROSIS		**INSERTION/REMOVAL**	
D71	**MUMPS**	R74	**NASOPHARYNGITIS (ACUTE)**	
D71	MENINGITIS	R83	CHRONIC	
D71	ORCHITIS			
		D09	**NAUSEA (DUE TO) (OF)**	
K81	**MURMUR, HEART NEC OR NYD**	W05	PREGNANCY	
N99	**MUSCULAR DYSTROPHY**	F91	**NEARSIGHTEDNESS**	
L18	**MYALGIA NEC**	—52	**NEEDLE BIOPSY**	
N99	**MYASTHENIA GRAVIS**	—67	**NEEDS SECOND OPINION**	
A78	**MYCOSES NEC**		**NEOPLASM**	
			BENIGN:	
—41	**MYELOGRAM**	U78	BLADDER	
		B75	BLOOD, BLOOD-	
B74	**MYELOMA (MALIGNANT) NEC**		FORMING ORGANS	
		L71	BONE	
K75	**MYOCARDIAL INFARCTION**	N75	BRAIN (ANY PART)	
	(ACUTE)		BREAST	
K76	HEALED	X79	—FEMALE (EXCLUDING	
K76	OLD		CHRONIC CYSTIC	
			DISEASE)	
K70	**MYOCARDITIS (ACUTE)**	Y79	—MALE	
K71	RHEUMATIC (CHRONIC)	R86	BRONCHUS	
		K72	CIRCULATORY SYSTEM	
L19	**MYOFIBROSIS**		(ANY PART)	
		L71	CONNECTIVE TISSUE	
X78	**MYOMA, UTERUS**	D78	DIGESTIVE SYSTEM (ANY	
			PART)	
F91	**MYOPIA**	H75	EAR	
		T73	ENDOCRINE GLAND NEC	
L18	**MYOSITIS NEC**	F74	EYE	
L70	EPIDEMIC		GENITAL SYSTEM	
L70	INFECTIVE	X80	—FEMALE NEC:	
		X78	FIBROMYOMA OF	
H71	**MYRINGITIS**		UTERUS	
H74	CHRONIC	Y79	—MALE (ANY PART)	
		U78	KIDNEY	
T86	**MYXEDEMA**	R86	LARYNX	
		L71	LIGAMENT	
	NAEVUS SEE NEVUS	R86	LUNG	
		B75	LYMPHATICS	
	NAIL	N75	MENINGES	
S22	BREAKING	L71	MUSCLE	
S22	BRITTLE	L71	MUSCULOSKELETAL	
S22	CRACKED		SYSTEM (ANY PART)	

NEOPLASM *contd*
L71   TENDON (SHEATH)
T73   THYROID
U79   URETER
U79   URETHRA
U79   URINARY SYSTEM

U88   **NEPHRITIS**

U88   **NEPHROPATHY**

K87   **NEPHROSCLEROSIS**

U88   **NEPHROSIS**

U88   **NEPHROTIC SYNDROME**

NERVE(S)
P01   BAD
N55   BLOCK
N55   INJECTION
N81   INJURY, PERIPHERAL

P01   **NERVOUS**
D09   STOMACH

N99   **NEURALGIA NEC**

P78   **NEURASTHENIA**

N99   **NEURITIS NEC**
L86   LUMBOSACRAL
F99   OPTIC
L86   THORACIC

S06   **NEURODERMATITIS**

N76   **NEUROFIBROMATOSIS (VON RECKLINGHAUSEN'S DISEASE)**

N99   **NEUROGENIC BLADDER**

P79   **NEUROSIS, NEUROTIC NEC**
P74   ANXIETY
P75   HYSTERICAL
P79   OBSESSIVE

S79   **NEVUS (BENIGN)**
S81   CAVERNOUS
S82   CONGENITAL
S77   MALIGNANT
K99   SPIDER

NEWBORN (LIVEBORN) INFANT
A94   ASPHYDIA
A94   DIARRHOEA
A94   HEMOLYTIC DISEASE
A93   IMMATURE
A94   JAUNDICE

A94   LIGHT FOR DATE
A94   MORBIDITY
A95   MORTALITY
A94   OMPHALITIS
A94   POSTMATURITY
A93   PREMATURE
A94   RESPIRATORY DISTRESS

F99   **NIGHT BLINDNESS**

P06   **NIGHTMARES**

S83   **NIPPLES, SUPERNUMERARY**

—69   **NO REASON FOR ENCOUNTER**

U02   **NOCTURIA**

NODULE(S) — *see also* **MASS**
B02   LYMPH (GLAND OR NODE)
T81   THYROID (WITHOUT THYROTOXICOSIS):
T85   THYROTOXIC
R85   VOCAL CORD

H85   **NOISE-INDUCED HEARING NOISE**

NON OBSTETRIC CONDITIONS AFFECTING:
W77   CHILDBIRTH
W77   PREGNANCY
W77   PUERPERIUM
X82   INJURY

NORMAL
W52   DELIVERY
A31   GROWTH ASSESSMENT

R06   **NOSEBLEED**

NOT EATING
T05   ADULT
T04   CHILD

NUCLEAR
—41   SCANNING
—41   TRACING

N06   **NUMBNESS**

F99   **NYSTAGMUS**

T82   **OBESITY**

—45   **OBSERVATION (OF)**
—45   HIGH RISK PATIENT

OBSTETRIC — *see also* PREGNANCY
W52 DELIVERY, VAGINAL

D12 OBSTIPATION

W92 OBSTRUCTED LABOUR

OBSTRUCTION
D99 ABDOMINAL
U99 BLADDER NECK
R07 NASAL

K92 OCCLUSION (ARTERY)
K90 CEREBRAL
K75 CORONARY
K92 PRECEREBRAL

—36 OCCULT BLOOD

—57 OCCUPATIONAL THERAPY

F39 OCULAR PRESSURE

X05 OLIGOMENORRHEA

U05 OLIGURIA

S94 ONYCHOGRYPHOSIS

S74 ONYCHOMYCOSIS

X74 OOPHORITIS

OPTIC
N81 NERVE INJURY
F99 NEURITIS

ORAL CONTRACEPTIVE
W11 (FROM PRACTICE)
W11 (PRESCRIBED ELSEWHERE)

Y74 ORCHITIS

A77 ORNITHOSIS

L99 OSTEITIS
L99 DEFORMANS
L70 PYOGENIC

L91 OSTEOARTHROSIS, OSTEOARTHRITIS NEC
L91 ANKLE
L91 ELBOW
L91 HAND
L89 HIP
L91 JOINT (OTHER)
L90 KNEE
L91 SHOULDER
L84 SPINE
L91 WRIST

L94 OSTEOCHONDRITIS, OSTEOCHONDROSIS
L94 DISSECANS
L94 INVENALIS

OSTEOMYELITIS
L70 ACUTE
L70 CHRONIC
L70 UNSPECIFIED

L95 OSTEOPOROSIS

L71 OSTEOSARCOMA

D45 OSTOMY TRAINING

—68 OTHER REFERRALS NEC

H71 OTITI MEDIA SUPPURATIVA (UNSPECIFIED

OTITIS
H70 EXTERNA
MEDIA:
H71 (ACUTE)
H74 —CHRONIC
H72 —NONSUPPURATIVE
H71 —PERFORATED
H72 —SEROUS
H71 UNSPECIFIED

H83 OTOSCLEROSIS

OUT OF
R02 BREATH
Z06 WORK

X80 OVARIAN CYST (BENIGN)

T83 OVERWEIGHT

X03 OVULATION PAIN

D22 OXYURIASIS

—56 PACKING
H56 EAR
R56 NOSE, NASAL FOR EPISTAXIS
D56 RECTAL
—56 VAGINAL

P09 PAEDOPHILIA

L99 PAGET'S DISEASE

A01 PAIN NEC
D01 ABDOMEN:
D01 GENERALIZED

PAIN NEC *contd.*

D06	LOCALIZED
D04	ANAL
L16	ANKLE:
L16	MUSCULOSKELETAL
L09	ARM NEC:
L09	MUSCULOSKELETAL
L02	BACK:
L03	LOW
L03	—MUSCULOSKELETAL
L02	MUSCULOSKELETAL
L03	—LOW
L86	WITH RADIATING
	SYMPTOMS
U13	BLADDER
A01	BODY
L29	BONE
X18	BREAST:
W19	LACTATING
Y16	MALE
R01	BREATHING
K01	CARDIOVASCULAR
	CHEST:
K01	CARDIOVASCULAR
K01	HEART
L04	MUSCULOSKELETAL
R01	RESPIRATORY
K03	CIRCULATION
D04	DEFECATION
H01	EAR
L10	ELBOW:
L10	MUSCULOSKELETAL
D06	EPIGASTRIC:
D06	LOCALIZED
F01	EYE
N03	FACE:
N03	NERVE
L12	FINGER:
L12	MUSCULOSKELETAL
L05	FLANK
L17	FOOT:
L17	MUSCULOSKELETAL
D06	GALLBLADDER
D08	GAS
D02	GASTRIC
A01	GENERALIZED NEC
	GENITAL:
X01	FEMALE
X03	—INTERMENSTRUAL
X02	—MENSTRUAL
	MALE
Y01	—PENIS
Y02	—SCROTUM
Y02	—TESTES
D19	GUMS
L12	HAND NEC:
L12	MUSCULOSKELETAL
N01	HEAD
K01	HEART
L13	HIP:

L13	MUSCULOSKELETAL
D06	HYPOCHONDRIUM
D06	ILIAC FOSSA
X03	INTERMENSTRUAL
D01	INTESTINAL
L07	JAW
L20	JOINT NEC:
L20	MULTIPLE
	SPECIFIED SITE — *see*
	PAIN, BY SITE,
	MUSCULOSKELETAL
U14	KIDNEY
L15	KNEE:
L15	MUSCULOSKELETAL
L14	LEG NEC:
L14	MUSCULOSKELETAL
L29	LIMB NEC:
L29	MUSCULOSCELETAL NEC
D06	LIVER
B03	LYMPH GLAND
H01	MASTOID AREA
D20	MOUTH
L18	MUSCLE NEC:
L18	MULTIPLE
	SPECIFIED SITE — *see*
	PAIN, BY SITE,
	MUSCULOSKELETAL
L01	NECK:
L01	MUSCULOSKELETAL
N29	NEUROLOGICAL
X01	PELVIC:
X03	INTERMENSTRUAL
X02	MENSTRUAL
Y01	PENIS
W18	POST-PARTUM
Y06	PROSTATE
D04	RECTAL
R01	RESPIRATORY
Y02	SCROTUM
L08	SHOULDER
R09	SINUS
S01	SKIN
	SPECIFIED — *see* PAIN, BY
	SITE
D02	STOMACH
L29	STUMP
Y02	TESTES
L14	THIGH:
L14	MUSCULOSKELETAL
R21	THROAT
L17	TOE:
L17	MUSCULOSKELETAL
D20	TONGUE
R22	TONSILS
D19	TOOTH, TEETH
D06	UMBILICAL REGION
U01	URINATION
X01	VAGINAL
L11	WRIST:
L11	MUSCULOSKELETAL

Z03   **PERSON LIVING ALONE**

    PERSONALITY
P80   AGGRESSIVE
P80   ASOCIAL
P80   COMPULSIVE
P80   DEPRESSIVE
P80   IMMATURE
P80   PASSIVE

A09   **PERSPIRATION EXCESSIVE**

R71   **PERTUSSIS**

L98   **PES PLANUS**

N88   **PETIT MAL (STATUS)**

R74   **PHARYNGITIS**

Y81   **PHIMOSIS (CONGENITAL)**

K94   **PHLEBITIS (SUPPURATIVE)**
N73   INTRACRANIAL
N73   VENOUS SINUS

—57   **PHOTOTHERAPY**

    PHYSICAL
—30   EXAMINATION (ROUTINE)
      COMPLETE
—39   FUNCTION TEST
—57   MEDICINE
—57   MODALITIES
—57   THERAPY, TRAINING

—57   **PHYSIOTHERAPY**

—59   **PIERCING, EARS**

L82   **PIGEON-TOED**

K96   **PILES**
K55   REDUCTION OF
K96   THROMBOSED EXTERNAL

S96   **PIMPLES**

D22   **PINWORMS**

S90   **PITYRIASIS (ROSEA)**
S99   RUBRA
S74   VERSICOLOR

    PLACENTA — *see also*
      PREGNANCY,
      COMPLICATED BY
      PLACENTAL
      ABNORMALITIES
W99   ABRUPTIO

W99   PRAEVIA

A78   **PLAGUE**

    PLAIN X-RAY
—41   ABDOMEN
L41   BONE
—41   CHEST
—41   SOFT TISSUE

B34   **PLATELETS**

R82   **PLEURISY (ALL TYPES)**
      (EXCEPT TUBERCULOUS)
R93   SEROUS
R70   TUBERCULOUS
R93   WITH EFFUSION NEC:
R70   TUBERCULOUS

H13   **PLUGGED FEELING, EAR**

R99   **PNEUMOCONIOSIS**

R81   **PNEUMONIA (BACTERIAL)**
      (INFLUENZAL) (VIRAL)

R99   **PNEUMOTHORAX**

    POISONING (BY)
      FOOD (INFECTIOUS):
D73   UNSPECIFIED
D70   SALMONELLA
D70   SPECIFIED
S88   IVY
A84   MEDICINAL AGENT
      (OVERDOSE) (WRONG
      DRUG)
A86   NONMEDICINAL
      SUBSTANCE
S88   OAK

N70   **POLIOMYELITIS**
N70   LATE EFFECTS

Z29   **POLLUTION (OF**
      ENVIRONMENT)

L99   **POLYARHTRITIS**

K99   **POLYARTERITIS (NODOSA)**

B99   **POLYCYTHEMIA, SECONDARY**

X07   **POLYMENORRHEA**

L99   **POLYMYALGIA RHEUMATICA**

L99   **POLYMYOSITIS**

—50	**PRESCRIPTION (REQUEST)**	T04	—NEC INFANT
	(RENEWAL) (PROVISION)	Z01	ECONOMIC
—65	PERSON OTHER THAN	Z07	EDUCATIONAL
	PATIENT	Z29	ENVIRONMENTAL
			CIRCUMSTANCES
—56	**PRESSURE, COMPRESSION NEC**		HAZARDOUS TO
K02	CHEST		HEALTH
K02	HEART		FEEDING
X17	PELVIC	T05	—ADULT
R09	SINUS	T04	—INFANT
S97	SORE	Z01	FINANCIAL
		Z02	FOOD
—44	**PREVENTIVE MEDICATION**	T10	GROWTH
			HEALTH CARE
W84	**PREVIOUS CESAREAN SECTION**		SYSTEM
		Z10	—ACCESS
Y04	**PRIAPISM**	Z10	—AVAILABILITY
		H02	HEARING
	PRICKLY	H86	—DEAFNESS
N05	FEELING	K29	HEART NEC
S92	HEAT	Z03	HOUSING
		—64	INITIATED BY
W84	**PRIMIPARE, ELDERLY**		PROVIDER
			INTERPERSONAL
	PROBLEM(S) NEC		(WITH) NEC
P24	(0F) (WITH) (*see also*	Z16	—CHILD (CHILD–
	SYMPTOMS) AGE-		PARENT) NEC:
	SPECIFI DEVELOPMENT	Z16	ABUSE (VIOLENCE)
	(OF):	Z18	CARING (FOR) ILL/
	(WITH) (*see also*		DISABLED
P09	—SYMPT0MS)	Z19	DEATH
	HOMOSEXUALITY	Z19	LOSS (SEPARATION)
	(MALE,FEMALE)	Z20	—FAMILY NEC:
A29	—SYMPTOMS)	Z15	DISRUPTION,
Z10	ACCESS TO HEALTH		SEPARATION
	CARE	Z24	—FRIENDS (C0
	ALCOHOL		WORKERS)
P16	—ACUTE	Z12	—MARITAL:
P15	—CHRONIC	Z15	SEPARATION OR
	APPEARANCE		DIVORCE
S24	—HAIR	Z24	—NON-FAMILY NEC
S22	—NAIL(S)	Z16	—PARENT–CHILD:
R08	—NOSE	Z19	SEPARATION
S29	—SKIN NEC	Z20	—PARENT/OTHER
Z11	BEING ILL		FAMILY MEMBER:
Z04	BELIEF SYSTEM	Z20	ABUSE (VIOLENCE)
K85	BLOOD PRESSURE NEC	Z21	BEHAVIOR
R04	BREATHING	Z22	CARING (FOR) ILL/
R01	—PAIN		DISABLED
R02	—SHORTNESS	Z23	DEATH
	CARE, CARING FOR	Z23	LOSS (SEPARATION)
	CHILD	Z12	—PARTNER
Z18	—DISABLED		(HUSBAND) (SPOUSE)
Z18	—GRAVELY ILL		NEC:
Z16	CHILD BEHAVIOR	Z12	ABUSE (VIOLENCE)
F18	CONTACT LENSES	Z14	CARING (FOR) ILL/
P19	DRUGS		DISABLED
	EATING	Z15	DEATH
P11	—PSYCHOGENIC	Z15	DIVORCE
	CHILDREN	Z15	LOSS (SEPARATION)

B34	**PROTHROMBIN TIME**	K04	RACING	
		K04	SLOW	
	PRURITUS			
D05	ANOGENITAL	—52	**PUNCH BIOPSY**	
D05	PERIANAL			
S02	SKIN	S18	**PUNCTURE (SKIN)**	
		—57	ARTERIAL	
A77	**PSITTACOSIS**			
		B83	**PURPURA**	
S91	**PSORIASIS**	B83	FIBRINOLYTIC	
		B83	FULMINANS	
P58	**PSYCHIATRIC COUNSELLING**			
			PUS (FROM) (IN)	
P43	**PSYCHOLOGICAL TESTING**	H04	EAR(S)	
		F73	EYE(S)	
P79	**PSYCHONEUROSIS**	R25	SPUTUM	
		D18	STOOL	
P98	**PSYCHOSIS, PSYCHOTIC NEC**	U07	URINE	
P73	AFFECTIVE			
P15	ALCOHOLIC		**PYELITIS**	
P70	ARTERIOSCLEROTIC	U70	ACUTE	
P72	CATATONIC	U99	CHRONIC	
P73	DEPRESSIVE	U70	UNSPECIFIED	
P19	DRUG			
P72	HEBEPHRENIC	U41	**PYELOGRAM (INTRAVENOUS)**	
P71	KORSAKOV'S		**(RETROGRADE)**	
	(NONALCOHOLIC)			
P15	ALCOHOLIC		**PYELONEPHRITIS**	
P73	MANIC DEPRESSIVE	U70	ACUTE	
P71	ORGANIC:	U99	CHRONIC	
P71	TRANSIENT (OTHER)			
P72	PARANOID	A03	**PYREXIA (UNKNOWN ORIGIN)**	
P98	PHENOMENA NEC	A76	WITH RASH NEC	
P70	PRESENILE			
P71	PUERPERAL	R74	**PYREXIAL COLD**	
P72	SCHIZOAFFECTIVE P			
P72	SCHIZOPHRENIC	R76	**QUINSY**	
P70	SENILE			
P98	SPECIFIED TYPE NEC	A77	**RABIES**	
—58	**PSYCHOSOCIAL COUNSELLING**	—59	**RADIATION THERAPY**	
	AND ASSESSMENT			
		L83	**RADICULAR SYNDROME,**	
—58	**PSYCHOTHERAPY**		**UPPER LIMBS**	
F99	**PTERYGIUM**	—41	**RADIOGRAPHY (CONTRAST)**	
			(DIAGNOSTIC)	
	PUERPERAL			
W70	PYREXIA (CAUSE	—41	**RADIOISOTOPE FUNCTION**	
	UNKNOWN)		**STUDY**	
W70	SEPSIS			
		R04	**RALES**	
H01	**PULLING AT EARS**			
		X82	**RAPE (INJURY)**	
R39	**PULMONARY FUNCTION TEST**			
			RASH NEC (SKIN)	
	PULSE (BEAT)	S89	DIAPER	
K04	FAST	S07	GENERALIZED	
K05	IRREGULAR	S92	HEAT	
K04	QUICK	D20	LIPS	

RENAL *contd.*
T88	GLUCOSURIA
U95	STONE

—50 **RENEW PRESCRIPTION**

REPAIR
—54	AND FIXATION NEC
L54	DISLOCATION
L54	FRACTURE
S54	LACERATION
W54	EPISIOTOMY

REQUEST (FOR)
—45	DISCUSSION REGARDING SURGERY
A20	EUTHANASIA
—67	SPECIALIST REFERRAL
—50	VITAMINS

K96 **RESIDUAL HEMORRHOIDAL SKIN TAGS**

R57 **RESPIRATORY THERAPY**

—59 **REST**

N04 **RESTLESS(NESS) LEGS SYNDROME**

Z03 **RESTRICTION OF SPACE**

RESULT(S)
—60	ALLERGY
—60	BACTERIOLOGY
	BLOOD:
—60	(CHEMISTRY) (COUNT) (CULTURE)
—60	PRESSURE
—60	CYTOLOGY
—60	FECAL
W60	FETAL MONITORING
—60	FLUID:
—60	AMNIOCENTESIS
—60	SPINAL
—60	LABORATORY NEC
X60	MAMMOGRAPHY
—61	OTHER PROVIDER
X60	PAP (SMEAR)
—60	PARASITOLOGY
W60	PREGNANCY TEST
—60	RADIOISOTOPE
—60	RADIOLOGY
—60	SCAN
—60	SENSITIZATION
—60	STRESS TEST
—60	TEST OR EXAMINATION OR PROCEDURE •
—60	TISSUE (EXCISED) (FROM BIOPSY):

—60	CYTOLOGY
—60	URINE (ANALYSIS) (CULTURE)
—60	X-RAY

RETAINED PLACENTA (WITHOUT HEMORRHAGE)
W93	DEADBORN(S)
W92	LIVEBORN(S)

P85 **RETARDATION, MENTAL**

D10 **RETCHING**

RETENTION
—53	CATHETER, INSERTION OR REMOVAL
U05	URINE

—34 **RETICULOCYTES**

B72 **RETICULOSARCOMA**

F82 **RETINAL DETACHMENT**

RETINOPATHY
F83	DIABETIC
F83	HYPERTENSIVE
F83	NOS

W95 **RETRACTED NIPPLE**

U41 **RETROGRADE PYELOGRAM**

RH
B33	ANTIBODY TITER
W92	ISO-IMMUNIZATION

L18 **RHEUMATISM (NONARTICULAR) NEC**
L92	SHOULDER

L33 **RHEUMATOID FACTOR**

R74 **RHINITIS**
R97	ALLERGIC
R97	PERENNIAL
R97	VASOMOTOR

R07 **RHINORRHEA**

T91 **RICKETS**

RIGHT
K77	HEART FAILURE
D06	LOWER QUADRANT PAIN (RLQ)
D06	UPPER QUADRANT PAIN (RUQ)

	SENILE
N99	DEGENERATION, BRAIN
H84	PRESBYACUSIS

| P05 | **SENILITY** |

	SENSATION (OF)
F13	ABNORMAL, EYE
S01	BURNING (SKIN)
N17	FALLING
R02	SUFFOCATION
N05	TINGLING OF EXTREMITIES

| —33 | **SEROLOGIC TEST FOR SYPHILIS** |

—44	**SERUM**
—44	INJECTION

| —58 | **SEXUAL COUNSELLING** |

| P09 | **SEXUAL DEVIATION** |

| N06 | **SHAKING** |

| D70 | **SHIGELLA ENTERITIS** |

| S70 | **SHINGLES** |

| A02 | **SHIVERING** |

	SHOCK
A12	ANAPHYLACTIC
A88	ELECTRIC
A87	POSTOPERATIVE

	SHORT(NESS) (OF)
P20	ATTENTION SPAN
R02	BREATH
F91	SIGHT
T10	STATURE

| —50 | **SHOT(S) (INJECTION)** |

| P22 | **SHYNESS, EXCESSIVE (CHILDREN)** |

| D83 | **SIALOADENITIS** |

| D09 | **SICK TO STOMACH** |

B34	**SICKLE CELL TEST**
B78	ANEMIA

	SICKNESS
A88	ALTITUDE
A88	MOTION
A88	MOUNTAIN
A88	TRAVEL

| D40 | **SIGMOIDOSCOPY** |

	SINUS
R09	DRAINAGE
R09	HEADACHE
S85	PILONIDAL
R09	PRESSURE

| R75 | **SINUSITIS (ACUTE) (CHRONIC)** |

	SITE
H—	ACOUSTIC NERVE
T—	ADRENAL (GLAND)
R—	ALVEOLUS (PULMONUM)
D—	ANUS
K—	AORTA
K—	AORTIC (VALVE)
D—	APPENDIX
X—	AREOLA
K—	ARTERY (ANY)
H—	AURICLE
L—	BACK
X—	BARTHOLIN'S GLAND
D—	BILE DUCT
U—	BLADDER (URINARY)
	BLOOD:
B—	(CELLS)
K—	—VESSEL
B—	FORMING ORGANS
N—	BRAIN
X—	BREAST
X—	BROAD LIGAMENT
R—	BRONCHIOLE
R—	BRONCHUS
K—	CAPILLARY
X—	CERVIX (UTERI)
F—	CHOROID
F—	CILIARY BODY
K—	CIRCULATORY SYSTEM
X—	CLITORIS
D—	COLON
F—	CONJUNCTIVA
F—	CORNEA
Y—	CORPUS CAVERNOSUM
D—	CYSTIC DUCT
D—	DIGESTIVE SYSTEM
D—	DUODENUM
H—	EAR
K—	ENDOCARDIUM
T—	ENDOCRINE (GLAND)
Y—	EPIDIDYMIS
D—	ESOPHAGUS
H—	EUSTACHIAN TUBE
F—	EYE
F—	EYEBALL
F—	EYELID
X—	FALLOPIAN TUBE
D—	GALLBLADDER
	GENITAL:
X—	FEMALE

Y— MALE
F— GLOBE, EYE
D— GUMS
K— HEART (VALVE)
X— HYMEN
T— HYPOTHALAMUS
D— ILEUM
D— INTESTINE
F— IRIS
T— ISLET CELL
D— JEJUNUM
L— JOINT
U— KIDNEY
X— LABIA
H— LABYRINTH
F— LACRIMAL (DUCT)
        (GLAND) (SYSTEM)
R— LARYNX
F— LENS
L— LIMB
D— LIPS
D— LIVER
R— LUNG
H— MASTOID (PROCESS)
R— MEDIASTINUM
K— MITRAL (VALVE)
D— MOUTH
L— MUSCLE NEC
L— MUSCULOSKELETAL
        SYSTEM
K— MYOCARDIUM
R— NASOPHARYNX
L— NECK
N— NERVE
N— NERVOUS SYSTEM
X— NIPPLE
R— NOSE
F— OPTIC NERVE
F— ORBIT
X— OVARY
D— PANCREAS
T— PARATHYROID (GLAND)
Y— PENIS
K— PERICARDIUM
D— PERITONEUM
R— PHARYNX
T— PINEAL (GLAND)
T— PITUITARY (GLAND)
R— PLEURA
Y— PREPUCE
Y— PROSTATE
K— PULMONARY (VALVE)
X— RECTOVAGINAL SEPTUM
D— RECTUM
R— RESPIRATORY SYSTEM
F— RETINA
Y— SCROTUM
Y— SEMINAL VESICLE
R— SINUS
S— SKIN

Y— SPERMATIC CORD
N— SPINAL CORD
B— SPLEEN
D— STOMACH
T— SUPRARENAL (GLAND)
D— TEETH
Y— TESTIS
T— THYMUS (GLAND)
T— THYROID (GLAND)
D— TONGUE
R— TONSIL
R— TRACHEA
K— TRICUSPID (VALVE)
Y— TUNICA VAGINALIS
H— TYMPANIC MEMBRANE
H— TYMPANUM
U— URETER
U— URETHRA
U— URINARY TRACT
X— UTERUS
X— VAGINA
Y— VAS DEFERENS
K— VEIN
F— VISUAL PATHWAYS
F— VITREOUS (BODY)
R— VOCAL CORDS
X— VULVA

L99 **SJOGREN'S SYNDROME**

SKIN
S79   TAGS
—32   TEST
—32   TUBERCULOSIS

P06 **SLEEP DISORDER**

SLIPPED
        DISC
L83   CERVICAL
L86   LUMBAR
L94   FEMORAL EPIPHYSIS

N70 **SLOW VIRUS INFECTION**

N19 **SLURRING**

A76 **SMALL POX**

Z29 **SMOG**

R05 **SMOKER'S COUGH**

P17 **SMOKING (TOBACCO)**
P17   ADDICTION
P17   PROBLEMS

R07 **SNEEZING**

R04 **SNORING**

SOCIAL
Z28   HANDICAP
Z28   ISOLATION
Z03   MIGRANTS
Z28   WITHDRAWAL

—41   **SOFT TISSUE IMAGING**

SORE, SORENESS — *see also*
   PAIN OR ABSCESS
S97   BED
L04   CHEST
B03   GLANDS
D19   GUMS
R08   IN NOSE
D20   LIPS
D20   MOUTH
Y01   PENIS
L04   RIBS
S01   SKIN
D19   TEETH
R21   THROAT
X01   VULVA

N06   **SPASM**
D93   ANAL
K89   CEREBRAL ARTERIES
L18   MUSCLE NEC:
L18   MULTIPLE
         SPECIFIED SITE — *see*
         SYMPTOMS, BY SITE
D02   STOMACH

      SPASTIC
D93   COLON SYNDROME
N99   PALSY (INFANTILE)

—31   **SPECIFIC HEALTH RISK**
         ASSESSMENT

      SPEECH
N19   DISTURBANCE
—57   THERAPY

N07   **SPELLS**

—38   **SPERM COUNT**

Y99   **SPERMATOCELE**

N85   **SPINA BIFIDA**

      SPINAL
N81   CORD INJURY
N51   TAP

N17   **SPINNING (HEAD)**

R39   **SPIROMETRY**

SPIT, SPITTING (UP)
R24   BLOOD
T04   FOOD, INFANT, CHILD

D93   **SPLENIC FLEXURE SYNDROME**

B87   **SPLENOMEGALY**

L54   **SPLINT APPLICATION**

L88   **SPONDYLITIS (ANKYLOSING)**

L84   **SPONDYLOSIS**
L84   CERVICAL:
L84   WITH MYELOPATHY
L84   KISSING SPINE
L84   THORACIC WITHOUT
         MYELOPATHY

F04   **SPOTS IN FRONT OF EYE**

L79   **SPRAINS, STRAINS NEC**
L77   ANKLE(S)
L79   BACK NEC
L79   ELBOW
L79   FINGER
L79   FOOT
L79   HIP
L78   KNEE(S)
L79   OTHER JOINTS
L79   SACROILIAC REGION
L79   SHOULDER
L79   WRIST

      SPUR
L99   BONE
L99   CALCANEAL

      SPUTUM
R25   GREEN/YELLOW
R25   PUS IN

F14   **SQUINT(ING)**

L28   **STAGGERING**

P10   **STAMMERING**

      STATE
P01   ANXIETY
P72   PARANOID
P79   PHOBIC

      STENOSIS
K83   AORTIC:
K71   RHEUMATIC
K71   MITRAL:
K73   CONGENITAL
K83   NONRHEUMATIC
K92   PRECEREBRAL ARTERIES:

P85	**SUBNORMALITY, MENTAL**		D20	TONGUE
P77	**SUICIDE, SUICIDAL (ACTS)**		H70	**SWIMMER'S EAR**
	(ATTEMPTS) (IDEAS)			
	(IMPULSES)		A06	**SWOON**
	(PERSONALITY)			
	(TENDENCIES)			**SYMPTOM(S), COMPLAINT(S)**
			X11	(OF) NEC MENOPAUSAL
S88	**SUNBURN**		A29	(OF) NEC:
			B04	BLOOD
A88	**SUNSTROKE**		B04	—FORMING ORGANS
			A17	GENERAL INFANT
	SUPPORT (FOR)		L16	ANKLE
D54	HERNIA (TRUSS)		K07	—SWELLING
L54	JOINT			(NONTRAUMATIC)
K56	VARICOSE VEIN		L09	ARM
			L06	AXILLA
W95	**SUPPRESSED LACTATION**		L02	BACK
			L03	—LOW
P78	**SURMENAGE**		U13	BLADDER
			X21	BREAST
	SUTURE (OF)		W20	—DURING PREGNANCY
—54	APPLY		Y16	—MALE
—54	INSERTION		R04	BREATHING
S54	LACERATION (SKIN)		R02	—SHORTNESS OF
—54	REMOVAL		K29	CARDIOVASCULAR
			L04	CHEST
	SWALLOWED, SWALLOWING		W29	CHILDBEARING
D21	DIFFICULTY		K29	CIRCULATORY
D79	FOREIGN BODY		K29	—HEART
D21	PROBLEMS		X11	CLIMACTERIC
			F18	CONTACT LENSES
A09	**SWEAT, SWEATING**		D29	DIGESTIVE
	(PROBLEMS)		H29	EAR
A09	COLD		L10	ELBOW
A09	EXCESSIVE		T29	ENDOCRINE
A09	NIGHT		F29	EYE
S92	RASH		F16	EYELIDS
			L12	FINGER
A08	**SWELLING, SWOLLEN NEC**		L05	FLANK
D25	ABDOMEN		L17	FOOT
K07	ANKLE (NONTRAUMATIC)		A29	GENERAL
F15	EYES			GENITAL
B02	GLANDS		X29	—FEMALE
D19	GUMS		Y29	—MALE
L20	JOINTS		D19	GUMS
D20	LIPS		S24	HAIR
B02	LYMPH GLANDS		L12	HAND
L19	MUSCULAR		K29	HEART
R08	NOSE		L13	HIP
Y04	PENIS		L07	JAW
X09	PREMENSTRUAL		L20	JOINT
Y06	PROSTATE		L20	—MULTIPLE
D29	RECTAL		U14	KIDNEY
Y05	SCROTUM		L15	KNEE
	SKIN:		W19	LACTATION
S04	LOCALIZED		L14	LEG
S05	MULTIPLE		L15	—KNEE
Y05	TESTES		D20	LIP(S)
R21	THROAT		B03	LYMPH (GLAND)

S29	**TATTOO (MARK)**	—34	GLUCOSE
S52	REMOVED	—34	—TOLERANCE TEST
		—34	HEMOGLOBIN
R60	**TB SKIN TEST RESULT**	—34	HORMONES
		—34	IRON
F03	**TEARING, EXCESSIVE**	—34	LIPIDS
		—34	MINERAL
Z03	**TECHNICAL DEFECTS IN**	N34	PHENYLHYDANTOIN
	HOME	—34	POTASSIUM
		—34	PROTEIN
D29	**TEETH GRINDING**	—34	THEOPHYLLINE
		—34	TOXIC SUBSTANCE
D19	**TEETHING**	—34	UREA NITROGEN
		—34	URIC ACID
A03	**TEMPERATURE, HIGH**	F39	GLAUCOMA
		H39	HEARING
	TENDER(NESS)	—38	LABORATORY NEC
	ABDOMEN — *see* PAIN,	W33	PREGNANCY
	ABDOMEN	W33	URINE
X01	PELVIC	P43	PSYCHOLOGICAL
Y01	PENIS	R39	PULMONARY FUNCTION
Y06	PROSTATE	—32	SCRATCH
Y02	SCROTUM	—32	SENSITIZATION
S01	SKIN	—36	STOOL FOR OCCULT
Y02	TESTES		BLOOD
		—33	SYPHILIS
L99	**TENDINITIS**	R32	TUBERCULIN
L92	AROUND SHOULDER	U33	URINE (CULTURE)
		H39	VESTIBULAR
	TENDON		VISUAL:
L54	FIXATION OR SUPPORT	F39	ACUITY
L55	INJECTION	F39	FIELD
L55	SHEATH INJECTION		
		—34	**TEST,TESTING BLOOD**
L93	**TENNIS ELBOW**		**THERAPEUTIC**
			SUBSTANCES
P01	**TENSE**		
		N72	**TETANUS**
	TENSION		
N02	HEADACHE	K73	**TETRALOGY OF FALOT**
X11	MENOPAUSAL		
X89	PREMENSTRUAL		**THERAPEUTIC**
		—57	EXERCISES
W83	**TERMINATION OF PREGNANCY**	—51	PHLEBOTOMY
		—59	PROCEDURE NEC (*see also*
	TEST, TESTING		THERAPY)
—32	ALLERGY		
—34	BLEEDING		
—34	BLOOD:	—59	**THERAPY NEC**
—34	ALKALINE	—57	COLD
	PHOSPHATASE	—57	HEAT
—34	AMINOPHYLLINE	—57	OCCUPATIONAL
—34	BILIRUBIN	—57	PHYSICAL
—34	CALCIUM	—59	RADIATION
B34	COAGULATION	—57	RESPIRATORY
—34	CREATININE	—57	SPEECH
K34	DIGITALIS	—57	ULTRAVIOLET LIGHT
—34	ELECTROLYTES		
—34	ENZYMES		
—34	GASES	—57	**THERMAL, HOT OR COLD**

R78	**TRACHEOBRONCHITIS**
R40	**TRACHEOSCOPY**
F86	**TRACHOMA**
—57	**TRACTION**

TRAINING (IN)
D57	OSTOMY
	USE OF
—57	CRUTCHES
—57	SPECIAL DEVICES

Z03	**TRAMPS**
—59	**TRANSFUSION, BLOOD (COMPONENTS)**

Z03	**TRANSIENT(S)**
K89	ISCHEMIC ATTACK (TIA)

K73	**TRANSPOSITION, GREAT VESSELS**
P09	**TRANSSEXUALISM**
P09	**TRANSVESTITISM**

TRAUMA, TRAUMATIC
see also INJURY)
A81	ABDOMEN, MULTIPLE
A81	CHEST
A82	LATE EFFECTS
A81	PELVIS, MULTIPLE
L99	— *see also* INJURY ARTHROPATHY

—39	**TREADMILL TEST**
D22	**TREMATODOSIS (OTHER)**
N06	**TREMOR**
D22	**TRICHINIASIS**
D22	**TRICHURIASIS**
Y99	**TRICHOMONIASIS MALE**
X73	**TRICHOMONIASIS, UROGENITAL, PROVEN FEMALE**
N92	**TRIGEMINAL NEURALGIA**

TRIGGER
N55	POINT INJECTION
L99	FINGER

TROUBLE (WITH) — *see also* **DIFFICULT**
K29	CIRCULATION
K29	HEART
Z12	PARTNER
Y06	PROSTATE
L28	WALKING

—54	**TRUSS**
A78	**TRIPANOSOMIASIS**
W52	**TUBAL LIGATION**
R32	**TUBERCULIN TEST**

TUBERCULOSIS
A70	BONE
R33	CULTURE
A70	GENERALIZED
A70	INTESTINAL
A70	JOINT
A70	KIDNEY
A70	LATE EFFECTS OF
A70	PRIMARY
A70	MENINGES
A70	OTHER
A70	RECENT POSITIVE CONVERSION OF TB SKIN TEST
R70	RESPIRATORY
R70	UNSPECIFIED SITE

A78	**TULARAEMIA**

TUMOR NEC — *see also* **NEOPLASM SKIN**
S04	LOCALIZED
S05	MULTIPLE

W84	**TWIN PREGNANCY**
F16	**TWITCH(ING) EYELIDS**
H39	**TYMPANOMETRY**
D70	**TYPHOID**

ULCER, ULCERATIVE (OF)
F85	CORNEAL
S97	DECUBITUS
F85	DENDRITIC
D85	DUODENUM
D84	ESOPHAGUS
D86	GASTRIC:
D86	PERFORATED
D86	GASTROJEJUNAL
D86	MARGINAL
D83	MOUTH
D86	PEPTIC

VARICOSE *contd.*
K99   SCROTUM
K99   SPECIFIED SITE NEC

—41   **VASCULAR ULTRASOUND**
          (DOPPLER)

Y52   **VASECTOMY**

K42   **VECTORCARDIOGRAM**

VEINS
K06   PAINFUL
K06   SWOLLEN

VENTOUSE EXTRACTION
W93   DEADBORN(S)
W92   LIVEBORN(S)

K73   **VENTRICULAR SEPTAL**
          DEFECT

VERRUCA
S03   PLANTARIS
S03   VULGARIS

K89   **VERTEBRO-BASILAR**
          INSUFFICIENCY

N17   **VERTIGO**
H82   AURAL
H82   MENIERE'S
H82   OTOGENIC

Y73   **VESICULITIS (SEMINAL)**

H39   **VESTIBULAR TESTING**

VIRAL
—33   CULTURE
A77   INFECTION UNSPECIFIED
N71   MENINGITIS DUE TO
          ENTEROVIRUS

VISION
F05   BLURRED
F05   CLOUDY/HAZY
F05   DIFFICULT
F05   DOUBLE
F05   POOR
F39   TESTING
F05   TROUBLED
F03   WET

VISUAL FIELD
F99   DEFECT
F39   TESTING

—50   **VITAMINS**

S99   **VITILIGO**

—57   **VOCATIONAL**
          REHABILITATION

D10   **VOMITING (OF)**
D14   BLOOD
W05   PREGNANCY

X84   **VULVITIS**

D99   **VOLVULUS**

P06   **WALKING IN SLEEP**

S03   **WARTS**
S99   SENILE (SEBORRHEIC)
          VENEREAL:
X91   FEMALE
Y76   MALE

L19   **WASTING, MUSCULAR**

—45   **WATCHFUL WAITING**

F03   **WATERY EYE(S)**

H81   **WAX IN EAR, EXCESSIVE**

A04   **WEAK, WEAKNESS**
          (GENERALIZED)
F05   EYE(S)
K29   HEART
L20   JOINT(S)
          MUSCULAR — *see* CHAPTER
          L, SYMPTOMS/
          COMPLAINTS, BY SITE
N18   NEUROLOGICAL (RIGHT-
          OR LEFT-SIDED)

WEIGHT (PROBLEM)
T31   CHECK
T82   EXCESSIVE
T07   GAIN
T08   LOSS

S04   **WELTS**

H04   **WET EAR**

R03   **WHEEZING**

L79   **WHIPLASH INJURY (NECK)**

—57   **WHIRLPOOL**

S93   **WHITEHEADS**

R71   **WHOOPING COUGH**

P15   **WITHDRAWAL PROBLEMS**
          (DRUG) ALCOHOL

15   ICPC desk copy

A. The ICPC rubric titles have maximally 32 positions and are designed for use in computer output.

B. The position numbers of all rubrics for which inclusion criteria („definitions") are given in ICHPPC-2-defined are added in bold print.

Co. 2 Diagnostic/prev. proc.
-30 MED EXAM/HEALTH EVALUA/COMPLETE
-31 MED EXAM/HEALTH EVALUA/PARTIAL
-32 SENSITIVITY TEST
-33 MICROBIO/OTHER IMMUNOLO. TEST
-34 OTHER BLOOD TEST
-35 OTHER URINE TEST
-36 OTHER FECES TEST
-37 HISTOLOGICAL/EXFOLIA. CYTOLOGY
-38 OTHER LABORATORY TEST NEC
-39 PHYSICAL FUNCTION TEST
-40 DIAGNOSTIC ENDOSCOPY
-41 DIAGNOSTIC RADIOLOGY/IMAGING
-42 ELECTRICAL TRACINGS
-43 OTHER DIAGNOSTIC PROCEDURES
-44 PREV. IMMUNIZATIONS/MEDICATIONS
-45 OBSERV/PREV. EDUCA/COUNSELING
-46 CONSULTATION PRIM. CARE PROVIDER
-47 CONSULTATION SPECIALIST
-48 CLARIFICATION/DISCUSSION OF RFE
-49 OTHER PREVENTIVE PROCEDURES

Co. 3 Medic/treatment/trera. proc.
-50 MEDICAT(SYSTEMIC DRUGS)/INJEC
-51 I&D/ASPIRATION/(EXCL. CATHET. 53)
-52 EXC/BIOPSY/DESTRUC/DEBRID/CAUT.
-53 INSTRUMENTA/CATH/INTUB/DILAT
-54 REPAIRSUTURE/CAST/PROS DEVICE
-55 LOCAL INJECTION/TREATMENT
-56 DRESSING/PRESSURE/COMPRESSION
-57 PHYSICAL MED/REHABILITATION
-58 THERA. COUNSELING/LISTENING
-59 OTHER THERA. PROC/MINOR SURG. NEC

Co. 4 Results
-60 RESULTS TEST AND PROCEDURES
-61 RESULTS EXAM./TEST/RECORD/LETTER

Co. 5 Administrative
-62 ADMINISTRATIVE ENCOUNTER

Co. 6 Referrals/other RFE
-63 FOLLOW-UP ENCOUNTER UNSPECIFIED
-64 ENCOUNTER INITIATED BY PROVIDER
-65 ENCOUN. INIT/OTHER THAN PT/PROV
-66 REFERRAL TO OTHER PROV (*excl.* M.D.)
-67 REFERRAL TO M.D./CLINIC/HOSPITAL
-68 ALL OTHER REFERRALS NEC
-69 OTHER REASONS FOR ENCOUNTER NEC

A--- General & unspecified
A01 PAIN:GENERALIZED/UNSPECIFIED
A02 CHILLS
A03 FEVER 291
A04 GENERAL WEAKNESS/TIREDNESS 295
A05 GENERAL DETERIORATION
A06 FAINTING(SYNCOPE) 264
A07 COMA
A08 SWELLING (*excl.* EDEMA K07)
A09 SWEATING PROBLEMS 290
A10 BLEEDING, SITE NOS
A12 ALLERGY/ALLERGIC REACT NOS
A13 CONCERN ABOUT DRUG REACTION
A14 INFANTILE COLIC
A15 EXCESSIVE CRYING INFANT
A16 IRRITABLE INFANT
A17 OTHER GEN SYMPT. INFANTS NEC
A20 EUTHANASIA REQUEST/DISCUSSION
A25 FEAR OF DEATH
A26 FEAR OF CANCER, NOS, NEC
A27 FEAR OF OTHER DISEASE,UNSPEC.
A28 DISABILITY/IMPAIRMENT NOS
A29 OTHER GENERAL SYMPT./COMPLT.

A70 TUBERCULOSIS, GENERAL. (EXCL.R70) 4
A71 MEASLES (*excl.* RUBELLA A74) 12
A72 CHICKENPOX 9
A73 MALARIA 21
A74 RUBELLA 13
A75 INFECTIOUS MONONUCLEOSIS 17
A76 OTHER VIRAL DIS. WITH EXANTHEMS

A77 OTHER VIRAL DISEASES NOS
A78 OTHER INFECTIOUS DISEASES NOS

A79 CARCINOMATOSIS (UNKNOWN PRIM.SITE) 39

A80 ACCIDENT/INJURY, NOS
A81 MULT. TRAUMA/INTERNAL INJ.
A82 LATE EFFECTS OF TRAUMA
A84 POISONING BY MEDICAL AGENT
A85 ADV.EFFECT MED.AGENT PROPER DOSE 377
A86 TOXIC EFFECT OTHER SUBSTANCES 335
A87 COMPLICAT.SURG/MED.TREATMENT
A88 ADVERSE EFFECTS PHYS.FACTORS
A89 EFFECTS PROSTHETIC DEVICE

A90 MULT.SYNDROMES/CONGENITAL ANOMALIES

A91 INVESTIG. ABNORMAL RESULTS,NEC 299
A92 TOXOPLASMOSIS
A93 PREMATURE/IMMATURE LIVEBORN INFANT
A94 ALL PERINATAL MORBIDITY
A95 PERINATAL MORTALITY
A96 DEATH (*excl.* PERINATAL)
A97 NO DISEASE
A99 OTHER GENERALIZED DISEASES

B--- Blood
B02 ENLARGED LYMPH GLAND(S) 266
B03 OTHER SYMPT. LYMPHATIC GLANDS
B04 SYMPT. BLOOD/BLOOD FORM.ORGANS
B25 FEAR OF AIDS
B26 FEAR, CANCER OF BLOOD/BLOOD-FORM. ORG.
B27 FEAR OTHER BLOOD/LYMPH.DISEASE
B28 DISABILITY/IMPAIRMENT
B29 OTHER SYMPT.BLOOD/SPLEEN NOS

B70 ACUTE LYMPHADENITIS 209
B71 CHRONIC/NON-SPEC. LYMPHADENITIS 63

B72 HODGKIN'S DISEASE 38
B73 LEUKEMIA 38
B74 OTHER MALIGNANT NEOPLASMS
B75 BENIGN NEOPLASMS

B76 RUPTURED SPLEEN
B77 OTHER INJURIES

B78 HEREDITARY HEMOLYTIC ANEMIAS 60
B79 OTHER CONGENITAL ANOMALIES

B80 IRON DEFICIENCY ANEMIA 58
B81 PERNIC./FOLATE DEFICIENCY ANEMIAS 59
B82 ANEMIA OTHER/UNSPECIFIED
B83 PURPURA/COAG.DEFECTS ABN.PLATE.
B84 ABNORMAL WHITE CELLS 64
B85 ABNORMAL UNEXPLAINED BLOOD TEST 51
B86 OTHER HEMATOLOGICAL ABNORMALITY 375
B87 SPLENOMEGALY 277
B90 HIV-INFECTION (AIDS, ARS)
B99 OTHER DIS./BLOOD/LYMPH/SPLEEN

D--- Digestive
D01 GENERALIZED ABDOM. PAIN/CRAMPS 279
D02 STOMACH ACHE/STOMACH PAIN
D03 HEARTBURN 275
D04 RECTAL/ANAL PAIN
D05 PERIANAL ITCHING
D06 OTHER LOCALIZED ABDOMINAL PAIN 279
D08 FLATULENCE/GAS PAIN/BELCHING 278
D09 NAUSEA 274
D10 VOMITING (*excl.* PREG. W06) 274
D11 DIARRHEA
D12 CONSTIPATION 161
D13 JAUNDICE
D14 HEMATEMESIS/VOMIT BLOOD 276
D15 MELENA/BLACK, TARRY STOOLS 276
D16 RECTAL BLEEDING 164
D17 INCONTINENCE OF BOWEL (FECAL)
D18 CHANGE IN FECES/BOWEL MOVEMENTS

019	SYMPT./COMPLT.TEETH,GUMS
020	SYMPT./COMPLT. MOUTH, TONGUE, LIP
021	SWALLOWING PROBLEMS
022	WORMS/PARASITES 28
024	ABDOMINAL MASS NOS 296
025	CHANGE IN ABDOM. SIZE/DISTENSION
026	FEAR OF CANCER OF DIGEST. SYSTEM
027	FEAR OF OTHER DIGESTIVE DISEASE
028	DISABILITY/IMPAIRMENT
029	OTHER SYMPT./COMPLT.DIGEST.

070	INFECTIOUS DIARRHEA, DYSENTERY 1
071	MUMPS 16
072	INFECTIOUS HEPATITIS 15
073	OTHER PRESUMED INFECTIONS

074	MALIG.NEOPL.STOMACH 32
075	MALIG. NEOPL. COLON, RECTUM 32
76	MALIG. NEOPL. PANCREAS 39
77	MALIG.NEOPL.OTHER/UNSPEC. 39
78	BENIGN NEOPLASMS

79	FOREIGN BODY THROUGH ORIFICE
80	OTHER INJURIES

81	CONGENITAL ANOMAL. DIGEST. SYSTEM

82	DISEASE OF TEETH/GUMS
83	DISEASE OF MOUTH/TONGUE/LIPS
84	DISEASE OF ESOPHAGUS
85	DUODENAL ULCER 151
86	OTHER PEPTIC ULCERS 152
87	DISORD.STOMACH FUNCTION 153
88	APPENDICITIS 154
89	INGUINAL HERNIA 155
90	HIATUS (DIAPH.) HERNIA 156
91	OTHER ABDOMINAL HERNIAS
92	DIVERTICULAR DIS.INTESTINES 158
93	IRRITABLE BOWEL SYNDROME 159
94	CHRONIC ENTERITIS/ULCERAT COLITIS 160
95	ANAL FISSURE/PERIANAL ABSCESS 162
96	HEPATOMEGALY 277
97	CIRRHOSIS/OTHER LIVER DISEASE 165
98	CHOLECYSTITIS/CHOLELITHIASIS 166
99	OTHER DIS.DIGESTIVE SYST.

Eye

EYE PAIN
RED EYE
DISCHARGE FROM EYE
FLOATERS/SPOTS
OTHER PROBLEMS WITH VISION
ABN.SENSATIONS OF EYE
ABN.EYE MOVEMENTS
ABN.APPEARENCE OF EYES
SYMPT. OF EYELIDS
SYMPT./COMPLT.GLASSES
SYMPT./COMPLT.CONTACT LENS
FEAR OF EYE DISEASE
DISABILITY/IMPAIRMENT
OTHER SYMPT./COMPLT. OF EYE

INFECTIOUS CONJUNCTIVITIS 18
ALLERGIC CONJUNCTIVITIS 92
BLEPHARITIS/STYE/CHALAZION 93
OTHER INFECTIONS OF EYE

NEOPLASMS OF EYE/ADNEXA 39

CONTUSION/ABRASIONS/BLACKEYE
FOREIGN BODY IN EYE
OTHER INJURIES

BLOCKED LACRIMAL DUCT OF INFANTS 251

OTHER CONGENITAL ANOMALIES EYES
DETACHED RETINA
RETINOPATHY
MACULAR DEGENERATION
CORNEAL ULCER (HERPETIC)

F86	TRACHOMA
F91	REFRACTIVE ERRORS 94
F92	CATARACT 96
F93	GLAUCOMA 97
F94	BLINDNESS,ALL TYPES 98
F95	STRABISMUS
F99	OTHER DIS.EYE

H— Ear

H01	EAR PAIN/EARACHE
H02	HEARING COMPLAINTS (*excl.* H84–86)
H03	RINGING/BUZZING/TINNITUS
H04	DISCHARGE FROM EAR
H05	BLOOD IN/FROM EAR
H13	PLUGGED FEELING
H15	CONCERN WITH APPEARANCE OF EARS
H27	FEAR OF EAR DISEASE
H28	DISABILITY/IMPAIRMENT
H29	OTHER SYMPT./COMPLT.OF EAR

H70	OTITIS EXTERNA 100
H71	ACUTE OTITIS MEDIA/MYRINGITIS 101
H72	SEROUS OTITIS MEDIA.GLUE 102
H73	EUSTACHIAN SALPINGITIS 103
H74	CHRONIC OTITIS, OTHER INFECT.EAR

H75	NEOPLASM OF EAR 39

H76	FOREIGN BODY IN EAR
H77	PERFORATION TYMP.MEMBRANE
H78	SUPERFICIAL INJURY OF EAR
H79	OTHER INJURIES

H80	CONGENITAL ANOMALIES OF EAR

H81	EAR WAX (EXCESSIVE) 106
H82	VERTIGINOUS SYNDROMES 104
H83	OTOSCLEROSIS
H84	PRESBYACUSIS
H85	ACUSTIC TRAUMA
H86	DEAFNESS/PARTIAL OR COMPLETE 105
H99	OTHER DIS. OF EAR/MASTOID

K— Circulatory

K01	PAIN ATTRIBUTED TO HEART 262
K02	PRESSURE,TIGHTNESS. ATTR.TO HEART
K03	OTHER PAIN ATTRIB. TO CIRCULATION
K04	PALPITATIONS/AWARE OF HEARTBEAT 263
K05	OTHER ABN./IRREG.HEARTBEAT/PULSE
K06	PROMINENT VEINS
K07	SWOLLEN ANKLES/EDEMA 265
K24	FEAR OF HEART ATTACK
K25	FEAR OF HYPERTENSION
K27	FEAR/OTHER DIS. CIRCU. SYSTEM
K28	DISABILITY/IMPAIRMENT
K29	OTHER SYMPT.HEART/CIRC.SYSTEM

K70	INFECTIOUS DIS. CIRC. SYSTEM

K71	RHEUMATIC FEVER/HEART DISEASE 108

K72	NEOPLASM CIRC.SYSTEM 39

K73	CONG.ANOMALIES HEART/CIRC.SYST.

K74	ANGINA PECTORIS 110
K75	ACUTE MYOCARDIAL INFARCTION 109
K76	OTHER AND CHRONIC ISCHEMIC HEART DIS. 110
K77	HEART FAILURE 112
K78	ATRIAL FIBRILLATION/FLUTTER 113
K79	PAROXYSMAL TACHYCARDIA 114
K80	ECTOPIC BEATS, ALL TYPES 115
K81	HEART MURMUR, NOS 116
K82	PULMONARY HEART DISEASE 117
K83	HEART VALVE DIS. NOS,NON-RHEUM 111
K84	OTHER DISEASE OF HEART
K85	ELEVATED B/P W/O HYPERTENSION 119
K86	UNCOMPLICATED HYPERTENSION 120
K87	HYPERTENSION WITH INVOLV.TARGET ORGANS 121

K88	POSTURAL HYPOTENSION (LOW B/P) **131**
K89	TRANSIENT CEREBRAL ISCHEMIA **123**
K90	STROKE/CEREBROVASC.ACC. **124**
K91	ATHEROSCLEROSIS *excl.* HEART/BRAIN **125**
K92	OTHER ARTER. OBSTR./PERIPH.VASC.DIS. **126**
K93	PULMONARY EMBOLISM **127**
K94	PHLEBITIS AND THROMBOPHLEBITIS **128**
K95	VARICOSE VEINS OF LEGS (EXCL.S97) **129**
K96	HEMORRHOIDS **130**
K99	OTHER DIS.CIRCULATORY SYSTEM

L—   Musculoskeletal

L01	NECK SYMPT./COMPLT. (EXCL. HEADACHE)
L02	BACK SYMPTOMS/COMPLAINTS
L03	LOW BACK COMPLT.W/O RADIATION
L04	CHEST SYMPTOMS/COMPLAINTS
L05	FLANK SYMPTOMS/COMPLAINTS
L06	AXILLA SYMPTOMS/COMPLAINTS
L07	JAW SYMPTOMS/COMPLAINTS
L08	SHOULDER SYMPTOMS/COMPLAINTS
L09	ARM SYMPTOMS/COMPLAINTS
L10	ELBOW SYMPTOMS/COMPLAINTS
L11	WRIST SYMPTOMS/COMPLAINTS
L12	HAND & FINGER SYMPTOMS/COMPLT.
L13	HIP SYMPTOMS/COMPLAINTS
L14	LEG/THIGH SYMPTOMS/COMPLAINTS
L15	KNEE SYMPTOMS/COMPLAINTS
L16	ANKLE SYMPTOMS/COMPLAINTS
L17	FOOT & TOE SYMPTOMS/COMPLAINTS
L18	MUSCLE PAIN/FIBROSITIS
L19	OTH.SYMPT.MULTIPLE/UNSPEC.MUSCLES
L20	SYMPT.MULTIPLE/UNSPEC.JOINTS **288/289**
L26	FEAR OF CANCER
L27	FEAR OF OTHER MUSCULOSKELETAL DIS.
L28	DISABILITY/IMPAIRMENT
L29	OTHER & MULT. MUSCULOSKELETAL SYMPT

L70	INFECTIONS

L71	NEOPLASMS **39**

L72	FRACTURE: RADIUS/ULNA **306**
L73	FRACTURE: TIBIA/FIBULA **310**
L74	FRACTURE: HAND/FOOT BONES **307/308**
L75	FRACTURE: FEMUR **309**
L76	FRACTURE: OTHER **301–305,311**
L77	SPRAINS & STRAINS OF ANKLE(S) **317**
L78	SPRAINS & STRAINS OF KNEE(S) **316**
L79	SPRAINS & STRAINS OF OTHER JOINTS **314** E.V.
L80	DISLOCATIONS
L81	OTHER INJURY

L82	CONGENITAL ANOMALIES **248**

L83	SYNDROMES OF CERVICAL SPINE **237**
L84	OSTEOARTHRITIS OF SPINE **237**
L85	ACQUIRED DEFORMITIES OF SPINE
L86	LUMBAR DISC,LESION,RADIATION **239**
L87	GANGLION JOINT/TENDON
L88	RHEUMATOID ARTHRIT/ALLIED COND. **228**
L89	OSTEOARTHRITIS OF HIP **229**
L90	OSTEOARTHRITIS OF KNEE **229**
L91	OTHER OSTEOARTHRITIS **229**
L92	SHOULDER SYNDROME **232**
L93	TENNIS ELBOW
L94	OSGOOD-SCHLATTER, OSTEOCHONDROS **242**
L95	OSTEOPOROSIS **243**
L96	ACUTE MENISCUS/LIGAMENT KNEE **312**
L97	CHR.INTERNAL KNEE DERANGEMENT **244**
L98	ACQUIRED DEFORMITIES OF LIMBS **245**
L99	OTH. DIS. MUSCULOSKELETAL SYSTEM **230/231**

N—   Neurological

N01	HEADACHE (EXCL.R09,N89) **258**
N02	TENSION HEADACHE **76**
N03	PAIN, FACE **258**
N04	RESTLESS LEGS SYNDROME
N05	TINGLING FINGERS/FEET/TOES
N06	OTH.SENSA.DISTUR/AB INVOL.MOV. **255/259**
N07	CONVULSIONS/SEIZURES **254**

N16	OTHER DISTURB. SENSE/SMELL/TASTE
N17	VERTIGO/DIZZINESS (EXCL.H82) **256**
N18	PARALYSIS/WEAKNESS (EXCL.A04)
N19	DISORDER SPEECH **257**
N26	FEAR OF CANCER OF NEURO.SYSTEM
N27	FEAR OF OTHER NEURO.DISEASE
N28	DISABILITY/IMPAIRMENT
N29	OTHER SYMPT./COMPLT.NEURO.SYSTEM

N70	POLIOMYELITIS/OTHER ENTEROVIRUS
N71	MENINGITIS/ENCEPHALITIS
N72	TETANUS
N73	OTHER INFECT.NEURO.SYSTEM

N74	MALIGNANT NEOPLASMS **39**
N75	BENIGN NEOPLASMS
N76	UNSPEC. NEOPLASMS
N79	CONCUSSION **322**

N80	OTHER HEAD INJ. W/O SKULL FX **322**
N81	OTHER INJURIES

N85	CONGENITAL ANOMALIES

N86	MULTIPLE SCLEROSIS **87**
N87	PARKINSONISM **88**
N88	EPILEPSY,ALL TYPES **89**
N89	MIGRAINE **90**
N90	CLUSTER HEADACHE **90**
N91	FACIAL PARALYSIS,BELL'S PALSY
N92	TRIGEMINUS NEURALGIA
N93	CARPAL TUNNEL SYNDR.
N94	OTHER PERIPHERAL NEURITIS
N99	OTHER DIS. NEURO. SYSTEM.

P—   Psychological

P01	FEELING ANXIOUS/NERVOUS/TENSE
P02	ACUTE STRESS/TRAN.SITUAT.DISTURB. **77**
P03	FEELING DEPRESSED
P04	FEELING/BEHAVING IRRITABLE
P05	FEELING/BEHAVING OLD/SENILE **297**
P06	DISTURBANCES OF SLEEP/INSOMNIA **75**
P07	INHIB./LOSS SEXUAL DESIRE **79**
P08	INHIB./LOSS SEXUAL FULFILMENT **79**
P09	CONCERN SEXUAL PREFERENCE
P10	STAMMERING, STUTTERING, TICS
P11	EATING PROBLEMS CHILD
P12	BEDWETTING,ENURESIS (EXCL.U04)
P13	ENCOPRESIS
P15	CHRONIC ALCOHOL ABUSE **80**
P16	ACUTE ALCOHOL ABUSE
P17	TOBACCO ABUSE **82**
P18	MEDICINAL ABUSE
P19	DRUG ABUSE
P20	DISTURB.MEMORY/CONCENTRATION
P21	OVERACTIVE CHILD, HYPERKIN.
P22	OTHER CONCERN BEHAV.CHILD
P23	OTH. S/C BEHAVIOR ADOLESCENT
P24	SPECIFIC LEARNING PROBLEMS
P25	PHASE OF LIFE PROBLEM ADULT
P27	FEAR OF MENTAL DISORDER
P28	DISABILITY/IMPAIRMENT
P29	OTHER PSYCHOLOGICAL SYMPTOMS

P70	DEMENTIA/SENILE,ALZHEIMER **66**
P71	OTHER ORGANIC PSYCHOSIS **66**
P72	SCHIZOPHRENIA, ALL TYPES **67**
P73	AFFECTIVE PSYCHOSIS **68**
P74	ANXIETY DISORDER/ANXIETY STATE **70**
P75	HYSTERICAL/HYPOCHONDRIACAL DIS. **71**
P76	DEPRESSIVE DISORDER **72**
P77	SUICIDE ATTEMPT
P78	NEURASTHENIA, SURMENAGE
P79	OTHER NEUROTIC DISORDER
P80	PERSONALITY DISORDER **84**
P85	MENTAL RETARDATION **85**
P98	OTHER/UNSPEC.PSYCHOSIS
P99	OTHER MENTAL/PSYCHOL. DISORDERS

R—   Respiratory

R01	PAIN:ATTRIB. TO RESPIR.SYSTEM **262**
R02	SHORTNESS OF BREATH,DYSPNEA **269**

R03 WHEEZING **269**
R04 OTHER BREATHING PROBLEMS **269**
R05 COUGH **270**
R06 NOSE BLEED/EPISTAXIS **267**
R07 SNEEZING/NASAL CONGESTION
R08 OTHER SYMPTOMS OF NOSE
R09 SYMPT./COMPLT. SINUS (*incl.*PAIN)
R21 SYMPT./COMPLT. THROAT
R22 SYMPT/COMPLT.TONSILS
R23 VOICE SYMPT/COMPLT
R24 HEMOPTYSIS **268**
R25 ABNORMAL SPUTUM/PHLEGM
R26 FEAR OF CANCER OF RESPIR.SYSTEM
R27 FEAR OF OTHER RESPIR.DISEASE
R28 DISABILITY/IMPAIRMENT
R29 OTHER SYMPT.RESPIR.SYSTEM NEC

R70 TUBERCULOSIS RESP (EXCL.A70) **4**
R71 WHOOPING COUGH **6**
R72 STREP.THROAT/SCARLET FEVER **7**
R73 BOIL/ABSCESS NOSE
R74 U.R.I. (HEAD COLD) **133**
R75 SINUSITIS ACUTE/CHRON. **134**
R76 TONSILLITIS ACUTE **135**
R77 ACUTE LARYNGIT./TRACHEIT. /CROUP **137**
R78 ACUTE BRONCHITIS/BRONCHIOLITIS **138**
R80 INFLUENZA (PROVEN)WO PNEUMONIA **139**
R81 PNEUMONIA **140**
R82 PLEURISY ALL(*excl.*R70) **141**
R83 OTHER INFECT.RESPIR.SYSTEM

R84 MALIGN. NEOPL. BRONCHUS/LUNG **33**
R85 OTHER MALIG.NEOPL. **33**
R86 BENIGN NEOPLASM

R87 FOREIGN BODY NOSE/LARYNX/BRONC.
R88 OTHER INJURIES

R89 CONGENITAL ANOMALIES OF RESPIR. SYSTEM

R90 HYPERTRO./CHRONIC INFECT.T & A **136**
R91 CHRONIC BRONCHITIS/BRONCHIECTASIS **142**
R93 PLEURAL EFFUSION NOS
R95 EMPHYSEMA/COPD **143**
R96 ASTHMA **144**
R97 HAYFEVER,ALLERGIC RHINITIS **145**
R98 HYPERVENTILATION
R99 OTHER DIS. RESPIR.SYSTEM

S— **Skin**
S01 PAIN, TENDERNESS OF SKIN
S02 PRURITUS, SKIN ITCHING
S03 WARTS **19**
S04 LOCAL SWELLING/PAPUL/LUMP/MASS
S05 GEN.SWELLING/PAPUL/LUMP/MASS
S06 LOCAL REDNESS/ERYTHEMA/RASH
S07 GEN.REDNESS/ERYTHEMA/RASH **292**
S08 OTHER CHANGES IN SKIN COLOR
S09 INFECTED FINGER/TOE/PARONYCHIA **207**
S10 BOIL/CARBUNCLE/CELLULITIS LOCAL **207**
S11 OTHER LOCALIZED SKIN INFECTION
S12 INSECT BITE
S13 ANIMAL/HUMAN BITE
S14 BURNS/SCALDS
S15 FOREIGN BODY IN SKIN
S16 BRUISE/CONTUSION INTACT SKIN
S17 ABRASION/SCRATCH/BLISTER
S18 LACERATION/CUT
S19 OTHER INJURY TO SKIN
S20 CORNS, CALOSITIES **219**
S21 SYMPT./COMPLT.OF SKIN TEXTURE
S22 SYMPT./COMPLT.NAILS
S23 BALDNESS/LOSING HAIR
S24 OTHER SYMPT./COMPLT.HAIR & SCALP
S26 FEAR OF CANCER OF SKIN
S27 FEAR OF HAVING OTHER SKIN DIS.
S28 DISABILITY/IMPAIRMENT
S29 OTHER SYMPT./COMPLT.SKIN

S70 HERPES ZOSTER **10**
S71 HERPES SIMPLEX (EXCL.F85,X90,Y72) **11**

S72 SCABIES AND OTHER ACARIASES **30**
S73 PEDICULOSIS/OTHER SKIN INFEST. **29**
S74 DERMATOPHYTOSIS **24**
S75 MONILIASIS/CANDIDIASIS(EXCL.GU) **25**
S76 OTHER INFECTIOUS SKIN DIS. **7**

S77 MALIGN.NEOPL. OF SKIN **34**
S78 LIPOMA OF SKIN **40**
S79 OTHER BENIGN NEOPLASM OF SKIN **41**
S80 OTHER/UNSPEC. NEOPLASM SKIN

S81 HEMANGIOMA/LYMPHANGIOMA **44**
S82 NEVUS/MOLE
S83 OTHER CONGENITAL LESIONS

S84 IMPETIGO **210**
S85 PILONIDAL CYST/FISTULA
S86 SEBORRHEIC DERMATITIS **212**
S87 ATOPIC DERMATITIS/ECZEMA **213**
S88 CONTACT DERMATITIS/OTHER ECZEMA **214**
S89 DIAPER RASH **215**
S90 PITYRIASIS ROSEA **216**
S91 PSORIASIS W/WO ARTHROPATHY **217**
S92 POMPHOLYX/ DIS. SWEAT GLANDS
S93 SEBACEOUS CYST **220**
S94 INGROWN TOENAIL/OTH.DIS.OF NAIL
S95 MOLLUSCA CONTAGIOSA
S96 ACNE **224**
S97 CHRONIC ULCER SKIN/INCL.VARICOSE
S98 URTICARIA **226**
S99 OTHER DIS.SKIN/SUBCUT.TISSUE

T— **Endocrine & metabolic**
T01 EXCESSIVE THIRST
T02 EXCESSIVE APPETITE
T03 LOSS OF APPETITE **273**
T04 FEEDING PROBLEM INFANT (EX. P11) **53**
T05 FEEDING PROBLEM ADULT (EX. T06) **53**
T06 ANOREXIA NERVOSA
T07 WEIGHT GAIN
T08 WEIGHT LOSS (EXCL.T06) **293**
T10 FAILURE TO THRIVE **294**
T11 DEHYDRATION
T15 THYROID LUMP,MASS
T26 FEAR OF CANCER OF ENDOCR.SYSTEM
T27 FEAR OF OTHER ENDOCR.NUTRI.DIS.
T28 DISABILITY/IMPAIRMENT
T29 OTHER SYMPT./COMPLT.ENDOCR.NUTRI.

T70 INFECT. DIS. ENDOCR.METAB.NUTRI.

T71 MALIGN. NEOPL. THYROID **39**
T72 BENIGN NEOPLASM THYROID
T73 OTHER/UNSPEC.NEOPLASMS **39**

T78 THYROGLOSSAL DUCT(CYST)
T80 OTHER CONGENITAL ANOMALIES

T81 GOITER/NODULE WO THYROTOX. **47**
T82 OBESITY (BMI >30)
T83 OVERWEIGHT (BMI <30)
T85 HYPERTHYROIDISM/THYROTOXICOSIS **48**
T86 HYPOTHYROIDISM/MYXEDEMA **49**
T87 HYPOGLYCEMIA
T88 RENAL GLUCOSURIA
T90 DIABETES MELLITUS **50**
T91 VITAMIN DEF./OTHER NUTR.DIS.
T92 GOUT **54**
T93 LIPID METABOLISM DISORDER
T99 OTHER ENDOCR. METAB. NUTR. DIS.

U— **Urology**
U01 PAINFUL URINATION **280**
U02 FREQUENT/URGENT URINATION **283**
U04 INCONTINENCE.(*excl.*P12) **281**
U05 OTHER URINATION PROBLEMS
U06 BLOOD IN URINE **373**
U07 OTHER COMPLAINTS OF URINE
U13 OTHER SYMPT./COMPLT.BLADDER
U14 SYMPT./COMPLT.KIDNEY
U26 FEAR OF CANCER OF URINARY SYST.
U27 FEAR OF OTHER URINARY DISEASE

U28 DISABILITY/IMPAIRMENT
U29 OTHER SYMPT.URINARY SYSTEM

U70 PYELONEPHRITIS/PYELITIS,ACUTE 169
U71 CYSTITIS/OTHER URIN.INFECT.NEC 170/198
U72 URETHRITIS, NON SPECIFIC 172/372

U75 MALIGN. NEOPL., KIDNEY 37
U76 MALIGN. NEOPL., BLADDER 37
U77 OTH. MALIG. NEOPL. URINARY TRACT 37
U78 BENIGN NEOPL.URINARY TRACT
U79 OTHER UNSPEC. NEOPL. URINARY TRACT

U80 INJURIES

U85 CONGENITAL ANOMALIES URIN.TRACT

U88 GLOMERULONEPHRITIS/NEPHROSIS 168
U90 ORTHOSTATIC ALBUMINURIA 173
U95 URIN.CALCULUS ALL TYPES/SITES 171
U98 ABN.URINE TEST FINDING, NOS 298
U99 OTHER DIS. URINARY SYSTEM

W— **Pregnancy & family planning**
W01 QUESTION OF PREGNANCY (EXCL. W02)
W02 FEAR OF BEING PREGNANT
W03 ANTEPARTUM BLEEDING
W05 VOMITING/NAUSEA OF PREGNANCY
W10 MORNING AFTER PILL
W11 FAMILY PLAN./ORAL CONTRACEPTIVE 344
W12 FAMILY PLANNING/IUD 345
W13 FAMILY PLAN./STERILIZATION 343/347
W14 FAMILY PLANNING/OTHER 346/347
W15 COMPLAINTS OF INFERTILITY 195
W17 HEAVY POST-PARTUM BLEEDING
W18 OTHER COMPLT. POST-PARTUM PERIOD
W19 SYMPT./COMPLT.LACTATION
W20 OTHER S/C BREAST(IN PREG.)
W27 FEAR OF COMPLICATIONS OF PREG.
W28 DISABILITY/IMPAIRMENT
W29 OTH SYMPT.PREG./FAMILY PLANNING

W70 PUERPERAL INFECTION, SEPSIS
W71 OTHER INFECTIOUS CONDITIONS†

W72 MALIGNANT NEOPLASM† 39
W73 BENIGN NEOPLASM†

W75 INJURIES† COMPLICATING PREG.

W76 CONG.ANOMALIES† OF MOTHER

W77 OTHER NON-OBSTET. CONDITIONS†
W78 PREGNANCY: CONFIRMED 350
W79 UNWANTED PREGNANCY: CONFIRMED 350
W80 ECTOPIC PREGNANCY 196
W81 TOXEMIA, (PRE)ECLAMPSIA 199
W82 ABORTION, SPONTANEOUS 201
W83 ABORTION, INDUCED 200
W84 PREG.HIGH RISK
W90 NORMAL DELIVERY LIVEBORN(S) 203
W91 NORMAL DELIVERY DEADBORN(S) 203
W92 COMPLICATED DELIVERY LIVEBORN
W93 COMPLICATED DELIVERY DEADBORN
W94 MASTITIS PUERPERALIS 205
W95 OTHER DISORDERS OF BREAST 205
W96 OTH.05 COMPLIC. OF PUERPERIUM
W99 OTHER DIS. OF PREG. DELIV. PUERPERIUM

X— **Female genital system**
X01 GENITAL PAIN
X02 MENSTRUAL PAIN 191
X03 INTERMENSTRUAL PAIN 191
X04 PAINFUL INTERCOURSE 374
X05 MENSTRUATION ABSENT/SCANTY
X06 MENSTRUATION EXCESSIVE
X07 MENSTRUATION IRREGULAR/FREQ.
X08 INTERMENSTRUAL BLEEDING
X09 PREMENSTRUAL SYMPTOMS
X10 POSTPONEMENT OF MENSTR.

X11 MENOPAUSAL SYMPT./COMPLT. 187
X12 POSTMENOPAUSAL BLEEDING 187
X13 POSTCOITAL BLEEDING
X14 VAGINAL DISCHARGE
X15 OTH.SYMPT./COMPLT.VAGINA
X16 SYMPT./COMPLT.VULVA
X17 SYMPT./COMPLT.PELVIS
X18 BREAST PAIN
X19 LUMP/MASS BREAST
X20 SYMPT./COMPLT.NIPPLE
X21 OTH. SYMPT./COMPLT.BREAST
X23 FEAR OF VENEREAL DIS.
X24 FEAR OF SEXUAL DYSFUNCTION
X25 FEAR OF GENITAL CANCER
X26 FEAR OF BREAST CANCER
X27 FEAR OTHER GENITAL/BREAST DIS.
X28 DISABILITY/IMPAIRMENT
X29 OTHER SYMPT./GENITAL SYSTEM.

X70 SYPHILIS, FEM.(GENIT.& NOS) 22
X71 GONORRHOEA, FEM. (GENIT. & NOS) 23
X72 UROGENITAL CANDIDIASIS.PROVEN 26
X73 UROGENITAL TRICHOMONIASIS, PROVEN 27
X74 PELVIC INFLAMMATORY DISEASE 183

X75 MALIGN.NEOPL. CERVIX 36
X76 MALIGN.NEOPL. BREAST 35/39
X77 OTHER MALIGNANT NEOPLASMS 36/39
X78 FIBROID/MYOMA (UTERUS/CERVIX) 43
X79 BENIGN NEOPL.BREAST (EXCL. X88) 42
X80 OTHER BENIGN NEOPL. FEM.GENIT.
X81 OTHER/UNSPEC.NEOPL. FEM.GENIT.

X82 INJURIES

X83 CONGENITAL ANOMALIES FEM.GENIT.

X84 VAGINITIS/VULVITIS,NOS 185
X85 CERVICITIS/OTHER CERV.DIS. 184
X86 ABNORMAL PAP SMEAR 376
X87 UTEROVAGINAL PROLAPSE 186
X88 CHRONIC CYSTIC DIS.BREAST 181
X89 PREMENSTRUAL TENSION SYNDROME 188
X90 HERPES GENITALIS 11
X91 CONDYLOMATA ACUMINATA 19
X99 OTHER DIS. OF FEMALE GENITAL SYSTEM

Y— **Male genital system**
Y01 PAIN IN PENIS
Y02 PAIN IN TESTIS/SCROTUM
Y03 DISCHARGE FROM PENIS/URETHRA
Y04 OTHER SYMPT./COMPL. OF PENIS
Y05 SYMPT./COMPLT.SCROTUM & TESTES
Y06 SYMPT./COMPLT.PROSTATE
Y07 SYMPT./COMPLT. POTENCY (EX.P07,P08)
Y08 OTHER S/C SEXUAL DYSF(EX.P07,P08)
Y10 INFERTILITY/SUBFERTILITY 195
Y13 FAMILY PLANNING/STERILIZATION 343
Y14 FAMILY PLANNING/OTHER 347
Y16 SYMPT./COMPLT. MALE BREAST
Y24 FEAR OF SEXUAL DYSFUNCTION
Y25 FEAR OF VENEREAL DISEASE
Y26 FEAR OF CANCER MALE GENITAL
Y27 FEAR OF OTHER GENITAL DISEASE
Y28 DISABILITY/IMPAIRMENT
Y29 OTHER SYMPT.MALE REPROD.SYST.

Y70 SYPHILIS MALE 22
Y71 GONORRHOEA MALE 23
Y72 HERPES GENITALIS 11
Y73 PROSTATITIS/SEMINAL VESICULI 176
Y74 ORCHITIS/EPIDIDYMITIS 178
Y75 BALANITIS 26/179
Y76 CONDYLOMATA ACUMINATA 19

Y77 MALIGN. NEOPL. PROSTATE 37
Y78 OTHER MALIGN. NEOPL. 35/37/46
Y79 BENIGN NEOPL. MALE GENITAL

Y80 INJURIES

'81   PHIMOSIS/REDUND. PREPUCE 179
'82   HYPOSPADIA
'83   UNDESC.TESTICLE/CRYPTORCHISM 249
'84   OTHER CONG.ANOMAL.

85   BENIGN PROSTATIC HYPERTROPHY 175
86   HYDROCELE 177
99   OTHER DIS.MALE GENIT.INCL.BREAST 26/27/31

—   **Social problems**
01   POVERTY/FINANCIAL PROBLEMS 356
02   PROBLEM FOOD AND WATER
03   PROBLEM HOUSING/NEIGHBORHOOD 357
04   PROB. SOCIAL/CULTURAL SYSTEM 365/366
05   PROB. WORKING CONDITIONS 367
06   PROB. WITH BEING UNEMPLOYED 367
07   PROBLEMS WITH EDUCATION 364
08   PROB. SOCIAL INSURANCE/WELFARE
09   PROB. LEGAL/POLICE 370

Z10   PROB. HEALTH CARE SYSTEM/ACCESS
Z11   PROB. WITH BEING ILL 358
Z12   RELATION PROBL.PARTNERS 359
Z13   PROBLEMS WITH BEHAV.PARTNER 358
Z14   PROB. WITH PARTNER BEING ILL 358
Z15   LOSS OR DEATH OF PARTNER 362
Z16   RELATION PROBL. WITH CHILD 360
Z18   PROB. W.CHILD BEING ILL 358
Z19   LOSS OR DEATH OF CHILD 362
Z20   RELAT.PROB. PARENT/OTHER FAMILY 361
Z21   PROBL. W. BEHAV. PARENT/OTH.FAMILY 361
Z22   PROB. W.PARENT/FAMILY BEING ILL 358
Z23   LOSS OR DEATH PARENT/FAMILY 362
Z24   PROBLEMS IN RELAT.W.FRIENDS
Z25   PROB. ASSAULTS/HARMFUL EVENTS
Z27   FEAR OF HAVING A SOCIAL PROB.
Z28   SOCIAL HANDICAP 366
Z29   OTH. SOCIAL PROBLEMS NEC 366

Computerized version of ICPC

The International Classification of Primary Care (ICPC) is available on disk for the IBM PC and compatibles, using MS-DOS, from Oxford Electronic Publishing. All enquiries concerning this version should be addressed to:

Ann Yates,
Oxford Electronic Publishing,
Oxford University Press,
Walton Street,
Oxford OX2 6DP,
UK.

Translations of ICPC

Translations are available in the following languages:

Dutch
French
German
Italian
Norwegian
Portuguese
Spanish

All enquiries about translated versions should be sent to Professor Lamberts at the following address:

Professor Henk Lamberts,
Instituut voor Huisartsgeneeskunde,
Universiteit van Amsterdam,
Meibergdreef 15,
1105 AZ Amsterdam,
The Netherlands.